Remoralizin

Continuum Resources in Religion and Political Culture
Series Editors: Graham Ward and Michael Hoelzl, The University of
Manchester, UK

Aimed at undergraduates studying in this area, titles in this series look
specifically at the key topics involved in the relationship between religion
and politics, taking into account a broad range of religious perspectives,
and presenting clear, approachable texts for students grappling with
often complex concepts.

The New Visibility of Religion, edited by Graham Ward and Michael Hoelzl

Remoralizing Britain?

Political, Ethical and Theological Perspectives on New Labour

Edited by
Peter Manley Scott
Christopher R. Baker
Elaine L. Graham

continuum

Continuum International Publishing Group

The Tower Building	80 Maiden Lane
11 York Road	Suite 704
London SE1 7NX	New York, NY 10038

www.continuumbooks.com

British Library Cataloguing-in-Publication Data
A catalogue record for this book is available from the British Library.

ISBN: HB: 0–8264–4414–8
     978–0–8264–4414–1
     PB: 0–8264–2465–1
     978–0–8264–2465–5

Library of Congress Cataloging-in-Publication Data
Remoralizing Britain?: political, ethical, and theological perspectives on
   New Labour/edited by Peter Manley Scott, Christopher R. Baker, and
   Elaine L. Graham.

    p. cm.
   Includes bibliographical references.
   ISBN-13: 978–0–8264–4414–1 (hb)
   ISBN-10: 0–8264–4414–8 (hb)
   ISBN-13: 978–0–8264–2465–5 (pb)
   ISBN-10: 0–8264–2465–1 (pb)

   1. Labour Party (Great Britain) 2. Political ethics – Great Britain.
   3. Religion and politics – Great Britain. I. Scott, Peter M., 1961–II. Baker,
   Christopher Richard, 1961–III. Graham, Elaine L.

JN1129.L32R43 2009
172.0941–dc22   2008036976

Typeset by Newgen Imaging Systems Pvt Ltd, Chennai, India
Printed and bound in Great Britain by Athenaeum Press Ltd, Gateshead, Tyne and Wear

Contents

Contributors

John Atherton is Canon Theologian Emeritus at Manchester Cathedral and hon. lecturer, the University of Manchester 1976–present, and secretary of the William Temple Foundation. He holds an M.Phil. and Ph.D. from Manchester University, and was awarded a Doctorate of Sacred Theology by the University of Uppsala, Sweden. He has published a number of books, including *Marginalisation* (SCM, 2003) and *Transfiguring Capitalism: An Enquiry into Religion and Global Change* (SCM, 2008). Currently he is organizing the Religion and Happiness research project, AHRC/ESRC, 2007–9.

Christopher R. Baker is director of research for the William Temple Foundation and part-time lecturer at the University of Manchester in Urban Theology. His research focuses on the impact of faith based engagement in UK Civil Society and Public Policy. His recent book *The Hybrid Church in the City – Third Space Thinking* was published by Ashgate in 2007.

Cynthia Burack is associate professor in the Department of Women's Studies at the Ohio State University. She is a co-editor (with Jyl J. Josephson) of *Fundamental Differences: Feminists Talk Back to Social Conservatives* (Rowman and Littlefield, 2003) and author of *Healing Identities: Black Feminist Thought and the Politics of Groups* (Cornell University Press, 2004) and *Sin, Sex, and Democracy: Antigay Rhetoric and the Christian Right* (State University of New York Press, 2008).

Mark D. Chapman is vice-principal of Ripon College Cuddesdon, Oxford, and a member of the Faculty of Theology at Oxford University. He is a Church of England priest and serves as honorary assistant curate at All Saints' Church, Cuddesdon. He has published widely in the fields of church history, political theology and many other aspects of theology. His most recent books are *Blair's Britain: A Christian Critique* (2005), *Anglicanism: A Very Short Introduction* (2006), *Bishops, Saints and Politics* (T & T Clark, 2007), and *Doing God: Religion and Public Policy in Brown's Britain* (DLT, 2008). Mark Chapman is publications officer for *Affirming Catholicism* and co-editor of the *Journal for the History of Modern Theology*.

Phil Edwards is the author of *More Work! Less Pay! Rebellion and Repression in Italy, 1972–77* (Manchester University Press, 2009). He is based at the School of Law in the University of Manchester, where he is an active member of the Regulation, Security and Justice Research Centre.

Doug Gay is lecturer in Practical Theology at the University of Glasgow and a Church of Scotland minister. His research interests span ecclesiology and political theology, with a particular interest in the relationships between theology and nationalism.

Anthony Giddens [Lord Giddens] is professor emeritus at the London School of Economics. He was educated at the University of Hull and the London School of Economics. He has taught at the University of Leicester and subsequently for many years at Cambridge, where he was professor of Sociology. He was director of the LSE from 1997 to 2003. He was made a peer in 2004. He is a Life Fellow of King's College, Cambridge. He has honorary degrees or comparable awards from 15 universities. He is an honorary fellow of the American Academy of Arts and Sciences and the Chinese Academy of Social Sciences. He was the BBC Reith Lecturer in 1999. His many books include *Capitalism and Modern Social Theory* (1971), *Beyond Left and Right* (1994) and *The Third Way* (1998). His most recent monograph is *Over to You Mr Brown* (2007). His books have been translated into some forty languages.

Elaine L. Graham is Samuel Ferguson Professor of Social and Pastoral Theology at the University of Manchester, UK. Her publications include *Making the Difference: Gender, Personhood and Theology* (1995), *Transforming Practice* (1996), *Representations of the Post/Human: Monsters, Aliens and Others in Popular Culture* (Rutgers University Press, 2002) and numerous articles and reviews. She is the co-author, with Heather Walton and Frances Ward, of *Theological Reflection: Methods* (SCM, 2005) and *Theological Reflection: Sources* (SCM, 2007). She was a member of the Commission on Urban Life and Faith and executive director of the Manchester Research Institute for Religion and Civil Society.

D. Emily Hicks, professor of comparative literature and director of the Border Institute, was born in San Francisco. In the early 1970s, as an undergraduate at UC Berkeley, while living in Oakland, she attended Black Panther Angela Davis' California Supreme Court pretrial hearing in Marin County. Hicks studied philosophy with Herbert Marcuse at UC San Diego. She has lectured and performed internationally and has served as faculty at institutions including USC, UC Irvine, the Universidad Autonoma de Baja California in Mexico and Banff Center for the Arts in Canada. Author of *Border Writing* (1991) and *Ninety-five Languages* (1999), she is completing a book on Magna Carta and the multiethnic state.

Will Hutton is chief executive of The Work Foundation, an independent, not for dividend research based consultancy which is the most influential voice on work, workplace and employment issues in Britain. Hutton has written several best-selling economic books including *The World We're In, The State We're In, The State to Come, The Stakeholding Society* and *On the Edge with Anthony Giddens.* In addition, he won the Political Journalist of the Year award in 1993. His latest book, *The Writing on the Wall: China and the West in the 21st Century,* was published in the UK in January 2007 by Little, Brown.

Inderjeet Parmar is professor of Government and Head of Politics at the University of Manchester. He is the author of two books on Anglo-American relations and think-tanks, the latest being *Think Tanks and Power in Foreign Policy* (Palgrave, 2004). He is currently writing a book on US philanthropy and foreign affairs titled *Foundations of the American Century: The Carnegie, Rockefeller and Ford Foundations in US Foreign Affairs, 1920–2003* (Columbia University Press, forthcoming 2009).

Peter Manley Scott is senior lecturer in Christian Social Thought and director of the Lincoln Theological Institute at the University of Manchester. He has researched extensively in the interactions between theology and politics. He is the author of *Theology, Ideology and Liberation* (CUP, paperback edition 2008), *A Political Theology of Nature* (CUP, 2003) and co-editor of *The Blackwell Companion to Political Theology* (Blackwell, paperback edition, 2006).

Stefan Skrimshire researches and teaches in the Lincoln Theological Institute at the University of Manchester, mostly on the subject of religious and political responses to future crises. He is author of *Politics of Fear, Practices of Hope* (London: Continuum, 2008), various journal and magazine articles, and is lead researcher on the interdisciplinary research project, Future Ethics: Climate Change, Political Action and the Future of the Human.

Jess Steele is head of Consultancy at the Development Trusts Association. She established and leads the DTA's consultancy service, the Pool, drawing on the grassroots expertise of practitioners throughout the development trust movement. Previously she was the deputy chief executive of the British Urban Regeneration Association. She has published extensively on local history, including *Turning the Tide: The History of Everyday Deptford* and edited *The Streets of London: The Booth Notebooks.* Her background as a community activist and entrepreneur in South East London included leading the award-winning Get Set for Citizenship SRB programme and establishing numerous social enterprises. She now lives in Hastings and is Treasurer of the Hastings Pier & White Rock Trust.

Gerry Stoker is professor of Politics and Governance at the University of Southampton, UK and director of the Centre for Citizenship and Democracy. His current research deals with issues of governance in complex settings, political disenchantment in Western democracies, citizen empowerment and strategies for encouraging civic behaviour among citizens. In his research work

Professor Stoker is committed to the use of pioneering methods and in particular to approaches that enable evidenced-based policy and practice.

Paul Vallely, CMG, has written about the developing world for more than two decades, with award-winning reporting from 30 countries. He has been chair of the development agencies Traidcraft and the Catholic Institute for International Relations and worked with Christian Aid and Cafod. He was seconded to Tony Blair's Commission for Africa and was co-author of its final report. He worked with Bob Geldof, deciding how to spend the money raised by Live Aid, assisting at Live8 and lobbying the Gleneagles summit with Geldof and Bono. He is now associate editor of *The Independent* where he writes on social, ethical and cultural issues.

Angelia R. Wilson is senior lecturer in Politics, University of Manchester, specializing in gender and political theory. Her research explores the intersection between feminist political theory, queer theory and policies regulating sexuality. Her book, *Below the Belt: Sexuality, Religion and the American South* (Cassell, 2000) articulates the tensions of US sexual politics around constructions of femininity, masculinity and issues such as abortion and homosexuality.

Foreword

New Labour might not do religion, but Tony Blair certainly does. Since stepping down as prime minister, he has become much more open about two convictions – his own religious faith and his belief that religion is a fundamental force in the world whether we like it or not. He has long been devout. Cherie Booth says in her memoirs that 'religion was more important to him than anyone I had ever met outside the priesthood'. Indeed, she adds, it was their mutual interest in religion that brought them together.

Blair kept his personal religious beliefs out of his politics while in power, but there seems no doubt that they played a part both in some of the decisions he made and in how he kept going in adverse circumstances. 'Doing the right thing', even when he was losing public support, is a phrase that constantly crops up when he is questioned about why he followed the policies he did – including the decision to participate in the ill-fated invasion of Iraq.

'Do the right thing' – on the face of it, this is an odd phrase, especially in the context of today's cultural pluralism. The oddity lies in the fact that someone who held diametrically opposed beliefs could claim the very same thing as the justification for their actions. Those who fiercely opposed the Iraq war were also 'doing the right thing', as are the Islamic radicals who are contesting what they see as the corrupt values of the West.

Blair's quest to encourage positive dialogue between people of different faiths is surely laudable, but will need more persuasive and developed foundations than he has managed to develop so far. It comprises most of the possibilities and problems of multiculturalism which we face nationally and globally today. In an era of instant communication and mass migration, identity politics has returned with a vengeance. It is usually far easier to get on with others who are like ourselves than those who are distinctively and visibly different. London is full of white South Africans, Australians and New Zealanders. The indigenous population scarcely seems to regard them as immigrants at all. It tends to be quite otherwise with migrants whose ethnic origins or culture clearly set them apart from the indigenous majority. Religion is certainly again highly important here – not just the type of faith, but the assiduousness with which it is practised. Muslims in Europe tend to be set apart by the character of their beliefs, but also by the fact of their religiosity in societies that have become largely secular.

Multiculturalism has come under widespread attack in recent years, but I see no other way forward at all in a world in which cultural diversity is now an everyday part of life. We should distinguish between naïve and sophisticated multiculturalism. Unfortunately, only the first of these has been practised in most European countries until recently (the UK under Labour is something of an exception).

Naïve multiculturalism consists in accepting religious ethnic and cultural diversity and leaving it at that. People should be free to live as they please, no matter what the social consequences; and specific cultural beliefs trump any attempt at setting up general values or universal moral prescriptions. One cannot have a single history of a nation – there are as many 'histories' as there are diverse cultural groups. It is usually naïve multiculturalism that people have in mind when they criticize and reject multiculturalism *tout court*. And they are correct; such a form of multiculturalism can lead to all sorts of troubles, including isolationism, conflict and an overall weakening of social solidarity.

Sophisticated multiculturalism is quite different, and to me it is what 'multiculturalism' as such should mean. Sophisticated multiculturalism, as originally developed particularly in Canada, emphasizes that all groups in a society (and to some extent in the larger world) have an obligation to accept a common framework of law and citizenship; that where cultural groups become isolated, efforts should be made to re-establish conventions with those in the wider community; and that sensitivity to cultural differences does not imply accepting that specific cultural beliefs cannot be questioned or overridden by more general norms.

New Labour, I would say, moved fairly far in the direction of sophisticated multiculturalism. Its critics have complained loudly of its authoritarianism and its attacks on civil liberties, and in some areas and some respects they certainly have a case. However, one could equally well say that Labour took important steps towards shoring up social cohesion, while still recognizing the rights of minorities. I think that a good case can be made, for example, for the citizenship tests and ceremonies that Labour introduced. Migrants must publicly declare their acceptance of a framework of citizenship rights and obligations, and of national identity; however, these declarations probably also help unite some of the strains and tensions affecting the welfare state. Welfare provision derives a lot of its legitimacy from the feeling that we are all in the same boat, all members of a single overall 'community of fate'.

Even in sophisticated multiculturalism there will always be problems at the edges where what is 'the right thing' as seen by different cultural groups clashes. When this happens by definition there are no simple answers and mutual accommodation of some sort is always needed. The dilemmas surrounding the wearing of the veil in public places are a very evident example of such a situation.

Immigration as a political issue has caused all sorts of problems to social democratic governments, anxious to maintain their traditional liberal attitudes. Many left-of-centre parties have fallen from power largely on the basis of this question alone, even in countries that seemed to have long-established traditions of tolerance. In terms of their social and economic development, countries like Denmark and the Netherlands in the late 1990s were the most advanced, not only in Europe but in the world. The former has seen the rise of a xenopobic, right-wing populist party that has gained over 20% support at the polls. In the Netherlands two political murders related to cultural and ethnic divisions have helped polarize the country.

New Labour had plenty of problems surrounding its struggles to cope with migration and its consequences – or what many of the public perceive as its consequences. Yet it could be argued that the party was better-prepared to cope with the issue than its counterparts in many Continental countries. The need to manage migration was on the Labour radar from the outset. So also was the acceptance that, although immigration can bring many benefits to a society, it can also create real problems and anxieties. For instance, immigrants moving into a particular area can have the effect of depressing wages, at least for a period. Immigration can put pressure on public institutions. Thus setting up schemes for training children or adults who have no English can be expensive and demanding on resources.

Migration has to be managed – a conclusion that all other social democratic parties have in the end arrived at. Especially important is control of illegal migration, which can create a situation in which large groups of individuals live without welfare protection, following a shadowy existence on the margins of society. Of course, governments do have a major responsibility to dispel myths about migrants – such as that they are inevitably scroungers on the welfare system, or that they bring with them higher levels of crime.

And what of interfaith dialogue? On the face of things, the idea looks impeccable. Surely we need the great religions of the world to be in discussion with one another, to clear up mutual misunderstandings? Surely we should try to harness the positive power of religion to social ends, to help create harmony rather than division?

Of course we should. However, such a task is far, far more difficult than it seems. Religion means faith, and faith can be refractory to the demands of reason and can breed fanaticism. The world's population is rising towards 9 billion, yet the Catholic Church still frowns on contraception. An even more fundamental problem is that religion is not autonomous, but reflects the conflicts and inequalities of the wider world. Those conflicts may in some part be expressed in religious terms, but can rarely if ever be resolved on the level of religion itself. Finally, religions themselves are almost always divided, and some of the bitterest conflicts happen between adherents of the 'same' religion – the phenomenon Freud famously referred to as the narcissism of small differences.

All these issues and far more are discussed by the contributors to this excellent book, which I commend to the reader.

Anthony Giddens
June 2008

Introduction

Christopher R. Baker, Elaine L. Graham and
Peter Manley Scott

Can an assessment be made of the moral character of a modern government? Of course, we are accustomed to evaluations of the moral character of an individual politician. Nonetheless, in this volume something more ambitious is attempted: in what ways did the New Labour administration (1997–2007) headed by Prime Minister Tony Blair contribute to the remoralizing of Britain? What are the moral character and the moral achievement of this government?

We know that politicians like to present themselves in moral terms. Any administration wishes to affirm its integrity and avoid sleaze. In addition, the appeal to morality may be part of the effort of winning elections and securing power. (One of the most remarkable things about Alastair Campbell's diaries is the revelation of the depth of Gordon Brown's and Tony Blair's desire for power, 1994–7.[1]) Yet this collection of essays emerges out of the conviction that New Labour's deployment of a range of moral discourses is more than the effort of trying to persuade an electorate of a political party's integrity and a tactic to win power; it formed a central element of New Labour's political strategy throughout the Blair decade. Indeed, Bill Clinton's characterization of the Third Way is relevant here: '[T]he Third way is fine, but it has to be a third way with liberal values. Don't just push a reform message. He [Blair] has to have good old-fashioned left causes too, for the poor, whatever. It's about values, not reform.'[2] Clinton thereby connects modernization with progressive or left-of-centre values as core to New Labour's governance. This, at least as a first approximation, is what is meant by 'remoralizing'.

And certainly, New Labour went to town in its appeal to morality. On seeking office and in coming to power, New Labour presented its vision for Britain in moral terms: moral rectitude; governance with integrity; a renewed ethical engagement in foreign policy; a commitment to social inclusion (Britain as a 'community'); education as a path to moral and economic development; and developing partnerships with 'the market' in the service of social justice. During the course of the New Labour administration, further moral themes have been introduced: responsibility and respect, the merits of local government and self-governance, and the moral imperative to confront threats of 'terror' at home and abroad. Throughout, New Labour has drawn on the language of faith and morals yet has done so cautiously.

In praise of values

Why a Labour Party in opposition, and after forming a government, should appeal to moral discourse is easily appreciated. As Stuart Hampshire has argued, the labour movement was an important moral force in its presentation of a set of socio-economic-political issues as moral issues.[3] Furthermore, it insisted that these issues should be treated with moral seriousness and be addressed to the movement that raised them. Social justice is here reflexive: it demands the amelioration of poverty and the increase in life-chances, and requires that any amelioration be checked by reference to the experiences of the labour movement. In a sense, then, New Labour's appeal to the language of morality has a sound pedigree. E. P. Thompson's famous jibe that British Labourism owes more to Methodism than Marxism merely underscores the point that Labourism raises issues of considerability and distribution in ethics.

Moreover, this situation was compounded by Tony Blair's successful campaign to abolish Clause 4. This fourth clause of the Labour Party's constitution committed the party to the goal of securing the nationalizing of the means of production, distribution and exchange with the aim of securing greater social justice. Such a programme had embedded within it a moral valuation: the goods of social justice were to be achieved by the enactment of this clause. Removing it from the constitution – or modernizing it to death, as the New Labourites might have preferred to put it – nonetheless created a problem for New Labour. If one ethico-political programme was to be abandoned, what was to replace it? The answer was: values; New Labour values. 'Community', equality understood in terms of equal worth, and responsibility were the leading values promoted by Blair himself. Yet the question is immediately raised: what is the relationship between political action and values? That this question causes much difficulty can be appreciated if we consider the following three questions. Where do these values come from? Must every political action be justified explicitly by reference to values, and can such appeals be divisive? Is there any danger that the declaration of values might substitute for political action?

That there is a question about where these values come from has provided the space for the deployment of Tony Blair's Christian faith. Or, perhaps more precisely, it has permitted a gesturing to Christian values as a way of saying that this person has integrity, is to be trusted. He may not be 'one of us' in religious terms – most of the electorate is neither Anglo-Catholic nor a convert to Roman Catholicism – but Blair has succeeded in communicating his moral seriousness. That these values were not necessarily also Labour values, and that Blair's appreciation of his faith changed during his premiership, have been the source of both confusion and conflict.

That there is the concern as to whether political action must be justified by reference to values has led of course to remoralizing. In this sense of remoralizing, policy options are not here presented as the outcome of a process of moral reasoning. Instead, a 'values' word – community, responsibility, respect, prudence, opportunity – is attached to policy and programmes with the result that such programmes are stabilized by the attachment. What is obscured by this attachment is the process of moral reasoning by which moral terms gain their interpretative weight. It thus remains unclear as to what these ethically charged words mean, and then it is possible to turn these terms in rather different – sometimes divergent – directions. Moreover, the proceduralism of the liberal polity tends also to work to unstick the attachment. If the liberal polity tends to referee conflict between moral values, then the appeal to such values leads to their being thinned. Such moral reconstruction is most confusing to religious communities who appreciate the persistent appeal to moral values but cannot fathom why such appeal makes little difference or why some find such appeals offensive.

Moreover, what are we to make of the question that reference to values may become a substitute for action? This is remoralizing in a second sense, of which a good example is the actions of Pilate in John's Gospel. Here we are presented by a very powerful actor – the power of brutal killing falls in his remit – who argues moral questions but refuses to apply any moral standards to his own decisions. He is content to discuss morality without allowing any moral reference to his own decisions. For him, nothing follows from moral reflection; it is not a self-involving discourse. From this point, it is a small step to saying that recipients of government programmes must be morally worthy recipients. Just as Jesus' innocence was not enough neither are the needs of the marginalized sufficient. At this point, remoralizing discourse becomes an insulating discourse: it identifies the weaknesses of recipients but not the pride of donors. For this reason, when the term 'morality' was mentioned to Karl Marx, it is reported that he would roar with laughter. Such remoralizing is always bourgeois: it is a substitute for help.

There is little doubt that this turn to faith and morals has had tangible political outcomes. Yet this moral agenda, with its apparently religious roots, has been much noted, but not much discussed. By drawing together social theorists, practitioners, ethicists and theologians, this book is an interdisciplinary effort at establishing the sources and effects of this remoralizing. In short, the political phenomenon of New Labour requires the disciplines of theology and ethics, as well as social theory and politics, to be properly understood and assessed. Drawing together for the first time theorists from a range of disciplines and commitments, this interdisciplinary collection offers a reckoning of this New Labour decade. As such, it has four central questions: What is the nature of this remoralizing? What are its sources? How effective has it been and what difference has this moral discourse made? What can be learned from Blairism about the relationship between faith, morals and governance?

Organization of this book

The volume has three core parts, plus opening and closing chapters. In the opening chapter, 'Doing God? Public Theology under Blair', Elaine L. Graham

examines the conventional wisdom that liberal democracy requires the maintenance of a neutral, secular, value-free public domain and the corresponding
'privatization' of religion, as well as indicating how the so-called secularization
thesis has been displaced as the dominant narrative of modernity. This test-
ing of conventional perspectives and knowledges allows for the re-situating of
religious belief in the public sphere. As such, this opening chapter serves to
introduce the efforts at understanding New Labour's remoralizing of Britain
that are explored in later chapters.

The first part, 'Ethics and Politics', seeks to understand Blair's and Brown's
contributions to the morality of politics, and explores the moral health of
British politics after ten years of New Labour. The first two chapters in this part
offer rather different assessments of the morality of politics under New Labour.
In 'Let Citizens without Sin Cast the First Stone: Judging the Moral Failings of
Blair and Politics', Gerry Stoker notes the high expectations regarding squeaky-
clean standards of governance that accompanied Blair into office and argues
that these expectations could never be met; and that against more reasonable
criteria, the Blair government has been worthy of the electorate's trust. By contrast, Stefan Skrimshire takes a more sceptical line: in 'Demoralizing Britain:
Ten Years of Depoliticization', he argues that the Blair government has consistently undermined the bases of democratic action through processes of depoliticization. This has involved the erosion of civic freedoms and civil liberties, and
the marginalizing of dissenting voices, including religious voices.

A second pair of chapters offers assessments of the contributions to polit-
ics of Tony Blair and Gordon Brown. In 'New Labour and a Liberal Labour
Tradition', Will Hutton argues that Blair's principal political-intellectual leg-
acy is the refounding of a liberal Labour tradition that marks New Labour as
neither Keynesian nor Marxist. What is distinctive about Blair's version of New
Labour, Hutton contends, is a liberal emphasis on intermediate institutions.
In the last chapter in this part, 'Gordon Brown and His Presbyterian Moral
Compass', Doug Gay argues that Brown's 'ethical capital' – that he could be
trusted; indeed, the very index of his trustworthiness – has been augmented by
New Labour in terms of his Presbyterian roots, and Gay proceeds to assess the
validity of this effort in the making of political-symbolic capital.

In the second part of the book, titled 'Justice and Community', the theme of
community is explored in a variety of contexts and from a range of perspectives,
and some comparison is offered with the US and continental Europe. In 'Are
We Happier, Mr Brown?', John Atherton draws on the emerging literatures on
Happiness to argue that economic indicators are not the only identifiers of a
nation's well-being, and that other non-economic indicators not much noticed by
the Treasury must be taken into account. The following chapter is complemen-
tary in that it also raises the question about how social inclusion is to be secured
and evaluated. In 'Social Justice, Social Control or the Pursuit of Happiness?
The Goals and Values of the Regeneration Industry', Jess Steele draws on her

experience as a practitioner to explore the different phases of community regeneration processes over the Blair decade (1997–2007), and offers a critical evaluation of regeneration policies and an assessment of the advances and defeats of regeneration as a builder of economic capacity and agent of social inclusion.

In the next contribution, Mark D. Chapman analyses the use of the concept of 'community' in New Labour rhetoric, and argues that its meaning is often vague. Furthermore, in 'But What is a Community? The Continuing Development of a New Labour Concept', he argues that recently it has been deployed alongside 'society' and 'cohesion' to identify strong, cohesive groupings with a vibrant culture that engender civic pride. The chapter concludes with an assessment of the impact of this discourse of community on debates on multiculturalism, and the strengthening of local democracy.

The three contributions that follow trace some of the ways in which the language of remoralization is divisive. In 'Constructing Christian Right Enemies and Allies: US, UK and Eastern Europe', Cynthia Burack and Angelia R. Wilson examine the translation of an ideological enemy – a foe conceptualized in moral/theological terms – into political discourses in the US, UK and Eastern Europe, and argues that in all these contexts, 'the homosexual' has functioned as an ideological, as well as a political, enemy. New Labour's reaction to this functioning is also explored. D. Emily Hicks, in 'The Moral Bases of the Black Panther Party's Breakfast Program, Johnson's Head Start and Blair's Sure Start: A Critical comparison', offers a comparative analysis of three different programmes in support of children in two different contexts (US, UK), and identifies moral deficiencies in the UK's Sure Start programme. Most particularly, she is concerned to challenge the notion of the 'deserving' or 'responsible' poor with which Sure Start has, she argues, become associated, and she compares the UK programme unfavourably with the Black Panther's Breakfast Program. Arguing from a jurisprudential perspective in ' "Putting the responsible majority back in charge": New Labour's Punitive Politics of Respect', Phil Edwards argues that Blair's fusion of Hobbesian liberal absolutism and Macmurray's moral communitarianism results in a model of a society permeated by an intrusive moralism, underpinned by state coercion.

In the third part of the book, titled 'Justice and International Order', two chapters on New Labour's foreign policy are offered. In 'Tony Blair and the Commission for Africa: A Fig Leaf for Iraq or a Moral Imperative?', Paul Vallely argues, from the perspective of participant observation and drawing on 'private' papers, that Blair's engagement with Africa's plight reveals both his moral idealism and political pragmatism. For Inderjeet Parmar in 'Soul Brothers? Blair, Bush and the Compact between Liberal Interventionism and Conservative Nationalism', there are two different bases of Bush and Blair's foreign policies, and he shows how the convergence of these policies is not based on any personal relationship but on the convergence of 'conservative nationalism' (Bush) and 'liberal humanitarian interventionism' (Blair).

In a closing chapter, titled 'When Remoralizing Fails?', the volume's editors revisit the trajectory of the deployment of Blair's personal faith and its political resonances during his premiership, the contribution of New Labour to the vitality of civil society, and address the issue of moralizing a society that is religiously plural. In this fashion, the critical evaluation of the methodological and substantive issues raised by this moral reckoning of the performance of New Labour is brought to a close.

Acknowledgements

The material collected in this volume was first presented at the conference, 'Remoralizing Britain', held in May 2007 to mark the first ten years of the Blair's New Labour government. Tony Blair announced his intention to resign as Prime Minister shortly after the conference – although we are making no claim regarding cause and effect! The conference was held at the University of Manchester, and was a joint venture of the Lincoln Theological Institute, The Manchester Centre for Public Theology, the William Temple Foundation and the Manchester Research Institute for Religion and Civil Society. We are very grateful for financial support from the Subject Area of Religions and Theology and the School of Arts, Histories and Cultures, both at the University of Manchester. We thank the Trustees of the Lincoln Theological Institute for further financial support. In addition, we are glad to acknowledge a British Conference Grant (BCG-44908) from the British Academy. Without such financial support, it would not have been possible to host the conference.

We would like to thank the contributors for their hard work in reworking their conference presentations for publication, and extend our appreciation to Anthony Giddens for writing a preface at short notice. It has been good to work with Continuum Publishing on this project, and we would like to thank our editor Rebecca Vaughan-Williams for all her work and Tom Crick for his help during the production process. Finally, we thank the series editors, Michael Hoelzl and Graham Ward, for their support.

Notes

[1] Alastair Campbell, 2007, *The Blair Years* (London: Hutchinson), especially 'Book one: Preparing for power'.

[2] Reported by Campbell, *The Blair Years*, p. 719.

[3] Stuart Hampshire, *Justice is Conflict* (London: Duckworth, 1999), p. 38.

Chapter 1

Doing God? Public Theology under Blair

Elaine L. Graham

God and New Labour: A joke or an enigma?

One of the most enduring portrayals of Tony Blair during his premiership was that depicted in *Private Eye* magazine, of 'the Revd. A.R.P. Blair', vicar of 'St. Albion's Parish Church'. Its representation was of Tony the trendy vicar, full of cheerful sincerity, guitar at the ready, instructing his flock with worthy homilies on education or the Third Way or extolling the virtues of the ecumenical alliance with 'Revd Dubya Bush of the Church of the Latter-Day Morons'. The column derived its satirical effect from its readers' knowledge that Blair's Christian faith was a key part of what defined him as an individual and a politician; but it also demonstrates the sense in which it was one of the most definitive and yet enigmatic aspects of his political personality. Blair himself made no secret of his faith, especially during his time as Leader of the Opposition, as New Labour worked to articulate its distinctive vision; in later years, however, flanked by advisers reluctant to 'do God', he seemed more diffident about being drawn into explicit statements of belief or conviction.

Yet despite this common knowledge of Blair's Christian profession, few evaluations of the Blair years have devoted serious or sustained attention to this dimension, or move much beyond the comic or the speculative.[1] One exception was Anthony Seldon's political biography, *Blair*, which is organized around a series of chapters listing Blair's leading influences and protagonists, and dedicates one such chapter to 'God'.[2] Yet disappointingly Seldon's latest and long-awaited edited collection, surveying the impact of New Labour between 1997 and 2007, contains no references to religion, Christianity or the church and only one on 'Islam'.[3] This is a startling omission, but demonstrates, perhaps, that political commentators are by and large as unaccustomed to 'doing God' as some political spin-doctors.

Startling, then, but not surprising, given the generally secular nature of British public life at the beginning of the twenty-first century, and given that Blair's references to religion, God and moral values in public nevertheless take place in a country where active participation in organized religion and the currency of Christian discourse is one of the lowest in the Western world.

But the very incongruity of Blair's personal religious convictions in relation to the largely secular trajectory of British public life of itself justifies critical attention. The fact is, the relationship between God and New Labour is not restricted to the private devotions of one former leader since Blair's successor, Gordon Brown, has frequently alluded to the formative influence of his upbringing within the Church of Scotland, going so far as to quote words from the New Testament in his first party conference speech as leader.[4]

Any analysis of the relationship between faith and politics in the Blair years, therefore, cannot simply be restricted to the personal convictions of one person. Nor can they be dismissed as irrelevant vestiges of superstition in an age of reason, since their very public currency attests to their ability to speak across the barriers of religious decline and cultural diversity. Yet what exactly do they represent as forms of public intervention into British political culture? It is one of the contentions of this volume that this lack of critical, informed and non-partisan attention to one of the defining elements of New Labour over the past decade is to 'bracket out' a significant dimension of the influences at work in British public life over the past decade.

To ask how 'faith' has been assimilated into the New Labour project, therefore, and how that has been mobilized as part of a *moral* project, we must insist on that being a matter of public discourse and not just private dispositions. While the personal convictions of political leaders are intriguing, not least as weather vanes of wider public sensibilities – in terms of what *can* be professed in public, and in what terms – this is also an issue about the legitimacy of religious belief and practice in the public sphere. However, since the new visibility of religion goes against the grain of religion as conceived, culturally speaking, as something best kept private, so this chapter will examine the conventional wisdom that liberal democracy requires the maintenance of a neutral, secular, value-free public domain and the corresponding 'privatization' of religion, as well as indicating how the so-called secularization thesis has been displaced as the dominant narrative of modernity. I will also review some possible frameworks by which the reappearance of religion in public life might be evaluated.

On 'doing God'

New Labour's invocation of the language of morality has been a major defining characteristic of its political agenda. Much of its reinvention after 18 years in opposition was conceived in terms of a new moral vision at the heart of British politics: the task of 'remoralizing Britain'. The party represented itself as restoring moral rectitude to government through its ambitions for an ethical foreign policy; the championing of social inclusion and the merits of active citizenship; and promoting the virtues of education and self-improvement. Latterly, the 'war on terror' has assumed the status of a moral crusade in defence of Western democracy.[5] The government has also been anxious to mobilize faith-based organizations as part of the so-called third sector in projects of neigh-bourhood renewal and regeneration, and may have yet more ambitious plans in terms of deploying the resources of religious groups in the restructuring of the welfare state.[6]

This has manifested itself more recently as a search for a common language by which to articulate and construct concepts of national identity, the rights and responsibilities of citizenship and the roots of social cohesion. This seems set to continue under Gordon Brown with his talk of 'Britishness'. Anthony Giddens' Foreword to this volume indicates how much of public debate in the UK about multiculturalism lacks conceptual or practical precision, however.

Yet if the past decade has been about 'remoralizing Britain' then we need to identify the genesis of that agenda. It is possible that it needs to be located in the late 1970s rather than the 1990s. Politics not simply as governance or management but as moral crusade, intended to transform British culture and the hearts and minds of the electorate, did not begin with New Labour. The turn to faith and morality over the past decade followed an earlier trend of so-called conviction politics in the 1980s under Margaret Thatcher. Often attributed to a reaction to postwar 'Butskellite' political consensus, the Conservative administrations of the 1980s and early 1990s advocated not only a clear reformist manifesto but a distinctive moral vision. Much of that was directed towards reversing the tide of liberalism in matters of sexual behav-iour and personal morality associated with the 1960s. Nor was Mrs Thatcher averse to deploying moral and religious language in the pursuit of her pol-itical vision, from her misquoting of the prayer of St Francis on the day of her election to the so-called Sermon on the Mound, delivered in May 1988 to the Church of Scotland General Assembly at New College, Edinburgh.[7] Henry Clark's *Church under Thatcher*[8] – after which I have titled this chapter – shows how those years were in many respects a struggle over values, and how the churches, especially the Church of England, found themselves cast in the role of unofficial opposition to the government when many other institutions of civil society were weakened.

The election of John Smith as leader of the Labour Party in 1992 ushered in a new era of a more explicitly values-based politics. It saw the introduc-tion of appeals to a legacy of 'ethical socialism' (with R. H. Tawney the most frequently invoked) with the reconstruction of New Labour after nearly two decades in opposition, and the need to rejuvenate core policy away from the extremes of welfare centralism or free market individualism.[9] The revival of the Labour Party after two decades of opposition was achieved partly through a rejuvenation of core principles, most particularly the relationship between the state and the individual and the renewal of the precepts of democratic socialism. And for Smith, and those around him, those values were those of

Christian socialism, and were articulated in a series of lectures and publications over the next few years of Labour's period of opposition, which extended beyond Smith's death in 1994 and the accession of Blair to party leader.

While Tony Blair was not alone in articulating the foundations of his political convictions in terms of religious values – and specifically a form of Christian socialism – he was one of the most articulate and prominent bearers of a new moral discourse within the Labour Party's process of reorientation in the early 1990s. Writing a Foreword to a collection of sermons and speeches by leading Labour politicians and published by the Christian Socialist Movement, Blair argued for the reconsideration of the party's core values in these terms:

> By rethinking and re-examining our values, and placing them alongside those of the Christian faith, we are able, politically, to rediscover the essence of our beliefs which lies not in policies or prescriptions made for one period of time, but in principles of living that are timeless. By doing so, we can better distinguish between values themselves and their application, the one constant and unchanged, the other changing constantly. To a Labour Party now undertaking a thorough and necessary analysis of our future, this is helpful.[10]

The appropriation of the moral vocabulary of Christian socialism may have been due to a combination of internal and external factors: a search for less politically fractious political principles as a way of renewing Labour's wider electoral appeal; a bid to be regarded as the party of moral probity against the Conservatives' growing reputation for 'sleaze'; and the retrieval of the heritage of ethical socialism as alternative to dogmatic State centralism. It was about articulating alternatives to individual morality and emphasis on personal freedom (Thatcher) in favour of the recovery of the language of 'common good' as the language of empowerment of grass-roots citizenry.

At the same time, religion was assuming a new visibility in public life in the UK. Throughout the twentieth century, the role of religion or questions of Church and state had steadily diminished as matters of political significance, and it did appear as if religious controversy was diminishing as grounds for public debate. Yet this began to change in the UK with the so-called Rushdie affair of 1989, in which British Muslim groups took to the streets in protest at the publication of what they regarded as scurrilous misrepresentations of Islam in the book *The Satanic Verses*. The emergence of such a concerted and politicized Islamic movement onto the political scene exposed dramatically the fault-line in classical liberal opinion between support for freedom of expression and toleration of cultural diversity. Since then, and since 9/11, there has been a modest but significant proliferation of cases involving religious groups clashing with mainstream liberal public opinion: Sikh protests against the play *Behzti*, which was critical of abuses of power in a gurdwara; the well-orchestrated campaigns of the group Christian Voice against the screening on national television of *Jerry Springer: The Opera*; attempts by Roman Catholic Bishops to influence legislation on same-sex parents' adoption entitlement; mobilization of conservative Christian groups to reform the abortion laws, and so on.

This is not to suggest that Britain is experiencing a religious revival. The continuing decline in institutional Christianity throughout Europe and certainly in the UK is undeniable, although much current debate in the sociology of religion is focused on the extent to which religion endures as a vestigial but influential cultural force through disaffiliated forms of religious practices and new spiritualities,[11] and how decline is tempered by the growth of British Islam and the vitality of some minority Christian groups due to the presence of migrants from Africa, the Caribbean and Eastern Europe.

So at a number of levels, we have been witnessing contradictory trends. There is a new prominence of matters of faith within the public sphere, not just in the rhetoric of individual politicians and the processes of government policy, but as religion influences aspects of law, economics, welfare and citizenship. On the other hand, however, despite the continued existence of national established churches in England and Scotland, the nature of British public debate has tended to fight shy of 'doing God' in public, a diffidence which extends throughout the political culture.

On *not* doing God

By his second term, Blair's earlier willingness to discuss his faith appeared to give way to a greater ambivalence about religion. Possibly he was bruised by his association with George W. Bush and jibes about them praying together; or perhaps he was reluctant to be identified with religion in the face of what might be termed the 'new secularism' among sections of the intelligentsia such as Richard Dawkins, Polly Toynbee or Christopher Hitchens.

For example, in the spring of 2003, when the allies were preparing to invade Iraq, some sections of the British media claimed that those close to Tony Blair had advised him not to end a televised address by saying, 'God bless you' on the basis that viewers would be alienated by its explicitly religious nature. Instead, he closed with the words, 'thank you'.[12] Similarly, Alistair Campbell is famously reported to have intervened in an interview to prevent Blair answering a question about his religious beliefs, allegedly with the comment, 'We don't do God'.[13] We might also think of the media attention occasioned by Tony Blair's remark that God would, ultimately, judge his decision to go to war with Iraq, when he appeared on the talk show *Parkinson* in March 2006.[14] And most recently, interviewed for a BBC TV series of retrospectives on his ten years in power, Blair offered the opinion that: 'you talk about [religion] in our system, and frankly, people think you're a nutter'.[15] This seems to be confirmation that while in office Blair walked what Callum Brown calls 'a political and cultural tightrope'[16] between an openness about his personal convictions and a reticence to expose his beliefs to public scrutiny for fear of misunderstanding or ridicule.[17]

Such diffidence about mixing religion and politics appears to have spread to some religious leaders. When challenged in an interview in the *Guardian* newspaper early in 2006 on his relative silence on moral questions, the Archbishop of Canterbury, Rowan Williams, questioned the assumption (often prevalent in sections of the conservative media), that it was the duty of religious leaders to provide moral leadership to the nation by making regular public pronouncements.[18] Yet part of Williams' argument against this was that this only added further fuel to public stereotypes of him as 'comic vicar to the nation'.[19] Clearly, the spire of St Albion's casts a long shadow. Yet Williams also expressed considerable scepticism towards the Church's ability to command automatic moral authority among the public at large:

> 'I think there is a bit of a myth, if you like, that Religious Leaders – "capital R capital L" – are, by their nature, people who make public pronouncements on morals.' Williams parodies this position as, 'Why doesn't the archbishop condemn X, Y, Z?' Because that's what archbishops do, you know, they condemn things. They make statements, usually negative, condemnatory statements. . . .
>
> I just wonder a bit whether, you know, when an archbishop condemns something, suddenly in, I don't know, the bedsits of north London, somebody says, 'Oh, I shouldn't be having premarital sex', or in the cells of al-Qaida, somebody says, 'Goodness, terrorism's wrong, the archbishop says so. I never thought of that.' I'm not sure that's how it is.[20]

Williams is caught between a rock and a hard place. Conservatives and traditionalists expect him to 'speak out' authoritatively; but in a society which is functionally secular, the majority of people regard religion 'as a very alien, very mysterious, rather malign force, which gives people ideas above their station'.[21] Even for the Established Church to speak into such a vacuum requires delicate negotiation, since any pronouncement could be mistaken as an attempt to colonize or monopolize the democratic process or to displace a rational, open field of discourse with an irrational and closed value-system. Williams' sensitivities seem consistent with a general perception of the marginalization of organized religion in Western culture, therefore, and the impossibility, or even desirability, of even religious leaders doing God, at least in public.

Indeed, many would argue that while Blair's 'shy and tangential'[22] professions of faith or Williams' self-consciousness may be due in part to a sense of the public relations aspect of 'doing God', attempts to offer religious reasoning to public debate are illegitimate since they breach basic principles of liberal democracy, which hold that religion and politics cannot mix. It is to this debate that I shall turn next.

Religion, secularism and modernity

It is a commonly held maxim of political liberalism that public debate should be underpinned by secular rather than religious principles. In some political settlements, such as the US, for example, this has meant the constitutional separation of Church and State. The classical position on this matter is expressed by the political philosopher Robert Audi when he argues that while in a healthy democracy the good citizen should 'try to contribute in some way to the welfare of others',[23] in a culturally or religiously diverse society this will require any policy to be founded on principles available to all citizens, regardless of their personal convictions: 'the ethics appropriate to a liberal democracy constrains religious considerations . . . because of its commitment to preserving the liberty of all'.[24] Even if political or policy debate concerns matters of ethical and moral significance – such as abortion, stem-cell research, euthanasia, civil partnerships, even going to war – no publicly stated political discourse should rest on principles that are only accessible to a partial section of the community.

Yet increasingly, such a separation is coming into question, on empirical as well as philosophical grounds. For a start, questions are raised about the self-sufficiency of the secular to furnish the public domain with sufficiently robust values for consensus. In what has been termed the 'Böckenförde dilemma', named after German Supreme Court Justice Ernst-Wolfgang Böckenförde, it is stated thus: 'The liberal secular state lives from sources it cannot guarantee itself.'[25] In other words, something which claims to be value-free in itself cannot summon the necessary basis for diverse communities and institutions to articulate a commitment to broad-based participation.

An alternative view argues that only if citizens, each from their own deep convictions, and on the basis of an overlapping consensus on basic human rights, engage in public debate on the basis of a more humane society, will a vibrant civil society and a healthy democratic process be fostered. In response to Robert Audi's perspective, therefore, Nicholas Wolterstorff questions whether the freedom of the citizen in a liberal democracy necessarily has to involve the effacement of religious reasons in public debate.[26] He argues against their 'bracketing out' since he believes that to require religious constraint of others amounts to a restriction upon their freedoms and civil liberties as equal citizens. Wolterstorff continues, 'I see no reason to suppose that the ethic of the citizen in a liberal democracy includes a restraint on the use of religious reasons in deciding and discussing political issues.'[27] In addition, it would be unrealistic for those with religious principles to leave them out of the picture, since 'there is no prospect whatsoever . . . of all adherents of particular religions refraining from using the resources of their own religion in making political decisions'.[28] If religious persons have religious reasons, it would be impossible not to include these, since 'we cannot leap out of our perspectives'.[29] There are no grounds for believing that a policy or piece of legislation will carry greater support on the grounds that religious reasons have been left out of the debate.[30]

Such a segregation of religion and politics represents a 'strong' form of secularism in which all partisan values and principles, especially theologically derived, are to be insulated from the public domain. Arguably, however, such a distinction could actually militate against any kind of public transparency. Neither secular states nor secularist public rhetoric are necessarily a protection against religiously motivated politics – quite the opposite, in fact – if a residue or minority of religious parties takes on a mission of actively shaping political or civic agenda.

Historically speaking, it may not even be a particularly accurate representation of the emergence of Western modernity and resulting settlements over the separation of Church and State. Stephen Toulmin argues that there never was such a polarization between 'secular humanism' and 'Christian orthodoxy': many of the early modern scientists and political theorists were devout believers, and the introduction of principles of free speech and tolerance were never intended to exclude religious reasoning from public debate.[31] An Enlightenment critique of religious authoritarianism and the compulsory conjunction of Church and State – and thus the enforcement of mandatory religious affiliation – should not be confused with the total redundancy of all religion. As Jose Casanova argues, 'secularization' in that respect was about the 'emancipation' of the secular from the religious, but willed as much in the name of religious freedom as the wish to see the end of all religion.[32]

What we need is an analysis that enables the coexistence of the facts of religious decline with the public visibility of religion in its many guises. Casanova has been critical of those versions of secularization theory which conceive the process of secularization as the inevitable and inexorable disappearance of religious beliefs and practices in the modern world. He questions such versions of the secularization thesis on both normative and empirical grounds, arguing that they simply perpetuate 'a myth that sees history as the progressive evolution of humanity from superstition to reason, from belief to unbelief, from religion to science.' This mythical account of secularization, says Casanova is itself in need of 'desacralization'.[33]

For purposes of greater clarity, Casanova has therefore identified what he regards as three main dimensions of the phenomenon of secularization: first, the decline of religious institutions, secondly, the separation of religion and the State or differentiation of religious and secular organizations and, thirdly, the 'privatization' of religion. These are largely independent variables, so it would be possible to see each of these features taking a different course in any particular society. Thus, it could be argued that in Britain, a model may be emerging of partial secularization in terms of decline and differentiation, but not of 'privatization' – indeed, that given the trends outlined above it may be necessary to speak of the 'deprivatization of modern religion'.[34] It also means that the best way of conceiving society – and therefore the nature of public discourse – might be certainly 'post-Christian' in that the authority of the Church and Christian culture are no longer predominant, but also 'post-secular' in that religious pluralism and the persistence of various kinds of practice and affiliation endure not simply as private options but as public realities.

The end result of this would be a society in which there was a divergence between a religiously indifferent (but not necessarily hostile or secularist) majority, and a series of religiously orientated minority groups. The latter would represent a wide range of opinion, from broadly supportive of the liberal pluralist agenda to those who strategically campaigned against specific pieces of legislation or cultural mores – such as abortion, blasphemy laws or civil partnerships – to those who were more virulently opposed to Enlightenment liberal values.

The deficiencies of much of the dominant drift of social scientific analyses of religion may however call for new tools and conceptual frameworks by which to examine phenomena such as New Labour's use of religious and moral discourse. Without departing from his central thesis of the irrevocable secularity of British society, the historian Callum Brown has called for a renewal of theoretical and empirical tools by which to evaluate the cultural and political currency of religion, not least because instances of exceptionalism or resistance to such a trend are of sufficient significance to occasion reappraisal of some of the established methods of analysis.[35]

> But one major thing needed is a workable narrative with which to tell the story of religion in the wider context of culture, politics and society. A new world order has been invoked in which, like it or not, religion is being restored after a long gap as a defining category of analysis. Having written religion out, it is not necessarily going to prove easy to reinsert it.[36]

This moves us on, therefore, to consider what theoretical and analytical perspectives may be available to scholars and commentators in trying to gain critical purchase on the resurgence of religion in the public domain.

Doing God in public: An agenda for debate

We are looking, therefore, for explanatory theories that enable that 'gap' to be rectified – the gap being, in Callum Brown's terms, the absence of religion from public debate and social analysis. It might require elements of discernment over the exercise of some degree of public accountability, such as when religious groups are in receipt of public funding; a measure of understanding from the inside what motivates religious groups and individuals; a means of critiquing, from a theologically informed vantage-point, how religious rhetoric is functioning in the public statements of political leaders.

What follows is a brief review of some possible perspectives.

1. Reconfiguring the public and the private

As we have seen, the demand that citizens in a liberal democracy must only use secular arguments in public discussion was contingent upon a particular configuration of modernity in the West. But strategically, the further danger is that such an insulation of public from private inhibits the extent to which any critical or rational scrutiny can be exercised over the activities of religious groups. It attenuates our capacity to examine the religious and theological foundations of public policy or political discourse. Intriguingly, of course, whereas the roots of such privatization of religion may have been motivated by a wish to protect religious minorities against a dominant majority which also defined itself theologically or ecclesiastically, the contemporary position in the West is to protect the rights of a non-affiliated majority against perceived breaching of a liberal consensus on the part of religious minorities. That may also require us to revisit the question of how the neutral or non-confessional public sphere is regulated.

Greater clarity on this dilemma may be brought if we distinguish between two different types of secularism. Sunder Katwala contrasts 'ideological' secularism with 'pragmatic' secularism which values the rights of all citizens but refuses to discriminate on the grounds of religion, just as it seeks to respect diversity of gender, sexuality and ethnicity.[37] This means it must respect the prerogative of religious participants to advance religious views in public. Rowan Williams has recently made a similar distinction between what he terms 'programmatic' and 'procedural' secularism. While programmatic secularism suspends any talk of value in a semblance of instrumental neutrality, procedural secularism engages with but attempts to adjudicate between, competing convictions:

> It is the distinction between the empty public square of a merely instrumental liberalism, which allows maximal private licence, and a crowded and argumentative public square which acknowledges the authority of a legal mediator or broker whose job it is to balance and manage real difference. The empty public square of programmatic secularism implies in effect that the almost value-free atmosphere of public neutrality and the public invisibility of specific commitments is enough to provide sustainable moral energy for a properly self-critical society. But it is not at all self-evident that people can so readily detach their perspectives and policies in social or political discussion from fundamental convictions that are not allowed to be mentioned or manifested in public.[38]

Similarly, Jose Casanova argues for the persistence of religiously motivated influences in the public sphere, and endorses the continuity of faith-based organizations' contribution to public life, so long as they are capable of acknowledging the pluralist nature of society. *If* religions react constructively to differentiation, *if* they do not work against the modern individual freedoms – Casanova argues – they can become legitimate public voices.

Although it takes us beyond the scope of this volume, this is an important implication of the recovery of religious dimensions to political life. It is all very well for religious groups to bring their convictions into the debate, but this implies that they already accept the terms of pluralist and public discourse as an appropriate ethic. However, the eruption of some countercultural religious groups has been on the basis of refusing to recognize such a compromise. But the problem is when some faith groups expect to enter the *political* arena to state *public* claims on the basis of *private* commitments.[39] I wonder, therefore, whether it is possible to move towards a consensus that is capable of differentiating between these three categories, respecting that what is contained within them requires translation into a common civil discourse that is not so much 'neutral' as 'mediated'.

2. Faith as public praxis

So far, we have concentrated on the public pronouncements of public figures and religious leaders, but we should not neglect a major area in which the moral and religious dimensions of public life are already active. This concerns the practical interventions of faith-based organizations, as part of local and national civil society. Faith-based organizations continue to exercise a significant influence in public life as political interest groups, as providers of social welfare, education and community services and they are increasingly being invited to consider themselves as an active and essential part of the 'third sector' of community and voluntary organizations and encouraged to participate in projects of welfare provision, neighbourhood regeneration, education and other forms of service delivery.[40]

> The 'third sector' comprises non-governmental organisations which are value-driven and which principally reinvest their surpluses to further social, environmental or cultural objectives. It includes voluntary and community organisations, charities, social enterprises, cooperatives and mutuals. Faith groups also play a very important role. The third sector is large and growing, and plays an increasingly vital role in both society and economy.[41]

In terms of New Labour's ambitions for welfare reform, faith-based organizations are regarded as rich in social capital, embodying the virtues of localism, altruism and community spirit. Indirectly, therefore, rather than fracturing the body politic, faith-based organizations are viewed as one means of enhancing social cohesion, and it is another contributory factor to the 'new visibility' of religion – with a distinctively local, practice-based flavour.[42]

Others sound notes of caution or criticism, however. First, of course, is the view already debated that religion has no legitimate place in the public domain, and certainly not in the delivery of essential welfare services. The assumption that faith is a reasonable and liberal set of values which engenders good citizenship and social cohesion is repudiated. The Cantle report on urban riots in Northern English cities in 2001, for example, spoke of communities living parallel but separate lives, of religion as a divisive rather than cohesive force. And of course any faith-group or interest group may be very effective at delivering services to its own constituency – in what would be termed 'bonding' social capital – while being indifferent to extending beyond its own boundaries.

Further studies of how faith-based organizations actually negotiate questions of public funding and accountability, therefore, might reveal more information on how the particular values of a religious tradition are mediated into the public domain in practice. Are there common values around neighbourhood renewal, social welfare, protection of the vulnerable, or local capacity-building which might form the 'pragmatic' basis of a shared *praxis* of realizing the common good?

3. Fostering 'religious literacy' in public life

One person who has spoken of the need for new sensibilities for public discourse in a 'post-secular' society is Jürgen Habermas, most famously in his acceptance speech for the German peace prize in 2001.[43] This followed on from a short monograph on bioethics in which he considered the contribution of religious values to concepts of human dignity.[44] He appears to be developing a new interest in the possibility of those who combine faith and reason to have some measure of contribution to make on matters of value. This joins with the voices of Williams, Casanova, Katwala and others, surveyed above, who conceive of a 'pragmatic' secularism which avoids privileging either religious or secular perspective, but seeks to engage them in shared debate in a conversational or communicative process. Such a model of debate seeks to 'honour the important public role of religion as a nurturer of reason and moral formation, while at the same time maintaining the religious impartiality of the state necessary for a pluralistic democracy.'[45]

Yet arguably we still need more concerted attention to the actual workings of religious discourse in shaping the moral and political outlooks of varied protagonists in the public domain. Here, the work of the British practical theologian Stephen Pattison may be helpful. Pattison is concerned with the relationship between ethics and organizations, and the search to develop a critical theory of corporate values. He is interested in the way 'secular' discourses and organizations bear many of the characteristics and functions of religion; not necessarily in terms of formal systems of moral guidelines, but in the form of the narratives, secular rituals or goals to which an organization subscribes and which constitute its corporate identity.[46] This seeks to offer a degree of 'religious literacy' to the public domain, by examining the theological roots of appeals to public and corporate values and subjecting them to critical scrutiny. Pattison's aim is to equip people 'as critical "theologians" of their own inhabited worldviews . . . to become critics of their faith positions'.[47]

Pattison argues that all organizational cultures carry appeals to more than just instrumental or pragmatic reasoning. He argues that this is not just of sectarian concern to those formally attached to religious bodies, but for all those involved in forging and implementing policy and service delivery. Theology has the capacity to identify, analyze and challenge the 'myths' by which people live; yet also it contends that the stories and symbols circulating throughout our public and institutional life are essential elements of culture, even though they may be deluded or life-affirming. 'Rather than live without faith and beliefs of any kind', says Pattison, 'the point is for us to recognize and critically assess our inhabited systems of faith, our beliefs, and our rituals.'[48]

This approach could be harnessed as a critical tool to systematize people's implicit value-commitments, as embodied in their managerial and organizational practices, thereby making explicit the relationship between the values people hold and the behaviours they engage in. In this respect, he stands in a longer tradition of those who seek to excavate the implicitly religious values at work in secular institutions and conventions, such as Max Weber or Paul Halmos.[49]

I wonder whether such a critical perspective might be put to work not only in relation to corporate institutions' 'mission statements' but the public pronouncements of political leaders like Tony Blair. To end, therefore, I have selected recent public statements by two rising politicians who have a personal Christian commitment yet are mindful of how best to reconcile openness about their own political and moral motivations with sensitivity towards a pluralist public realm.

Kevin Rudd, elected Prime Minister of Australia in November 2007, went against the grain of predominantly secularist public debate in that country[50] when still leader of the opposition in 2006, by writing about the connections between faith and politics. This was more than a personal confession of faith, however, being quite overtly party-political in criticizing what Rudd called 'the political orchestration of various forms of organized Christianity in support of the conservative incumbency' on the part of George W. Bush in the US and John Howard in his own country.[51] Rather than bolstering the interests of the powerful within a conservative programme that stresses family values and personal morality at the expense of social justice, Rudd argues that the instincts of Christianity are prophetic and countercultural. He regards Dietrich Bonhoeffer as a potential role model for those seeking an alternative model of political engagement, and hints that in a secular pluralist world Christianity may move more towards 'a counterculture operating within what some have called a post-Christian world'.[52]

This is not a bland homily. Rudd is invoking theology to deliver a sustained attack on his rival, John Howard, but his argument is developed via a detailed engagement with Bonhoeffer's political theology of speaking truth to power and the Biblical principle of the preferential option for the poor. Yet one of the linchpins of Rudd's attack on Howard is the latter's attempt to construct a discourse of Australian national identity premised on a 'clash of civilizations' which Rudd regards as implicitly anti-Islamic.[53]

> A Christian perspective on contemporary policy debates may not prevail. It must nonetheless be argued. And once heard, it must be weighed, together with other arguments from different philosophical traditions, in a fully contestable secular polity. A Christian perspective, informed by a social gospel or Christian socialist tradition, should not be rejected contemptuously by secular politicians as if these views are an unwelcome intrusion into the political sphere. If the churches are barred from participating in the great debates about the values that ultimately underpin our society, our economy and our polity, then we have reached a very strange place indeed.[54]

When Barack Obama, at the start of his presidential campaign, was asked what he had been reading recently in an interview with *The New York Times*, he quoted the unlikely choice of the liberal Protestant public theologian and ethicist Reinhold Niebuhr. While public discourse and political campaigning in the US – especially for President – is altogether more comfortable with public professions of faith than Australia or the UK, the Democrats have struggled in the past to capture the religious vote and have fought shy of campaigning on 'Christian moral values'. Yet here is a politician whose political roots are in church-related broad-based organizing in Chicago, and who has been a member of Trinity United Church of Christ. It is of course possible that he knew the question was coming in advance of the interview, but it is still significant that he chooses to indicate an interest in the moral legacy of twentieth-century Christian Realism for contemporary international politics. When asked what he takes away from his reading of Niebuhr, Obama's answer is once again superficially measured but is of course directed against his political opponents both within and beyond his own party, with particular censure aimed at those who allow an excessively doctrinaire world-view to inform their political decisions:

> I take away . . . the compelling idea that there's serious evil in the world, and hardship and pain. And we should be humble and modest in our belief we can eliminate those things. But we shouldn't use that as an excuse for cynicism and inaction. I take away the sense we have to make these efforts knowing they are hard, and not swinging from naïve idealism to bitter realism.[55]

Both are examples, I contend, of deliberate attempts to communicate across gulfs of religious and moral pluralism into a shared public discourse in ways which manage both to respect the pluralism of their intended audience without selling short these politicians' integrity. In neither case, either, did the theological sources diminish the sharply political intentions of such statements!

Conclusion

One characteristic of British society over the past decade has been how controversial and sensitive the reintroduction of religion into public life has become, whether that is measured in terms of the personal values of a new generation of conviction politicians, the pronouncements on current affairs by established faith leaders, or the political mobilization by particular religious bodies in order to influence public opinion.

Within all this, once again, is the vexed question of what legitimacy religion and religious identity should play within any such debate. It is no longer about the primacy of one, Established, Christian tradition as definitive of national identity and the moral basis of something called 'the common good', and nor is it any longer a matter of evacuating matters of religious belief and affiliation from public life and civil society altogether. It is, perhaps, a matter of articulating a new settlement within a population that comprises a majority of people largely indifferent but not hostile to organized religion, alongside a small but increasingly self-conscious and well-mobilized minority made up of a heterogeneity of religious groups.

I stated at the beginning of this chapter that it wasn't about Tony Blair, and in one sense it isn't. But in other ways, of course it *is*. Of *course* it is, given our fascination with political figures and celebrities. On one hand, with Blair's departure – which this conference was called to mark – we are seeing the end of an era, where the enduring significance of one man's personal values will be subjected to the hindsight of posterity. On the other, however, it is also undeniable that religion and morality have featured significantly as part of the 'soul' of New Labour, and so further interrogation is necessary in order to gain a better sense of the coherence of such values and the reasons for their deployment, and as a case-study of what legitimacy there may be in 'doing God' in public. This volume seeks to encourage these debates.

Notes

[1] The latest in this latter category being the revival at the end of 2007 of the persistent rumours predicting Blair's imminent admission into the Roman Catholic Church. See *Times, Guardian*, 9 Nov. 2007. When news of his eventual

confirmation just before Christmas 2007 was announced it was hardly unexpected, therefore, despite media attempts to portray it otherwise.

2 London, Free Press, 2004, pp. 515–32. See also Chapman, Mark (2005), *Blair's Britain*. London: Darton, Longman and Todd, which offers a critique of New Labour's appropriation of moral and religious discourse from a theological, and specifically a Christian socialist, perspective.

3 Seldon, Anthony, ed. (2007), *Blair's Britain 1997–2007*. Cambridge: Cambridge University Press.

4 Brown, Gordon (2007), *Courage: Eight Portraits*. London: Bloomsbury; Wintour, Patrick (2007), 'I will not let Britain down', *Guardian* (25 September), online, www.guardian.co.uk/frontpage/story/0,,2176532,00.html [accessed 30 Sept. 2007]. For a perspective challenging the connection between Brown's political convictions and religion, however, see Doug Gay, this volume.

5 See this volume, Chapters 3 and 13.

6 During 2007 no fewer than three government departments – the Treasury, the Department of Work and Pensions and the Department of Communities and Local Government – have published reports on the role of the 'third sector' in the delivery of welfare provision, social services and economic and social regeneration. See Blitz, James and Hall, Ben (2007), Brown to press on with welfare reforms. *Financial Times* (2 March) online, www.ft.com/cms/s/2ac75c26-c863-11db-9a5e-000b5df10621.html [accessed 27 June 2007].

7 Raban, Jonathan (1989), *God, Man and Mrs. Thatcher*. London: Chatto Counterblasts No. 1.

8 Clark, Henry (1993), *The Church under Thatcher*. London: SPCK.

9 Ormrod, David, ed. (1990), *Fellowship, Freedom and Equality*. London: Christian Socialist Movement; Bryant, Chris, ed. (1993), *Reclaiming the Ground: Christianity and Socialism*. London: Hodder & Stoughton; Haslam, David and Dale, Graham, eds (2001), *Faith in Politics*. London: Christian Socialist Movement.

10 Blair, Tony (1993), Foreword. In *Reclaiming the Ground: Christianity and Socialism*, ed. Chris Bryant, London: Spire, pp. 9–12, p. 11.

11 Garnett, J., Grimley, M., Harris, A., Whyte, W., and Williams, S., eds (2006), *Redefining Christian Britain: Post 1945 Perspectives*. London: SCM Press.

12 Brown, Colin (2003), *Daily Telegraph* (4 May) online, www.telegraph.co.uk/news/main/jhtml?xml=news/2003/05/04/nblair04.xml [accessed 11 May 2007].

13 Ibid.

14 White, Michael (2006), 'God will judge me, PM tells Parkinson', *Guardian* (4 March), online, www.guardian.co.uk/frontpage/story/0,,1723164,00.html [accessed 11 May 2007]. When Parkinson asked Blair, 'Does [religion] still inform your view of politics and of the world?' Blair replied, 'Well I think if you have a religious belief it does, but it's probably best not to take it too far.' Later, when Parkinson said, 'So you pray to God when you make a decision like that?' Blair countered with, 'Well, you know, I don't want to go into sermons . . .' Brown, Callum (2006), ' "Best not to take it too far": how the British cut religion down to size.' *Opendemocracy.net* (8 March), online, www.opendemocracy.net/xhtml/articles/3335.html [accessed 11 May 2007], p. 1.

15 BBC Television (2007), *The Blair Years*, 2 December.

16 Brown, 'Best not to take it too far', p. 2.

17 Ibid.
18 Rusbridger, Alan (2006), 'I am comic vicar to the nation', *Guardian*, 21 March. In fact, Williams has spoken on a number of matters, including the nature of childhood in a consumerist society, the future of legislation on abortion and the morality of the invasion of Iraq.
19 Ibid.
20 Ibid.
21 Ibid.
22 Brown, 'Best not to take it too far', p. 1.
23 Audi, Robert and Wolterstorff, Nicholas (1997), *Religion in the Public Square: Debating Church and State.* Lanham: Rowman and Littlefield, p. 16.
24 Ibid. p. 174.
25 'Der freiheitliche, säkularisierte Staat lebt von Voraussetzungen, die er selbst nicht garantieren kann.' (Böckenförde, Ernst-Wolfgang (1967), *Säkularisation und Utopie.* Ebracher Studien. Ernst Forsthoff zum 65. Geburtstag, Stuttgart, p. 93.)
26 Audi and Wolterstorff, *Religion in the Public Square*, pp. 111–12.
27 Ibid.
28 Ibid. pp. 11–12.
29 Ibid. p. 113.
30 Ibid. p. 3.
31 Toulmin, Stephen (1990), *Cosmopolis: The Hidden Agenda of Modernity.* Chicago: University of Chicago Press, pp. 24–5.
32 Casanova, José (2006), 'Rethinking secularization: a global comparative perspective'. *The Hedgehog Review* Spring/Summer, 7–22.
33 Casanova, José (1994), *Public Religions in the Modern World.* Chicago: University of Chicago Press, p. 17.
34 Ibid. p. 215.
35 See also Brown, Callum (2007), 'Secularization, the growth of militancy and the spiritual revolution: religious change and gender power in Britain, 1901–2001', *Historical Research*, 80, no. 209, 393–418.
36 Ibid. p. 394.
37 Katwala, Sunder (2006), 'Faith in democracy: the legitimate role of religion'. *Public Policy Research*, December–February, 246–251.
38 Ibid.
39 See Neuhaus, Richard (1984), *The Naked Public Square: Religion and Democracy in America.* Grand Rapids, MI: Wm. B. Eerdmans, p. 36.
40 Farnell, Richard et al. (2003), *'Faith' in Urban Regeneration: Engaging Faith Communities in Urban Regeneration.* Bristol: Polity Press; Timmins, Nicholas (2007), ' "Bigger Role" for private sector in welfare-to-work.' *Financial Times* (14 February), online, www.ft.com/cms/s/8bf51726-bbd0-11db-afe4-0000779e2340.html [accessed 27 June 2007].
41 www.hm-treasury.gov.uk/documents/public_spending_reporting/charity_third_sector.html [accessed 14 June 2007].
42 Farnell, Richard et al., *'Faith' in Urban Regeneration?*; Furbey, Rob (1999), 'Urban "regeneration": reflections on a metaphor', *Critical Social Policy*, 19, no. 4, 419–45.

[43] Habermas, Jürgen (2001), *Glauben und Wissen*. Frankfurt am Main: Suhrkamp. See also Harrington, Austen (2007), 'Habermas' Theological Turn?' *Journal for the Theory of Social Behaviour*, 37, no. 1, 45–61.

[44] Habermas, Jürgen (2003), *The Future of Human Nature*. Cambridge: Polity Press.

[45] Bedford-Strohm, Heinrich (2007), 'Nurturing reason: the public role of religion in the liberal state'. *Ned Geref Teologiese Tydskrif*, 48, nos 1 and 2, March–June, 25–41, p. 35.

[46] See especially, *The Challenge of Practical Theology* (London: Jessica Kingsley, 2007), Part 1: Ethics and Values and Part 2: On Organization and Management.

[47] Ibid. p. 69.

[48] Ibid. p. 80.

[49] See Pattison, S. (1997), *The Faith of the Managers: When Management Becomes Religion*. London: Cassell; Halmos, P. (1965), *The Faith of the Counsellors*. London: Constable.

[50] See Maddox, Marion (2007), 'Religion, secularism and the promise of public theology. *International Journal of Public Theology*, 1, no. 1, 82–100.

[51] Rudd, Kevin (2006), 'Faith in politics'. *The Monthly* (October) online, www.themonthly.com.au/excerpts/issue17_excerpt_001.html, p. 5 [accessed 12 June 2007].

[52] Rudd, 'Faith in politics', p. 3.

[53] Ibid. p. 10.

[54] Ibid. p. 7.

[55] Brooks, David (2007), 'Obama, gospel and verse'. *The New York Times* (26 April), online, http://select.nytimes.com/search/restricted/article?res=FA0810FD3E5 A0C758EDDA [accessed 12 June 2007].

Part I

Ethics and Politics

Chapter 2

Let Citizens without Sin Cast the First Stone: Judging the Moral Failings of Blair and Politics*

Gerry Stoker

Introduction

There has been for some time a ready market for the idea that all politicians lie and that none are to be trusted. As Colin Hay puts it, politics in today's understanding is 'synonymous with sleaze, corruption, and duplicity, greed, self-interest and self-importance, interference, inefficiency and intransigence. It is, at best, a necessary evil, at worst an entirely malevolent force that needs to be kept in check.'[1] Popular political culture is deeply anti-politics and politicians. People do not trust politicians in the UK.

Tony Blair when elected as Prime Minister, for a few months, floated above our dominant understanding of politicians but was soon drawn back into our default negative understanding of politics and its practitioners. A YouGov opinion poll in April 2007 provided a damning judgement on ten years of New Labour in government. When asked if Blair had cleaned up politics, as he promised, ten years on eight out of ten of us were clear that he has not. When asked if he could be trusted only two out of ten agreed. As Professor Tony King, writing about the poll, puts it: 'A decade ago Tony Blair was a political genius, a man who could walk on water. Now a large majority of voters dismiss him as just another politician: ineffectual, untrustworthy and out of touch.'[2] The story of the rise and fall of a political leader is hardly a unique piece of history but what is particularly noteworthy about Tony Blair's downfall is the way it has been framed in terms of a morality tale. It is Blair's moral failings that are seen as at the heart of his fall from grace. And I use the phrase 'fall from grace' deliberately because in the language of his critics Tony Blair is a sinner.

At the end of his premiership Blair found himself condemned for his moral failings not only by enemies but also by friends, as well as official watchdogs.

* This chapter was written with the support of an ESRC professorial fellowship RES-051027–0067.

Right-wingers such as Peter Oborne, a *Daily Mail* journalist, displayed an intense moral outrage. In his book *The Rise of Political Lying*, Oborne spends many pages exposing the lying and sleaze of New Labour and concludes that 'in recent years mendacity and deception have ceased to be abnormal and become an entrenched feature of the British system' and as a result: 'Britain now lives in a post-truth environment.'[3] But even the generally friendlier Mary Ann Sieghart writing in *The Times* in an otherwise reasonably favourable review of the Blair years comments:

> For me, Blair's worst sin has been to make the entire political class seem deceitful, and so erode people's trust in politics. After . . . a habitual economy with the truth, voters began to believe that 'they're all the same'. From there it is but a short step to political disengagement. This should not have happened. It is entirely Blair's fault that it did.[4]

The assault on Blair's political style can be rounded off with words from Britain's official watchdog on political ethics. According to Sir Alistair Graham, the former Chairman of the Committee on Standards in Public Life, Blair is 'personally responsible for a collapse in public trust on a par with the dying days of the last Conservative Government'. He added that 'confidence in the morality of those who govern the country was as low as it was a decade ago when Labour came to power on the back of Tory sleaze'.[5]

The chapter does not take issue with the argument that politicians are not trusted or the objective fact that many observers, commentators and citizens have a low opinion of Tony Blair. What it does suggest is that it is difficult to see in the behaviour of politicians – including Mr Blair – anything that could justify the scale and range of the negative feelings and attitudes about politics that have come to characterize our political culture. The fervour of moral condemnation that surrounded Blair on his departure from office tells us at least as much about our uneasy relationship with the business of politics in modern democracies as it does about Tony Blair's character.

The first section of the chapter lays out the perceived moral failings of New Labour and Blair in a little more detail and then tries to judge whether the case against Blair is fair. Blair emerges as no saint but I argue that the case against him is overblown. A second section of the chapter accepts that Blair's reputation for spin and sleaze is not entirely undeserved but argues that its grip on popular consciousness reflects the low trust environment in which politics operates and has operated for some time. Blair did not invent a lack of trust in politics; rather that lack of trust was ingrained and in turn created a climate for a focus on sleaze and spin. A third section of the chapter explores how the crisis of trust and morality surrounding our politics has rather deeper roots than the actions of one individual and one party. There are things wrong with the way our politicians supply politics to us but there are also issues on

the demand side of the chain in terms of the way we approach and understand politics. We orientate towards politics in a way that encourages moral
outrage and cynicism in equal measure. These are destructive rather than
helpful ingredients in the mix of a modern democracy given the extent they
have become magnified. A final section of the chapter asks whether anything
can be done to get us out of the current destructive approach to the conduct
of democratic politics.

Blowing our trust? Assessing the failings of Mr Blair

The most comprehensive and 'official' critique of Blair's political style comes
from Alistair Graham, the Chairman of the Committee for Standards in Public
Life. He condemns him as a guilty sinner who let himself down. This accusation came in March 2007 as part of a widely reported and damning attack on
the Blair years which coincided with the news that Alistair Graham's term as a
watchdog was not to be renewed. He cites[6] seven 'mortal sins' that the Prime
Minister was guilty of committing:

1. The cash-for-peerages scandal, which arose from the 'personal decision' by
   Blair to take secret loans;
2. Iraq, where the case for war 'undermined trust on a key issue where the
   lives of British soldiers were at risk'; basically Graham appears to share the
   widely held view that Blair lied over Iraq;
3. Blair's 'sofa-style' of decision-making which overrode the practices of
   Cabinet government;
4. 'Shocking political interference' in a fraud investigation by ending the
   inquiry into alleged corruption over BAE's arms deal with Saudi Arabia;
5. The failure to properly investigate alleged breaches of the ministerial code –
   involving David Blunkett, John Prescott and Tessa Jowell;
6. Postal voting, which despite public concerns was made a 'central plank of
   the electoral system and so leaving our system open to fraud';
7. An 'undue reliance on spin' and special advisers.

The nature of these sins are for Graham 'seven serious accusations that can
be personally made against the prime minister where he's failed on ethical
standards and he has to take responsibility for that'.[7]

What are we to make of these accusations of Alistair Graham? Graham,
rather like Kenneth Starr who dogged President Clinton during his presidency
of the US, appears to be a man on a moral mission. Should we share his view
that Blair is guilty of seven mortal sins? The literal meaning of mortal sin is
that it involves a total loss of grace on the part of the person committing sin.
I am sure I am not qualified to comment on the state of Blair's soul but I can

look at the substantive issues behind the accusations. Is Graham right to claim what he does about Blair and present it in the language of moral indignation and outrage?

Without going into the accusations in great depth, I suggest that we can divide them by two broad headings. First, there are issues where no moral fault could reasonably be laid at Blair's door since there are no moral issues at stake. Plainly, Graham can legitimately say he disagreed with Blair's hand-ling of these matters but to couch his views in a tone of moral condemnation is risible. There are other issues where some moral judgement is appropriate but that we need to remind ourselves that rarely in politics are there straight forward black and white issues.

In the first category where no moral judgement is relevant I would place Graham's concerns over the sofa-style of decision-making and the overuse of specialist advisers. His anxieties over these issues will find some support among, for example, constitutional traditionalists but others could reasonably hold the view that Blair's actions and those of his ministers were those of polit-ical leaders rightly attempting to make more responsive a civil service that was failing to grapple with issues of delivery and change. These are matters of effi-ciency and effectiveness of government rather than morality. Further, all of us would regard postal voting fraud as a concern but equally few would argue that in principle there is anything wrong with postal voting or the willingness of the Blair government to trial it, although you could question the way the trials were set up. The problems surrounding postal voting are issues of competence so common to much of government rather than matters of high morality. The language of mortal sin is therefore wholly inappropriate and misapplied in these cases.

I would place the remaining issues under the second heading where moral judgement is proper but where I am not so certain that the case can be made that Blair is a sinner and regard accusations about mortal sin as close to histri-onic. Given the messiness that surrounds the rules about party funding in the UK the issue of taking out loans needs more discussion about what would be a fair system of funding and less reference to mortal sins. As it turned out – one assumes to the disappointment of Graham – there was insufficient clear-cut evidence to pursue the 'money for peerages' case through the courts. Plainly the existing funding regime for our political parties is unsatisfactory – as the embarrassment of surrogate loans to Labour in November–December 2007 confirmed – but I think it is reasonable to suggest that it is the system that is at fault rather than Blair's moral character. Parties need money to fight elec-tions and if your opponents have wealthy donors and supporters then, in the absence of sufficient state party funding, we can expect party leaders to carry on making pragmatic decisions about where funding might come from.

The case of interference in the BAE case is a matter where the evidence is unclear. Therefore the choice over whether to continue the corruption investigation or not is premised on a judgement call over whether the evidence would become clearer or whether the unfair damage to employment and commercial interests in the UK would continue or increase. As for ministerial transgressions not being properly investigated, it is reasonable to suggest that a more independent system of investigation might be desirable. But this matter is more about impression management than substance as even under current arrangements we do get to know the detail of alleged examples of misbehaviour and it is difficult to see what more we would want to know about the love-life of Prescott. Moreover, all measures to introduce ethical rule into politics tend to get snarled up in partisan politics as whatever accusation or investigation takes place can be used by one side as a stick to beat the other.

The issue of Iraq deserves specific consideration as it is a matter where opinion is strongly held. Given the interests of this chapter, the focus of attention is whether debate should be over whether the heart of the issue is one of moral failure or a failure in judgement and foresight. With hindsight it's difficult to see the invasion of Iraq as anything other than a relative failure since many of the original objectives of the proponents have not been realized. But a debate remains between those who see it as a misjudgement caused by lack of foresight and those who see it as policy planned and executed through a deliberately constructed campaign of manoeuvres and propaganda by Blair and his entourage.[8]

So did Blair lie to us over Iraq? Calling someone a liar is a grave charge; saying that someone used evidence selectively to bolster their case is still a significant challenge but perhaps is not so morally loaded. You can deceive through a falsehood uttered in good faith that is not a lie: a distinction that goes to the heart of the debate over whether the public were lied to over weapons of mass destruction in Iraq. In the case of Iraq I suspect we are again in the world of grey rather than black and white. Giving a misleading impression by stressing certain truths and omitting others, by appearing to be listening but having already made up our mind, is not necessarily an attractive practice but it is a practice common to everyday exchanges in our world. Impression management is a central part of the art of influence and persuasion that is central to politics. To say you object to communication constructed in this way is almost the same as saying you would rather that humans did not communicate at all. The point is that lying is a strong word and in the current debate its scope is pushed too far in order to bolster an attack on politicians and Blair in particular.

From the perspective of this review Blair emerges as no saint but rather a human being doing a politician's job. He is not uniquely prone to lying or sleaze and his failings are by no means unusually large or disproportionate when viewed in a dispassionate way and the light of history. Several prime ministers within the living memory of many appear to have headed governments with similar problems including Margaret Thatcher, John Major and Harold Wilson.

Lack of trust begets lack of trust

Politicians make judgements and we hold them to account but it seems difficult to justify the high tone of moral indignation that surrounds the criticism
of Blair. Why then do so many of us appear to be keen to judge him as a sinner?
Why are frustration, irritation and moral indignation so commonly our reaction to a politician doing a politician's job? For those of us whose values and
ideologies are very different and vehemently opposed to the centrism that is at
the heart of New Labour then a certain amount of moral outrage towards Blair
would appear to be very easy to understand. Moral indignation is not automat-
ically how those on the ultra-left or right will react but if they did it would not
be surprising to see their angst at Blair's perceived failings expressed with a
certain moralistic vigour. But given what we know about the vast bulk of the
UK public and what they demonstrate in elections over and over again, most
citizens are in the same broad political space as New Labour – that after all was
part of the secret of its success and why the present leader of the main opposition party, David Cameron, has moved the Conservative Party on to much the
same ground. So why do so many of us still see Blair as untrustworthy, deceit-
ful and sleaze-ridden? The answer lies less in Blair's actions and more in our
pre-existing disposition to see all politicians as untrustworthy.

That British citizens do not now trust Blair is clear but to blame him for the
decline of trust in politics more generally is an opinion not easy to defend. As
Table 1 shows, we have had at least from the early 1980s a low opinion of politicians and government ministers. It's possible to see some slight rise in trust in
the early Blair years but even in that period still half the population remained
convinced that politicians could not be trusted. The spread of distrust in UK
politics cannot solely be put down to Blair's impact since there is strong evidence of its presence prior to his emergence as a leading politician.

Commenting on an earlier period of moral panic about political sleaze
and wrong doing in the early 1990s under a Conservative government, Roger
Mortimore notes that 'an existing general disdain and distrust of politicians
has made the public consciousness a fertile ground for sowing more specific
suspicions'.[9] In short, lack of trust begat a sense of sleaze and Mortimore argues

Table 1 Trust in politicians in Britain

Year	1983	1993	1997	1999	2001	2003	2005
% Public trust in politicians[a]	−57	−65	−63	−49	−57	−57	−51
% Public Trust in Government ministers[a]	−58	−70	−68	−47	−53	−53	−51

Note: [a] % expressing trust minus % expressing distrust

Source: Adapted from C. Hay, *Why We Hate Politics*, Oxford: Polity Press, 2007, Table 1.7, p. 35.

that a feedback loop driven by the media further undermined the confidence of the public in democratic politics as a result. It would appear that we may be seeing history repeating itself.

Why do we not trust politicians?

Why do we have a sustained, long-term lack of trust in politics? According to Meg Russell in her thoughtful pamphlet, the answer is that we have failed to come to terms with mass democracy in our culture. She argues that 'the ways that our political culture has adapted itself to modern life have, over time, conspired to erode faith in political rule'.[10] The adversarial style of our politics has, when combined with the sense that politicians must permanently campaign, fed distrust. The culture of consumerism has led politicians to offer promises to the public on which they struggle to deliver effectively. Single issue pressure groups add to the demands made on the political system to deliver without aiding any understanding of the need to balance competing demands. Citizens are given a constant message that suggests that politics is failing and the cynical and simplistic approach of the modern media has also 'played a key part in feeding all these problems'.[11]

I would agree with much of that analysis and add that the way that politics is practised today leaves too great a gap between governors and governed. Most of us are judging politicians from afar and through a distorted lens. The sense of moral outrage that pervades our reaction to politics I think reflects the fact that in most mature democracies most people have little if any direct involvement in politics.[12] Most people experience politics as spectators and through the eyes and ears of the media. The result of this alienated disengagement is that many citizens are able to combine a substantial level of cynicism about politics with occasional outbursts of moral indignation as to its failings and frustrations. On his departure it appears that many hated Blair but in the future it will be some other hapless politician.

The political class in the UK stands apart from us in our increasingly specialized society. Politics is the sphere of professionals where we are the amateurs. Our elected politicians may lack the specialist or technical knowledge about the areas of public policy they take responsibility for but they are 'expert' politicians, coached, trained and mentored to take on local and national roles of democratic leadership. The cohesion brought by parties, the advocacy of special interests through lobbying and the challenge and dissent presented through various forms of protest, offer vital links in the democratic chain between governors and governed. But they all are failing to engage citizens-at-large in politics. As parties have lost membership, they have become reliant on professional campaigners and organizers and operate in a way that treats citizens as passive political observers who just need to be mobilized at

election times to back the party.[13] Party politics is not the only arena of spe-
cialization. Citizen lobby organizations – such as Friends of the Earth – have
large-scale passive memberships and they too rely on professional organizers
and experts.[14] Members fund but the professional politicos in the lobby organizations decide what to campaign on. Citizens are a passive audience to be
talked to about particular campaigns through the media and occasionally galvanized to send in letters or cards of support or join a public demonstration
based often on rather simplistic messages. Citizens are offered little in terms
of depth of analysis or understanding of the issues at stake by these organizations. Even more radical protest organizations tend to be professionalized in
the style of behaviour and their use of the media. The occasional engagement
by a wider group of citizens in a protest 'event' or rally is in danger of being
more a lifestyle statement than a serious engagement with a political debate.[15]
We behave as consumers of politics; we buy into those campaigns we support
and boycott those goods and companies we don't. Our engagement is thin,
sporadic and often ill-informed.

Alienation and distance from the practice of politics provides a fertile ground
for cynicism about politics. The actions and moves of politicians are constantly
interpreted by the media through a lens that emphasizes their instrumental,
self-interested motivation.[16] We have no immediate or direct experience to provide a counterweight to that judgement. We are happy to question the morals
of politicians and judge them as morally bankrupt in a way that in other walks
of our life, where we know the people involved and their circumstances, we
would be more circumspect about rushing to a judgement.

Knowing little about how politics is done we are left to judge it by its results.
We constantly trip into moral consequentialism when judging politics.[17] Fair
enough you might say since that is all the politicians ask of us. 'Judge me on
my performance' they demand. But the difficulty is that we have, with their
encouragement, created a blame game that offers a thin and inadequate diet
of politics. Every aspiring politician convinces themselves they can deliver what
people want and every citizen wonders if this time they are going to get the
real thing: a politician who keeps his promises. But all know that it will, every
time and on every cycle, end in disappointment.

Blame – allocating it and avoiding it – appears to be the dominant political
game. We call for public inquiries and investigations into some blunder or mistake. Our perspective is provided by looking back on an action or inaction and
judging it by its results. But such a perspective needs to be tempered by recognizing the perspective of the decision-maker at the time. In the former case we
have the advantage of known outcomes, in the latter case the decision-maker
is faced by uncertainty and must engage in speculation. We should be under
no illusions about the ability of our representatives. They are not all-seeing
and often are in the business of making hard choices in the semi-dark. Our
moral judgements should reflect that fact. We could chastise them for taking

unnecessary risks on some occasions, for being too cautious on others but we should not morally condemn for failing to see the future with full clarity.

And because politicians are an 'alienated other' we priggishly contrast our private morality with their public immorality. People can and should use their own conscience to guide their decisions in their private lives, but in the sphere of politics soul searching has to be a collective endeavour. It is not enough for us to hide behind our consciences, stay out of politics and in so doing claim a moral purity. Obligations in the public sphere in democracies have to be decided in communication with others, not within the private conscience of each. We share a responsibility above all to maintain the sound institutions that protect all in our democratic practices. Moreover involvement in that wider public sphere may require us from time to time to engage in actions that cannot be entirely squared with our private consciences. In extreme cases, we might support violence to protect or promote denied political rights. More mundanely, and I hope more frequently, we have to be prepared to dirty our hands with the hard slog, grimy compromises and messiness of politics. Rigid moral formulas cannot be our guide in this world of public politics; rather morality comes from careful thought and the making of decisions in the light of the circumstances that present themselves and in communication with others. To act in this world 'we do not need to be saints . . . we do not need to wait for a moral revolution . . . all that is necessary is that we should be committed to political solutions to political problems'.[18] Politics is often an arena of grey rather than black and white when it comes to making choices.

Our disappointment with the performance of politicians is often accompanied by a general sense that if we cared to we could do better. People often find it difficult to think beyond their own experiences and therefore tend to judge political decisions according to their own interests and circumstances. Naïve aspirations and assumptions about politics often flow from these preconceptions. People can assume that most other people agree with them (or would do if only the issue was explained to them properly) and that the ideal outcome is one that suits them in every detail.

If you don't like something you see in a shop you can go elsewhere but in politics the only way to get something is to use voice – express your concerns in concert with others – and that carries far more costs than the exit mechanism available to us in market transactions.[19] People generally don't like making a lot of effort for little reward. Accordingly off-loading responsibility on to others as we have seen is a very common coping mechanism in political exchanges. But expressing your interest or opinion is only the start of a more general challenge in politics. You have not only to make your views known, you also have to listen. Politics is not about individual choice; it is about collective decision. Politics often involves a stumbling search to find a collective response to particular problems. It is not the most edifying human experience. It's rarely an experience of self-actualization and more often an experience of accepting second-best. The results tend to be messy, contingent and inevitably create a mix of winners and losers.

The negative response to politics that many of us share is I think a very human reaction to the way politics works. As an intricate mechanism in our multifaceted and complex societies politics exists because we don't agree with one another. Politics is about choosing between competing interests and views. It often demands incompatible allocations of limited resources. Crucially because it is a collective form of decision-making, once a choice has been made then that choice has to be imposed on us all. There is no point having a rule that vehicles on a road must stop when a traffic light turns red unless it is generally observed and enforced. Politics at the level of today's large-scale, interconnected and diverse societies is on a tough beat. Our collective will – which is what politics is supposed to express – is not easy to fathom or always comfortable to accept once it is decided upon.

We should not consider that we can do without politics. You might argue that politics persists only because humans make the wrong choices. If they followed the right path, set down by religion or some other moral guide, they would all choose the same thing and as a result politics would not be neces-sary. You might alternatively argue that politics operates only in societies that are structured so that people's interests are fundamentally opposed but that it might be possible to structure a society where people's interests were always aligned and as a result politics would not be required. The former argument has at various times been made by some religious and other moralizing opin-ion leaders. The latter is one used by some radicals and utopians of various hues. Neither is particular convincing to me and neither can take much suc-cour from the historical record to date. There is little to suggest that human beings or human societies are perfectible as implied by these contrasting understandings.

It is difficult to be certain about human nature. But I think it is reasonable to take as a starting point the idea that people are capable of terrible deeds and also capable of great acts. It is equally difficult to be entirely sure what is in someone's best interests and so it seems impossible to establish for cer-tain a society where interests do not clash. Given human society as it has been and as it might reasonably be expected to be in the future, we could argue that people will make judgements about what is right for themselves and for others and that there is no reason to assume that those judgements will be shared. Equally it is clear that as humans we need to find ways to act together, to engage in collective action, to resolve the problems and challenges of living together. It is an integral part of human nature to value the opportunity to be involved in decisions about issues that affect you. We will differ about what the outcomes could or should be but somehow in a democracy we need to sustain a commitment to the process and institutions of politics. We may not like its outcomes but we should be willing to support the complex expression of collective will that in our democracies politics is attempting to deliver.

Can we make politics better?

Cynicism mixed with moral outrage is our default response to a democratic politics. It is a caustic and disabling mix and its grip needs to be broken. I am not about to argue that we all need to become new model active citizens. Democracy should be about providing opportunities to get involved and engaged in a whole range of institutions and decisions from neighbourhood to the global. But it is important to recognize that for most people politics is not their first choice of activity. There are trade-offs between time spent on politics and the joys of private life. We should be cautious in our expectations about the extent and depth of engagement that people want. In this light two reform strategies stand out. The need to offer viable ways for people to engage in politics directly and the need to make representative politics work better. Some form of representative politics is therefore likely to remain at the heart of everyday politics in mature democracies. The challenge rests on reconnecting representative politics to its participative roots and in so doing making it a more plausible and effective arena for resolving conflicts and choosing pathways to coordination.

There are ways of re-engaging people in politics. The 'Make Poverty History' (MPH) protest in the summer of 2005 connected campaigning with formal representative politics in a powerful way and did so in ways that reached out to millions of people who were relative novices in the political process over an issue of high moral import. There are lessons that can be drawn from that campaign if we are interested in a remoralizing of politics and restoring trust in the political process.[20] The first is that hope sells rather than guilt. MPH convinced people that they could do something to make a difference to improve the lot the world's poor. Second, it built very deliberately from the bottom-up and then tried to link visionary leadership to that base but the base was around the local school-gate, bus stops, places of work rather than the elite institutions of politics. Finally its message was one of rehabilitation and renewal as converts to the cause were welcomed from all quarters and not derided for making a U-turn or because they were latecomers.

Not all politics can be packaged in the same way as the MPH campaign but it stands out as a politics that successfully brought together the formal institutions of governance and the informal power of civil society. There are other examples from across the globe. Graham Smith[21] shows how there has been innovation in forms of public engagement worldwide and offers the following categorization for these schemes: consultative, deliberative, co-governance, direct and e-democracy schemes. The range of options for engaging people is considerable (see Table 2). The goal should be to take examples of effective practice from several countries and test them further.

As Gordon Brown argues, 'to build trust in our democracy, we need a more open form of dialogue for citizens and politicians to genuinely debate problems and solutions'.[22] He is interested in some of the new forms of democratic practice and deliberation that enable citizens to become more fully engaged. He also recognizes the need for representative politics to be conducted in a more open and accountable way. He comments: 'Government must be more open and accountable to Parliament – for example in decisions about peace and war, in public appointments and in a new ministerial code of conduct'.[23] More details of this programme are presented in 'The Governance of Britain' Green Paper.[24]

A strategy of greater openness also makes some sense while not denying the reality of modern governance that much of the initiative and power rests with its executive rather than representative arms. As Fred Ridley[25] argued in the light of the earlier scandals of the Thatcher and Major years when the public has decided that politicians have 'feet of clay', politicians will need to make an extra effort to present themselves and their decision-making in a better light. So a greater openness to parliamentary scrutiny on decision-making, appointments and others issues would be welcome as would a more independent monitoring of the ministerial code.

But given all that has gone before can we believe that these measures will be enough to restore trust? It's difficult to think that a combination of some more engagement or greater openness – even if given some constitutional backing – will do the trick. Both strategies have been followed in the previous ten years of New Labour and it seems doubtful if a fuller, stronger commitment to their delivery although welcome is likely to turn the issue of lack of trust in politics around.

Some call for a wider remoralization of politics but these proposals tend to require taking the politics out of politics. Richard Ryder[26] argues that politicians should be required to promote public policies by reference to moral objectives and through open moral argument. Others, even some in the Brown camp, appear to favour taking more issues out of politics and handing over decisions to independent bodies or institutions.[27] The line of argument appears to be that these independents will make decisions based on objective information and widely accepted criteria and that therefore their decisions will be easier to justify. A different strategy for removing decision-makers from politics is suggested by Alex Rubner, namely a return to more independence for Members of Parliament and less public scrutiny and lobbying so that legislators can respond to proposals with their considered views and not have to adopt strategies of benevolent lying. The problem of the current system in this analysis is that 'in order to do good, politicians are often compelled to be dishonest. They engage in benevolent lying for otherwise, because of the likely

Table 2 New forms of engagement

Form	Description	Illustrative Case	Web Resource
Consultative innovations	Informs decision-makers of citizens' views through a combination of methods to explore public opinion.	Public debate on the future of GM technology in the UK in 2001.	www.gmnation.org.uk/
Deliberative methods	Enabling a cross-section of citizens to have the time and opportunity to reflect on an issue by gathering opinion and information in order to come to a judgement about an issue or concern.	The British Columbia Citizens' Assembly in Canada was established in 2004 and over 11 months, 160 were given the task of reviewing the province's electoral system.	www.citizensassembly.bc.ca
Co-governance Mechanisms	Arrangements aim to give citizens significant influence during the process of decision-making, particularly when it comes to issues of distribution of public spending and implementation practice.	Participatory Budgeting started its existence as a form of engagement in Porto Alegre, Brazil in the late 1980s but by 2004 it is estimated that over 250 cities or municipalities practiced some version of it.	www.pgualc.org
Direct democracy	Referendums called by citizens that come in two broad forms. Popular initiatives – allow the recall of decision made by elected representatives. Citizens' initiatives – allow citizens to set the agenda and put an issue up for public decision.	Quite widely practised in Switzerland and the US.	www.iandrinstitute.org/
E-democracy	The use of information and communication technology to give citizens new opportunities to engage.	MN-POLITICS is run by a non-partisan, independent organization established in 1994 that aims to enable internet-based dialogue and debate between citizens and groups in Minnesota.	www.e-democracy.org

Source: Developed from material in Graham Smith, *Democratic Innovations*, London: Power Inquiry, 2005.

obstruction of stupid voters, they cannot advance the national interest as they
see it.'[28]

None of the proposed additional strategies are of great value because
they all in different ways are trying to take the politics out of politics. As
Michael Walzer puts it political decisions are inherently and permanently
conflictual.

> Very few political decisions are verdicts in the literal sense of that term. I
> don't mean that we can't sometimes insist that it is morally right and perhaps
> imperative to do X; but even people who agree on the necessity of doing X
> are likely to disagree about how to do it, or how soon, or at whose expense. . . .
> Permanent settlements in politics are rare in political life because we have no
> way of reaching a verdict on contested issues.[29]

As noted earlier, politics as a result often requires messy compromises that
are presented through 'smoke and mirrors' to bridge conflicting interests and
values. Deliberation and the open exchange of different ideas are part of politics
but they do not capture the roundness of its practice. Politics is a sustained battle
of interests and ideas and claims for influence, accountability and scrutiny. It is
an inherent reflection of our plurality and difference as human beings. Its nobil-
ity is in its capacity to enable us to manage our mutual interdependence but its
practice is often laboured, dull and untidy, muddled and occasionally dirty.

Meg Russell[30] offers an optimistic view of the way forward in her idea that
those who do politics – activists through parties, lobby groups or protest
movements – need to conduct their business in a different way. She proposes
a new political charter in which they are more honest about their mistakes,
the hard choices that need to be made and the constraints faced by decision-
makers and more generous to their opponents in not making exaggerated or
unnecessary attacks and campaigning responsibly and in a way that does not
exploit citizens' distrust. She adds that media coverage and citizens' attitudes
to politics will also need to change. Her optimism that such a new political culture could take hold needs to be tempered by a recognition that when activists
do their politics they do so with a mix of motives from passion for a cause to
self-interest. But above all they campaign, demonstrate, bargain, organize and
do the mundane work of filling out envelopes and making phone calls in order
to win. There are no neutrals in politics and to ask activists to forgo potentially winning strategies may be asking for too much. Gordon Brown's political
opponents are unlikely to give up the sleaze attacks, allow him to show falli-
bility without sanction or forgo the chance to argue they could avoid the hard
choices he will be forced to make.

So do I end with a position of despair? People don't trust politics but without
some trust it's difficult to see how democracy can be sustained. No, my position
is rather that we don't know enough about the problem is to know what the

answer might be. Even if political activists did behave better (and I doubt how much advance we can reasonably expect on that front) and even we did find ways of drawing in to a degree more citizens into decision-making, the bulk of citizens would still remain observers rather than practitioners of political practice. The big unknown is how these observers come to understand politics and whether they could develop a complex and nuanced understanding of its practices. As Colin Hay argues in terms of the silent majority we

> know very little . . . about the cognitive process in and through which [they] come to attribute motivations to the behaviour [they] witness, or how [they] come to develop and revise assumptions about human nature [they] project on to others. If politics depends ultimately on our capacity to trust one another . . . then there can be no more important questions for political analysts than these.[31]

We need a political culture that is able to live with and manage contradictory forces. Citizens should engage directly in politics and be engaged by the mainstream representative political process. Yet even if that occurs they will differ about what the outcomes of democratic politics could or should be. So somehow we citizens need to be willing to support the multifaceted expression of collective will that we call politics even when the outcomes may not be to our liking. Politics in a democratic context demands a complex moral universe. One that grants you the freedom to challenge authority, criticize all actors and actions and cajole others to support your views but at the same time demands from you a collective responsibility to uphold a system that may produce outcomes that you may strongly object to or find morally dubious or even repugnant.

The tensions of our current political culture are often resolved by citizens opting out and condemning politics with a mix of cynicism and high moral fervour. Politics demands a better response than that and if we understood it more we would give it more leeway and scope. Politics is a human tool for dealing with conflicts and interdependence. We need to recognize its continuing capacity to enable us to live together in a complex world and learn to accept its lack of perfection. We should not be throwing stones at politics but recognize in the failings and limitations of its star practitioners a true reflection of ourselves.

Notes

1   C. Hay, *Why We Hate Politics* (Oxford: Polity, 2007) p. 153.
2   Anthony King, 'Mediocre or worse: voters' verdict on Blair' *The Daily Telegraph*, 1 May 2007.

3 Peter Oborne, *The Rise of Political Lying* (London: Free Press, 2005).

4 Mary Ann Sieghart, ' I'll give Blair six and a half out of ten' *The Times*, 10 May 2007.

5 'Blair's seven sins which will tarnish his legacy' *ThisisLondon.co.uk*, 18 March 2007.

6 Ibid.

7 Ibid.

8 John Lloyd's book on the media takes the view that the Iraq war was more a mess up rather than a conspiracy (J. Lloyd, *What the Media Are Doing to Our Politics*, (London: Constable, 2004)). For a carefully and well-argued work that takes a more critical line on Blair's actions see Steven Kettell, *Dirty Politics? New Labour, British Democracy and the Invasion of Iraq* (London: Zed Books, 2006).

9 R. Mortimore, 'Politics and public perceptions' in F. F. Ridley and A. Doig (eds) *Sleaze: Politicians, Private Interests and Public Reaction* (Oxford: OUP, 1995) p. 31.

10 M. Russell, *Must Politics Disappoint?* (London: Fabian Society, 2005) p. 4.

11 Ibid. p. 5.

12 See Gerry Stoker, *Why Politics Matters* (Basingstoke: Palgrave Macmillan, 2006).

13 P. Webb, D. Farrell and I. Holliday, eds, *Political Parties in Advanced Industrial Societies* (Oxford: Oxford University Press, 2002).

14 G. Jordan and W. Maloney, *The Protest Business? Mobilizing Campaign Groups*, (Manchester: Manchester University Press, 1997).

15 W. de Jong, M. Shaw and N. Stammers, eds, *Global Activism, Global Media* (London: Pluto, 2005).

16 C. Hay, *Why We Hate Politics*.

17 For a discussion of this point see Margaret Canovan, *Hannah Arendt. A Reinterpretation of Her Political Thought* (Cambridge: CUP, 1992) p. 188.

18 Canovan, *Hannah Arendt*, p. 200.

19 The discussion in this section of the chapter draws extensively on material from Stoker, *Why Politics Matters*.

20 Kirsty McNeill, 'Can we restore trust?' *Fabian Review*, Winter 2006/7, vol. 118, no. 4, 16–17.

21 Graham Smith, *Democratic Innovations* (London: Power Inquiry, 2005).

22 Gordon Brown, speech on 17 May 2007, from www.gordonbrownforbritain.com/2007/05/17/gordon-brown-formally-accepts-nomination-as-leader-of-the-labour-party/ [accessed on 29 May 2007].

23 Gordon Brown Speech 11 May 2007 launching his campaign for the leadership of the Labour Party, 11 May 2007 from www.gordonbrownforbritain.com/2007/05/11/gordon-brown-launches-leadership-campaign/ [accessed 29 May 2007 at 9.20 a.m.].

24 *The Governance of Britain*, Cm 7170, 3 July 2007. The Stationery Office ISBN 9780101717021.

25 F. F. Ridley, 'Feet of clay' in F. F. Ridley and A. Doig (eds) *Sleaze: Politicians, Private Interests and Public Reaction* (Oxford: OUP, 1995).

26 Richard Ryder, *Putting Morality Back into Politics* (Exeter: Societas, 2006).

27 For a development of this argument see F. Gains and G. Stoker, *How Politics Works: Understanding the New Realties of the Political Process in Public Management*, Paper for the Work Foundation, forthcoming, 2008.

[28] Alex Rubner, *The Mendacious Colours of Democracy* (Exeter: Imprint Academic, 2006) p. 3.

[29] Michael Walzer, *Politics and Passion* (New Haven: Yale, 2004) p. 103.

[30] Russell, *Must politics Disappoint?*, pp. 55–8.

[31] Hay, *Why We Hate Politics*, p. 162.

Chapter 3

Demoralizing Britain: Ten Years of Depoliticization

Stefan Skrimshire

Introduction

In many ways Tony Blair's exit was as typically 'New Labour' as his ten years of leadership had been. In his resignation speech to his constituency in Sedgefield, the rhetoric of grand vision was mixed with personal, 'hand on heart' morality. By way of summarizing the challenges of his premiership he extolled the virtue of 'doing what you genuinely believe to be right . . . to act according to your conviction'. Over the decision to invade Iraq in particular, 'I ask you to accept one thing. Hand on heart, I did what I thought was right.'[1] Should we view this approach with suspicion? For Blair to declare that he did what he thought was right at the time is both banally true and ethically without content. It tells us only that he did what he *wanted to do* given the ethical norms that inform his decisions. It is those norms we should wish to investigate, not the sincerity by which Tony Blair adopts them. The media, of course, have been complicit in drawing attention predominantly to Tony, the man, the moral individual. Thus the Observer's Andrew Marr could speak of the 'moral courage' of Blair's decision to bomb Serbia in 1999. Sion Simon in the Telegraph similarly could call that same war 'the most heroically disinterested intervention in history. . . . This was a uniquely philanthropic war. . . . Blair is now a war leader . . . resolute, decent, brave.'[2] On his leaving, no matter what people had made of his policy decisions, Blair was, in words expressed by many contributors to this volume, a 'passionate' politician; moved by 'moral conviction' (Elaine L. Graham); a natural 'activist' (Paul Vallely) and a 'role model' for young aspiring politicians (Will Hutton). This emphasis on the morality of the individual is definitive of discussions over New Labour's 'faith' and 'morals'. It is a highly significant intervention, since it appeals to one of the very facets of political style which features as a constant critique of New Labour. The media gushing over Blair's moralism demonstrates very clearly, in other words, a preference for presentation over substance. For how else might we actually judge Blair's self belief than by hearing his passionate voice and being swept along in the praise of its delivery? It represents an appeal to the value of the *private* in lieu of evoking any faith in the *public*.

It may well be impossible to judge Blair on whether the decreases in voter turnouts since he took power are attributable to him personally. But it *is* possible to show that this trend highlights a steadily diminishing sphere of public political engagement. If political disinterestedness is, as Gerry Stoker would have us believe, part of a generally chaotic democratic 'environment',[3] then New Labour is at very least a pioneer of that chaos. For the consequence is what is becoming more popularly termed a system of 'depoliticization', or in other words, the removal of the political from the public sphere. The following study offers some aspects of New Labour's role in these transformations. Of particular interest to me is New Labour's rhetoric of defending freedom and civil liberties in its war against fundamentalist ideologies. There is now a formidable and widespread critique of New Labour's erosion of precisely those liberties since it came to power. For all the encouragement that is offered citizens to 'make democracy work', therefore, we must never forget the huge efforts made by government to prevent this from happening. I offer some evidence for this by highlighting two aspects of the past ten years of depoliticization: the privatization of norms of citizenship; and the criminalization of protest and dissent. Lastly, I offer some suggestions for a further debate on how these relate to a crisis of 'faith' in political life. I argue that today the political is privatized much in the way that religious belief, under the pretext of protection from 'fundamentalism', has been over the past five years. Any dissenting voices, political or religious, that now make unwarranted incursions into the public sphere, that 'dare to take seriously their beliefs' to use Zizek's phrase,[4] are consequently a threat to democracy, not, as was once expressed by the authors of modern democracy, a guarantee of its existence.

Who can we blame for our loss of faith?

[Tony Blair] is the least political person I've dealt with. And I say that out of respect.
George W. Bush[5]

[Tony Blair] is taking the politics out of politics.

Roy Hattersley[6]

Political disaffection, particularly among young people, is today almost taken for granted in critiques of the contemporary 'health' of Western democracies. This is assumed of Blair's Britain as much as anywhere else. General election turnouts dropped dramatically after Labour's landslide victory, with 5 million less people voting in 2001 (59.4%) than had in 1997 (71.4%), and only 61.4% voting in 2005.[7] Party membership in the UK has halved since 1980.[8]

Commentators relish comparisons between the success of voting for reality TV shows like *Big Brother* with the poor turnouts for local and national elections.[9] But what do these statistics actually tell us about what 'politics' actually means to people? Equally common, for example, are the suggestions that the phenomenon of poor voter turnout does not necessarily imply that people in Britain are disengaged from politics. It means, to some, that new forms of engagement have emerged – for various reasons – to take the place of traditional forms of democracy. These typically include the rise of single issue campaign organizations, local community associations and internet-based forms of political interaction in the form of political blogs.[10]

While these observations no doubt have some truth in them, they fail to question how those alternative modes of political expression actually function as modes of participation. Might they not be themselves, for instance, acts of protest and critique at popular disenfranchisement from political life? When over one million people marched in London on 15 February 2003 to oppose war against Iraq, many lauded the event as a triumph for participative democracy. It led to the term 'Second Superpower' being coined by the *New York Times* in reference to the influence of global civil society. Madeleine Bunting of *The Guardian* was even moved to say that 'the decline of democracy has been overstated. What has changed is the pattern of participation; political parties and turnouts may be declining, but intense episodic political engagement is on the increase.'[11] The optimism may have been welcome, but today many look back to that event as symbolic of the new 'Superpower's' impotence, and with some reason. Blair not only ignored the demands of the protesters, but attacked them directly with his inimitable style of moralism. Protesters would have blood on their hands, he preached on the day of the largest public demonstration in British history, if they opposed military action.[12]

What, then, can we say about alternative modes of engagement by civil society outside of the ballot box? Are they born of hope, desperation or mere symbolism? What does it mean to be political in such a paradoxical climate of passion and disenfranchisement? Gerry Stoker has argued that while widespread mistrust of politics and politicians in the UK is commonly placed at the feet of Tony Blair, equal if not greater blame is also due to citizens' inability to use what is available to them. Citizens should not blame government, in other words, but themselves for not participating enough. For reasons that 'predate Blair',[13] critical engagement with politics in Britain is experienced through an environment of 'alienated disengagement'.[14] Stoker is clearly not alone in believing that Blair's government simply stumbled into a political climate of post-modern, disengaged political life. There is a widespread interest, for instance, in the changing face of democratic participation in an environment of media-driven cultural life. Such analyses shed some light on the government's obsession with 'managerial' approaches to policy changes as opposed to the 'old style' of political polarization of political alternatives (such as left and right). As Malcolm Todd and Gary Taylor put it,

> Politics today has little in common with the passions and conflicts that have shaped people's commitments and hatreds over the past century. . . . This is the age of 'micro-politics'. Politics has adopted the language of technocracy and presents itself through a depoliticised language of managerialism.[15]

Stoker may thus be justified in discrediting arguments that the 'corruption' or 'economic incompetence' of individual politicians leads directly to a disengagement from mainstream politics.[16] He is also right to observe that Britain has seen a reduction of 'activist' political engagement to a minimum of protest and campaigning elites. To a large extent participation in contestational politics is fragmented and 'erratic', delegating responsibility and active critique to designated experts or lobbyists in 'an environment that seems capable of supporting only the most individualized and privatized forms of engagement.'[17] But does the legacy of New Labour not bear *any* responsibility for this state of affairs? Is it enough to declare that our erratic activist behaviour 'puts a burden on the political system and does little to build a wider sense of engagement in, or understanding of, a political process'?[18]

I would like to suggest in response that some trends in governance have been critical in the creation of this atomized political environment. Not only has it been instrumental in silencing 'deep' engagement with the subject of politics itself, but also its replacement with an illusory 'surface' effect of engagement within civil society. It is thus closely associated with the concept of depoliticization, defined by Peter Burnham as 'a process of placing at one remove the political character of decision-making'.[19] Burnham makes the case with reference to New Labour's economic policy of market liberalization,[20] its shift towards decentralized 'micromanagement' and the appointment of an unprecedented number of non-governmental PR experts, advisers and lobbyists. In essence this has meant, Burnham argues, a 'reassignment of tasks away from the party in office to a number of ostensibly "non-political" bodies as a way of underwriting the government's commitment to achieving objectives'.[21] But depoliticization can also be seen as a more broadly *cultural* transformation: a strategy of removing questions of policy and governance from the arena of political engagement. Government may, in other words, give the impression of greater transparency at the same time as reducing the sphere of exchange between itself and the electorate. Depoliticization is also a principle of New Labour's political rhetoric. Timothy Bewes for instance observes the rhetoric of 'one nation' politics (not favouring any one section of society), the replacement of 'policies' with 'values' and the constant oscillation between the language of community and individual, rights and responsibilities, public and private.[22] We can talk of the 'removal of the political character of decision-making'

here because the sphere of political leverage, or polarization between positions (left and right, for instance) is simply removed, leaving only a managerial
style, or the governance of appearances. New Labour were early pioneers of
the manipulation of a 24-hour news culture, a style of news management that
takes its cue from the market logic of the entertainment industry. In the context of the declining faith in electoral favour, it has meant only that politicians
have become masters of 'infotainment'. They have achieved this by employing
the experts of those industries which invented the very idea – PR companies,
media management experts and other 'non-political actors' that lurk behind
the scenes. Shouldn't an increase in communications experts lead to greater
transparency and hence increased opportunity for popular engagement?
There has, allegedly, been a 'tenfold rise in press officers to more than 3,200'
in government since Blair came to power.[23] But it is the paradoxical 'dumbing
down' process of the mainstream media *product* to a lowest common denom-
inator that once again protects genuine political choice or authority from
entering the domain of public participation. Given the global dominance of a
handful of media corporations (in the UK, News Corporation owns BskyB, *The
Times* and *The Sun* newspapers as well as its many international companies) it is
little wonder that New Labour made a strategic decision to court their favour,
principally by befriending Rupert Murdoch.[24]

The depoliticization process through dumbing down of political information is twofold. Not only is the status of the politician as the guardian of
political truth greatly diminished, but the competence of the public is also
vastly underestimated. This leads to dimmed expectations and the reduction
of its role to a passive observer of the spectacle of social events. *Involvement* is
replaced with *observation*. We can now know more than was ever possible about
current affairs and government strategy, but do less than ever about it. It is also
characteristic of a style of neo-liberal governance that seeks the relatively new
terrain of 'commercial citizenship'. In a market economy governed more by
unelected bodies such as the WTO, International Monetary Fund (IMF) and
World Bank, the role of the citizen and the expectations of his or her involvement in policy is necessarily tied to relations of public and private ownership.
And if public life is increasingly dominated by the interests of private enterprise, the ability for people to intervene is confined to their consumer power.
The result is a democracy of sorts, but we should define it not, as Stoker would
like, simply to a politics that is 'tougher'[25] for being fragmented and chaotic,
but to one that is essentially toothless. As Crouch more realistically puts it,
today

> the mass of citizens plays a passive, quiescent, even apathetic part, respond-
> ing only to the signals given them. Behind this spectacle of the electoral
> game, politics is really shaped in private by interaction between elected
> governments and elites that overwhelmingly represent business interests.[26]

Making politics history: How New Labour tamed the development movement

I am also fond of Tony Blair and Gordon Brown. They are kind of the John and Paul of global development . . . Lennon and McCartney changed my interior world – Blair and Brown can change the real world.

Bono[27]

One of the redeeming moments for the state of political activism in Britain has been, Stoker claims, the 2005 Make Poverty History Campaign (MPH), which he says 'successfully brought the formal institutions of governance and the informal power of civil society together'.[28] Stoker is absolutely right to state that there are 'important lessons' that can be drawn from MPH, but for the opposite reasons to those he has in mind. For MPH, I will argue, is paradigmatic of the depoliticized form of political engagement introduced above. Looking in some detail at its organization therefore raises important questions about the scope of 'informal power' available to citizens. It also reveals the subtle but observable production of the *model activist*. The model activist is he or she who, by an extraordinary manipulation and mediatization of the function of civil society, comes to represent an image of the radical residue of government itself, rather than a democratic pressure upon it.

MPH was officially launched in 2004 as the result of a series of meetings between charities, NGOs and campaign groups in Oxford wishing to formalize a UK wing of the Global Call to Action Against Poverty. Their intention was an anti-poverty coalition that would coincide with the G8 summit in Scotland in 2005, the 5-year evaluation of the UN Millennium Development Goals, and the 20th anniversary of Live Aid.[29] On paper, at least, its progress from those humble beginnings represented an astonishing success. By 2005 MPH could boast 540 member organizations and the mobilization of a historic number of participants in its march in Edinburgh. Like the Jubilee 2000 campaign and, to an extent, the Stop the War Coalition, MPH was also significant for bringing to the campaigning table charities, NGOs, churches, trade unions, activists and politicians. And, at least in its original intent, it represented some relatively radical demands: MPH called for increased aid budgets, debt cancellation and fairer trade rules ('fair trade not free trade'). It also arguably forced the G8's rhetoric of change for Africa into popular discourse and scrutiny where before the economic analysis was the preserve of experts. Headed by the two celebrity heavyweights of development campaigns, Geldof and Bono, a star-studded cast of performers in London's Live 8 concert ensured global media coverage.

The white wrist-banded participants in MPH's march in Edinburgh 2005 could thus be forgiven for thinking at the time that they were taking part in an unprecedented incursion of civil society into the corridors of power. Sadly, its demands met a hollow reception at Gleneagles. As MPH itself admitted at

the time, the £25 billion promised in 'increased aid' was not new money but
the same promised at finance ministers meetings a month before Gleneagles.
Two years on we see how far those limited promises were kept, provoking even
Geldof and Bono themselves into calling the 2007 G8 meeting in Germany
a 'total farce'.[30] But even putting aside these quantitative failings of MPH's
demands, what can be said of its mobilization of a million voices in the name of
the poor across such diverse social boundaries? Was this not a direct answer to
the charge of popular political apathy? The reality behind the image suggests a
more cynical approach. Fronted by celebrities notorious for their allegiance to
Blair and the G8, MPH organizers were clear from the start that their strategy
was not so much a critique of their economic policies as a demand for more of
what they were promised already with the added pressure that the world was
watching (though many people, if they were honest, were really watching the
historic Pink Floyd reunion). On these terms, unsurprisingly, MPH had the
endorsement of New Labour, including Gordon Brown's own participation in
the Edinburgh march. Big businesses set to profit from enterprises related to
the G8's proposed 'structural adjustment programmes' were of course not ruf-
fled either.[31]

Emphasizing that the biggest historic international mobilization against
poverty was in essence a welcome to party to the Group of Eight wealthiest
nations is extremely significant. It suggests that mainstream modes of register-
ing disaffection are more like petitioning agencies than democratic voices of
critique. Bruce Whitehead, a press officer for MPH put it unambiguously when
he said of their 'big day':

> [ours] is not a march in the sense of a demonstration, but more of a walk . . .
> the emphasis is on fun in the sun. The intention is to welcome the G8 lead-
> ers to Scotland and ask them to deliver trade justice, debt cancellation and
> increased aid to developing countries.[32]

The essence of the strategy adopted by Bono and Geldof – to ensure influence
over the G8 by keeping in their good books – may have been well intentioned.
But the consequences for the possibility for restoring faith in critical, participative democracy in this country are damaging and far-reaching. MPH had clearly
learnt nothing from the mistakes of Live Aid 20 years ago, now widely criticized
for portraying Africa as the paradigm of misfortune and wretchedness. Live Aid
required philanthropist Westerners to throw their money at them out of a sense
of pity, not justice or basic human rights. Despite MPH's rhetoric this time not
on giving money but on pressuring world leaders for political change, the sentiment had not changed. By legitimizing the G8 its sphere of action was bound to
agendas set by rich nations. It is of no great surprise then, that MPH attracted
immediate criticism from some of its potential beneficiaries in the global south.
Despite Stoker's description of MPH as a truly 'bottom-up' campaign, starting

from the grass-roots voices, many southern campaign groups distanced them-selves from the Global Call for Action Against Poverty itself. Kofi Maluwi Klu, international coordinator of Jubilee 2000 Africa Campaign condemned its lack of southern consultation: 'The campaign is overwhelmingly led by Northern NGOs and its basic message is about white millionaire pop stars saving Africa's helpless. The political movements still fighting for liberation on the ground are completely erased.'[33] Anti-capitalist southern campaigners know only too well that the neo-liberal policies crippling Africa as much as debt had created an excuse for the entire northern development movement to wash its hands of the roots of the problem and create the illusion of instigating real 'grass-roots' change. MPH had transformed the energy of millions into a 'movement calling for the relaxation of the terms of oppression'.[34]

It should be clear that all of these criticisms of MPH strategy relate not only to its stated aims but to its self-decoration as a triumph for political participa-tion. The deeper problem, in other words, with an event like MPH was that it used the legitimation bestowed by the established political order. Worse, it used this legitimacy to demarcate the proper sphere of protest for civil society. Bono and Geldof had, as George Monbiot pointed out, illegitimately assumed on behalf of millions of well-intentioned campaigners around the world the role of 'arbiters: determining on our behalf whether the leaders of the G8 nations should be congratulated or condemned for the decision they make'.[35] The damage for a truly radical development movement was thus twofold. First, a genuine critique of power, by delegitimizing the power of the hegemony of the G8 through political gestures, had been denied. Second, the G8 themselves won a captive audience for their own PR campaign of being benign philanthropists to the starving world.

The result for hundreds of thousands of protesters who fell outside of this remit of collective action was silence, exclusion, or, as I shall describe later, criminalization and physical violence. MPH proved itself to be authoritarian in guarding the monopoly it had achieved in the message of anti-poverty. It denied the right for other protest groups to stand alongside them – notably Stop the War Coalition, under the naive pretext that 'issues of economic justice and development are separate from that of war'.[36] MPH liaised very carefully with police to form strategies for evicting undesirable activists who might wish to act under banners other than the MPH slogan.[37] What began as a triumph for mass mobilization of people power thus proved in the end to be collusion between celebrity, media and the political elite to stifle the diversity of dissent already operative against the G8. Mobilization against the G8, representing a diverse political cross-section such as the Dissent! network, G8 alternatives and numerous autonomous protest groups, became quickly stigmatized as disrup-tive by introducing the 'wrong' kind of protester.

The emphasis on Live 8, the organization of concerts around the world to raise awareness for the MPH cause, is also highly significant. Far from encouraging people to take their voices and protest to the site of power, Live 8 confined their energy to a celebration of celebrity. Once again, maximizing PR came above representing the voice of the poor themselves. Geldof's initial refusal to stage African musical acts in London, consigning them instead to a park in Cornwall was justly cited by the BBC's Andy Kershaw as 'musical apartheid'.[38] Geldof's defence was that the concert was a 'political', not 'cultural' event. The irony is that precisely the reverse was true. Live 8 represented the almost irresistible transformation of the image of 'legitimate protest' into one of the global consumption of 'cultural' media images. The replacement of *involvement* with *observation*, discussed above, is nowhere more evident than in the way that broadcasting dominated proceedings of Live 8. Live 8 was predicted by its organizers to be 'the biggest global broadcast in history', reaching, according to the advertising industry, one-third of the world's population.[39] Geldof's TV company, Ten Alps, which provided the huge screens for Hyde Park, enjoyed 400% increase in profits following Live 8. One of the PR firms organizing Live 8, Freud Communications, is run by Matthew Freud, son-in-law to Rupert Murdoch and one of the most influential PR companies in the UK according to the *Financial Times*.[40] But the PR role in MPH goes beyond mere profit-making (itself a telling indictment of the outcome of mass political participation). It suggests a far more sinister proximity of PR organizing with New Labour itself.[41] Symbolic of this proximity was the appointment of the comedy director Richard Curtis in developing the PR image of the MPH campaign. Curtis, well-known personal friend of Gordon Brown, was deeply opposed to the campaign appearing to criticize Blair or Brown, and instead encouraged the image of Britain leading the way on the campaign's concerns, bravely attempting to bring the other countries on board.[42]

We should, without any doubt, remind ourselves of the positive implications of the MPH mobilization. It showed that people, as Stoker rightly points out, are willing to go beyond a politics of guilt to one of political hope. The public political debate about G8 legitimacy and transparency was amplified and genuine. The subsequent fall from grace of the G8 for Bono and Geldof in Germany, 2007 may show them to be human after all, for having placed too much faith in the promises of world leaders. And yet, we should also remember what exactly MPH achieved in the name of political participation. MPH was fundamentally *not a protest*, not even a show of popular force, but a show of the power of the media. That mobilization harnessed, above all, a conventionalized message on behalf of the powerful and replaced genuine critique with it. Rather than celebrate a diversity of strategies of dissent (from the most symbolic to the most physical, including civil disobedience) in the representation of people power, it called for a unified voice through the image of the concert crowd. The metaphor is a powerful one: through the performance of the rock star the moment of participation is iconized through the person of the celebrity him- or herself. It is through watching, consuming and mirroring the sentiment of the rock star that the spectator contributes. In her scream of 'revolution!' Madonna communicates perfectly its new significance. The assurance is that not only will the revolution be televised (and on a scale never seen before) but that the televisation itself will *be* the revolution. As an incursion of the 'informal power of civil society', therefore, MPH confirms the most cynical of Jean Baudrillard's critique of post-modern society: the reality of social communication has been replaced by communication itself. The signified is overrun by the mass format of the signifier. The substance of dissent is replaced by its communication.

Criminalizing dissent

The world should apply what Natan Sharansky calls the 'town square test': if a person cannot walk into the middle of the town square and express his or her views without fear of arrest, imprisonment, or physical harm, then that person is living in a fear society, not a free society. We cannot rest until every person living in a 'fear society' has finally won their freedom.

Condoleeza Rice[43]

MPH may well represent New Labour's successful monopoly on legitimate protest. If so, the experience of the alternative Edinburgh protests was also typical of its delegitimizing of the kind of protest that falls outside of this format. Not content to stand obediently in front of a TV screen, several different protest groups came to Scotland with a different emphasis. They came to protest at the very meeting of the G8, symbol for many people of the unaccountable 'management' of world poverty through exclusive business deals.[44] Significantly, they did not demand that every other campaigner adopt their confrontational tactics. While MPH events were encouraged within the ranks of these groups, no mention was made by MPH of these alternative events. While the MPH 'demonstrators' enjoyed the sanction of state and law, other peaceful protestors were subject to the latest of a wave of draconian criminal justice and anti-terror legislation. Everywhere 'unauthorized' protesters congregated, travelled and demonstrated, they met with new stop and search powers, arbitrary arrests and detainment. In a particularly symbolic instance, around four thousand people were placed under temporary siege by riot police at the eco-village protest camp in Stirling.

The uncovering of these police tactics for criminalizing peaceful protest is beginning to attract wider attention with the success of documentary films such as *Taking Liberties* (Chris Atkins et al., 2007). But civil rights campaigners have seen it coming for some years. Since coming to power, New Labour has created over 3,000 new offences, an unprecedented number passed at twice the rate as the previous Tory government.[45] Much of the emphasis for criminal legislation under Blair's tenure has been on strengthening summary justice against 'anti-social behaviour'. But more significantly it has become a systematic abuse of anti-terror legislation. The Terrorism Act 2000 came into effect for the first time in Scotland for the G8 summit, allowing police to detain protesters in purpose-built cells for up to a week without charge. It allows police officers to 'stop and search a person whom he reasonably suspects to be a terrorist'.[46] Applied over 36,000 times in 2006 alone, it has been used overwhelmingly in legitimate protests, something Blair's government promised would never happen. Because the individual orders are authorized from above, individual officers need provide no good reason to stop and search – proving an irresistible temptation to police officers. In a notorious case, anti-war protesters at the Fairford RAF base, in Yorkshire, found themselves stopped and searched consecutively as many as 11 times.[47] Police at that same demonstration stopped, searched, and then forced 3 coach loads of protesters to return to London, an action the High Court subsequently found in a landmark case to be unlawful. Having breached human rights legislation with their legislation on indefinite detention of suspects without trial in 2004, Blair's government then rushed through (parts of it weren't even complete at the time of passing) the 2005 Prevention of Terrorism Act which allowed the Home Office to place anyone it wanted under 'control orders' – effectively house arrest.

A stifling of the right to protest may not provide a direct causal explanation of a lack of political engagement in the UK. But it surely contributes to a normalization of passive, acquiescent society. Security legislation under New Labour has been enacted strategically within a climate of paranoia. Definitions of 'terrorism', like those of 'harassment' and 'anti-social behaviour' are notoriously and perhaps purposefully ill-defined. Corresponding legislation thus provides a green light to the criminalization of virtually anyone the government doesn't like. The eviction and detainment of 82-year-old Walter Wolfgang for saying 'nonsense' during Jack Straw's speech on Iraq at the 2005 Labour Party conference has become just one notorious example. It includes, of course, the policing of speech, with The Terrorism Act 2006 extending the outlawing of free speech to include any speech that 'glorifies' terrorism. The inability for any international consensus over what terrorism means, has led some to suggest that congratulating Nelson Mandela's achievements as a revolutionary or wearing a Che Guevara T-shirt might even break this new law.

New Labour's approach to crime and punishment does more than push the country ever nearer to a police state. It fundamentally undermines an environment of increasing alienation from the process of democratic expression. The parameters of political expression become unavailable and undesirable to the majority. We should see, in other words, the application of new terror laws a style of governance long in the making. Within this style the 'process of placing at one remove the political character of decision-making' is applied to the sphere of civil engagement itself. For what is the nature of democratic expression in this climate of paranoia? It is the gradual disaffection with politics that

shows no dramatic underwriting of democracy but the continual transformation of normal civil life as one that has no concern with political critique. As
George Monbiot puts it, 'democracies such as ours will come to an end not with
the stamping of boots and the hoisting of flags, but through the slow accretion
of a thousand dusty codicils'.[48] We might add that for some this 'slow accretion'
means in practice the sudden shocking application of new draconian police
measures, as peaceful protesters around the world are discovering. For the
rest of us, however, the point is that these experiments in quashing civil liberties means a gradual and almost imperceptible shrinking of the parameters of
action for civil society itself. Dissent, while becoming merely clandestine for
the minority brave enough to pursue it, simply ceases to be an option for the
vast majority. And with the persistence of the former, antagonistic style of protest as the meetings of the G8 has attracted, the stakes are simply raised higher
and higher. Thus, two years after MPH, the summit in Germany saw the police
forces using water cannons, CS gas and baton charges to deter protesters from
even approaching the perimeter fence that housed the G8 meetings.

Over thirty years ago Michel Foucault suggested that social institutions (more
generally 'technologies of power') describe not only power from above, but a
horizontal production of subjects, norms and behaviours. Furthermore subjects learn to discipline themselves, removing the need for traditional modes
of repression.[49] Noticing the criminalization of dissent over the past ten years
reveals, similarly, that *more* than civil liberties are at stake in the traditional
sense of upholding certain 'rights' against state control. It means critiquing
carefully the production and acceptance of a style of publicness, appropriate
political interaction and citizenship. This is an important approach to many
facets of New Labour's 'security' agenda that goes largely unchallenged. The
intensification of surveillance technology in the UK, itself unparalleled in
comparison to other EU countries, is often justified for deterring new and
unprecedented threats to national security. It is also defended against criticism by assurance that the only people who have cause to oppose it are criminals, or at least potential criminals. It is a common argument that if you're
not 'guilty' your life won't be affected by the proliferation of CCTV cameras
or the impending compulsion to carry ID cards. This is of course entirely
counter-intuitive, since as a method of deterrence, saturation of surveillance
techniques is designed precisely to create an environment in which crime is
unthinkable. But this is only possible through the perception that every movement is *potentially* watched, assessed and stored as data for future prosecution.
Producing a nation of citizens that are under permanent observation, cata-
loguing and instant identification is not only an act of centralized authority
or policing. It is also a process within a wider manufacturing of an illusion of civic cohesion by means of mutual mistrust and fear. This includes the
fear, of course, that we are all, as individuals, potentially guilty until proven
innocent. Like Bentham's 'panopticon' design for 24-hour surveillance in the

eighteenth century, the exercise of power on the individual is today to produce a self-disciplining social subject. How does this relate to the policing of dissent within the wider legacy of New Labour? The right kind of protester is arguably produced, reproduced, congratulated and empowered to be once again part of the political process. And in the same move, those protesters who breach these carefully demarcated boundaries are portrayed as *illegal* and therefore a threat to social order by definition.

The production of good and bad protesters is thus not only operative in the heavy-handed removal of dissent – as Walter Wolfgang discovered. It is also in the distancing of protest from sites traditionally associated with power and therefore as much symbolic as practical. It is telling that world leaders must today meet behind temporary fortresses, requiring massive investment in security, policing and surveillance, in order to keep the public away from the site of political decision-making. It is also telling that the new wave of anti-protest legislation aims specifically at this *spatial* aspect of social order. In 2001 the peace campaigner Brian Haw went into his fourth year of permanent protest outside the houses of Parliament against sanctions and war against Iraq since 2001. His constant application of the right to protest had become an intolerable embarrassment to the image conscious New Labour and it responded in the only way it knew how – by legislating. The Serious Organised Crime and Police Act (SOCPA) was introduced in 2005 – in direct response to Haw's protest – to criminalize 'unauthorized' protest in designated areas. Section 132 specifically relates to a 1 kilometre exclusion zone around Parliament Square in London.[50] Its ostensible purpose is to remove the publicness of protest. Just before the Chinese Premier visited Britain in 2004, Brian Haw was beaten, arrested, and had his peace camp confiscated in a midnight police operation that he later successfully contested. The price for illegally removing the public sign of dissent from the public glare had obviously been worth the price for Blair's government. Like the Terrorism Act, SOCPA has never been used to arrest or detain actual terrorists. The first people to be arrested and charged under its legislation were two peace activists, Milan Rai and Maya Evans. They were arrested for reading out the names of Iraqi civilians and British soldiers killed in the war on Iraq next to the cenotaph, while ringing tiny Tibetan bells.

The strategy has proved highly effective. As physical spaces of dissent diminish, so does the government's democratic accountability. The appropriate place for critique becomes increasingly privatized spheres of interaction – opinion blogs, televised debates and Prime Minister's Question Time. Tony Blair's favoured personal response to public, explicit protest has been to insinuate that one should be grateful for the principle of democratic freedoms, and leave it at that. During an address to the Labour Party conference in 2004, Blair responded to a lone anti-war heckler, 'That's fine, sir. You can make your protest. Just thank goodness we live in a democracy and you can' at the same time as that heckler was handcuffed, arrested, and taken away to a police cell.[51] The point about free protest is precisely not one of gratitude but of demanding and prosecuting an active democratic principle. This is also the significance of Brian Haw's symbolic protest. It is a reminder that freedom of speech is a right that must be exercised tirelessly, not only acknowledged in principle. That New Labour has been so bent upon denying the public its spaces of open dissent shows its unwillingness to acknowledge the alternative forms of political participation that so many have argued is replacing traditional forms such as voting.

Conclusion: Privatizing belief

The shrinking of public sites of dissent discussed in this chapter reveals a dangerous paradox within New Labour's general rhetoric of 'security'. The government's challenge has been to acknowledge terrorism as a threat not only from outside the UK but also within its very communities. At the same time, I have argued, it wishes to create a greater distance than ever between private belief and public political expression. This lends itself very well to the criminalization of dissent under the pretext of the 'necessary' unfreedom of a state of emergency. But there is good evidence to suggest that a feeling of alienation from democratic debate and the antagonism of British foreign policy for the lives of its citizens (with particular reference to, though not exclusively, British Muslims) is fuel for the very thing it fears – 'politicized' or 'radicalized' dissent. The question of depoliticization explored above is thus related to this further question: what forms of dissent *can* contemporary liberal democracies tolerate? What risks are tolerable to it?

Important lessons can be learned here from the privatization of religious belief in the secularization process. For the crisis at the heart of secular liberalism today is this: there is a desire to invite tolerance towards a diversity of faiths on the condition that they are *easily* ostracized from social discourse as soon as they begin to deviate from the dominant one. This goes some way to explaining the incompetence of many public leaders, politicians and journalists at understanding in any meaningful depth the grievances of young Muslims. Without doubt, this is a hugely complex task. How does one engage with those *so far* outside a dominant political ideology that they are able to take their own lives and hundreds of others with them in opposition to it? In the UK, many reactions to the bombings on 7 July 2005 reflected an incredulity that such an atrocity could emerge from British society itself. The overwhelming desire in that instance was to be able to cast the perpetrators as mad, fundamentalist and bearing no communicable relation to the world-view of the rest of us. This desire for defining the enemy as a complete *outsider* is inseparable with the affirmation of what remains on the *inside* – that is, the rational, universalizing

discourse of tolerant liberals 'like us'. As I have tried to argue, today in liberal
society the public sphere is pushed into a space that is, for many people, literally uninhabitable. It is out of bounds, accessible in principle alone. Within
this environment policies that criminalize and punish dissent can only encourage anger and alienation among those most affected by its policy decisions.

Here the crisis in understanding a *locus classicus* of the West's 'outside', the
figure of 'radical Islam', relates to a much more general crisis in the acceptance
of difference in UK society in general, and thus the criminalization of dissent.
For New Labour's reaction, much like that of the US and other prosecutors of
the 'war on terror' to the enigma of religiously motivated terror has been characteristic of a rush to 'explain away' the threat of a radically oppositional and
public ideology. This is done by reference to a private, spiritual version from
which the radical version must deviate. Blair, like Bush, was quick to condemn
in the wake of the London bombing not Muslims but those whose faith had
become radicalized, politicized and 'gone public'. Ever since the birth of war
on terror rhetoric, the truth underlying both Bush and Blair's insistence that
'this is not a war on Islam' has been that, on the contrary, Islam has simply
become a term suited to reduce complex social grievances to something sim-
pler in their view: 'radical Islam' or 'political Islam'. The presupposition that
there is such a thing as good, tamed, universally acceptable Islam such that
the bad alternative – fundamentalist, violent Islam – can be universally and
uncontroversially rejected has been a powerful effective form for the focus
of a new global offensive. It makes dealing with the problem of religious violence a powerfully simple one: religious extremism is a madness which those
from a secular liberal persuasion will simply never understand. Thus, Polly
Toynbee could write that religious terrorism is 'not about poverty, deprivation,
or cultural dislocation' but only about 'religious delusion'.[52] On the contrary,
the two might well be more inseparable than liberal secularists would like to
admit. For the imagination of religion as something that is acceptable as long
as it does not threaten to 'go public' springs, as Russell McCutcheon argues in
Religion and the Domestication of Dissent, from a desire to avoid messiness in our
society. It is the refusal to live in 'less than perfect' societies.[53]

The past few years have seen the emergence of self-appointed experts on religious violence, extremism and fundamentalism.[54] Fundamentalist terrorism
therefore represents the nightmare that is triggered when religion breaks out
of its private realm and defames its 'timeless principles' with 'sadly degraded
forms of subsequent *practice*'.[55] But the misnomer of 'political Islam' is therefore synonymous with our perception of fanaticism itself, or the tendency for
any belief to turn violent given its incursion into public life. McCutcheon's analysis thus greatly illuminates my critique of New Labour and the depoliticization
of the public sphere in general. I have asked where it is that dissenters may
take their grievances without being tarred with the same brush as 'fundamentalists', 'fanatics' and 'terrorists'. For such, of course is the farcical experience of

anyone who has been arrested under terror legislation for acts as symbolic and peaceful as reading out the names of war dead or for wearing a peace T-shirt. It is also the challenge that confronts every protester that faces the popular castigation of their actions as 'helping the cause of terrorists'. This indistinction between public acts of protest and dangerous incursions upon state security is the same for religious beliefs as it is for secular ones. In both cases there is at play a very powerful manufacture of political 'authenticity' and 'normal' citizenship in social discourse. As McCutcheon puts it: 'Whether in academia, the courts, or on street corners, the discourse on faith, principles, authenticity, and belief act as but one cog in virtually any wheel, making a particular world possible only by allowing marginal groups to gain some sort of acceptance if only they idealize and privatize themselves, thereby simultaneously reproducing and putting up the conditions of their own marginality.'[56] The increasing attitude in our societies is that dissent is acceptable as long as it doesn't take itself too seriously.

Where does this bleak picture leave the possibility for a healthy, dissenting democratic society in the future? Professor Stoker may be right to observe, through quantitative data, that incursions of genuine public political dissent through such mobilizations as anti-capitalist or anti-war protest are rare and erratic, though there is reason to believe even this trend is changing. What those practices also represent, however, is a rejection of depoliticized protest and the symbolic protest of the mediatized 'event'. Unfortunately this may only be possible by *deepening* people's mistrust and scepticism towards political parties in today's 'post-democratic' environment. To redeem a sense of morality in contemporary politics by reference to swearing 'hand on heart' that those in charge believe in what they are doing will do nothing to re-engage the electorate. This approach only strengthens the privatization of 'political faith'. And the debate over morality in politics is vastly poorer if the most we can offer the electorate is to say that politicians, like all of us, make mistakes and sometimes fudge the facts. As I hope this chapter has demonstrated, the point is precisely that politicians *do not* operate by the same rules of moral engagement as we do everyday, and should not be judged by them. Most of us do not make decisions over waging war or criminalizing certain types of behaviour, and if we *did* then we should expect a far more rigorous analysis of how we came to those decisions. For to do these things requires in reality, as is continually revealed to the public, much more than the bluffing, half-truths and white lies of our everyday moral grey areas. It involves a complex and strategic process of shielding truth, debate and protest from the public domain. In the context of the moral half-truths that has so far led to over a hundred thousand Iraqi deaths, Stoker's observation that 'not telling the truth is not necessarily cheating; it can be a way of getting on in a complex society'[57] is both offensive and dangerously misleading.

Genuine democratic participation demands that political life is lifted outside of the private sphere. This might mean that its moral demands of politicians move beyond those of the 'merely human', to reaffirming once again those political ideals that seem practically impossible, such as the ideal of democracy itself. And at the heart of the principle of democracy is the demand that *dissent* is not only acknowledged in principle but practiced freely, peacefully and without fear. Without it, the fight for a renewed sense of citizenship will always remain on two levels: for the majority, remaining at the level of passive spectators; and for the minority of 'believers', being alienated from the mainstream and viewed as utopians and extremists.

Notes

[1] Tony Blair's resignation speech, transcribed by *BBC News*, 10 May 2007 [http://news.bbc.co.uk/1/hi/uk_politics/6642857.stm] [accessed 10 July 2007].

[2] Charles Glass, 'Top drawer', *Zmag*, 13 June 1999 [www.zmag.org/ZSustainers/ZDaily/1999-06/june_13glass.htm] [accessed 2 Oct. 2007].

[3] Gerry Stoker, *Why Politics Matters: Making Democracy Work* (Hampshire: Palgrave Macmillan, 2006) p. 47.

[4] Slavoj Zizek, 'Passion: Regular or Decaf?' *In These Times*, 27 February 2004 [www.lacan.com/zizek-passion.htm] [accessed 27 June 2007].

[5] Quoted by *BBC News 24* [http://news.bbc.co.uk/1/hi/uk/3269605.stm] [accessed 26 June 2007].

[6] John Pilger, 'Kebabing the Tonier-than-thou club', *The New Statesman*, 7 March 2005 [www.newstatesman.com/200503070013] [accessed 27 June 2007].

[7] The Electoral Commission, 'Election 2005: Turnout – How many, who, and why?' (London: The Electoral Commission, 2005).

[8] Jack Straw, 'The future for democracy – Politics in a spectator society', *The Fabian Society*, 28 June 2006 [www.fabian-society.org.uk/press_office/news_latest_all.asp?pressid=558] [accessed 19 June 2007].

[9] Frank Furedi, 'Foreword' in Malcolm J. Todd and Gary Taylor (eds), *Democracy and Participation: Popular Protest and New Social Movements* (London: Merlin Press, 2004) p. xii.

[10] Anthony Giddens, interview with Polity Press, 2007 [www.polity.co.uk/giddens5/news/sociology-and-politics.asp] [accessed 21 June 2007].

[11] Madeleine Bunting, 'We are the people', *The Guardian*, 17 February 2003. [www.guardian.co.uk/print/0,,4607202-103677,00.html] [accessed 20 June 2007].

[12] Colin Brown and Francis Elliott, 'Blair warns that marchers will have "blood on their hands"', *The Sunday Telegraph*, 15 February 2003 [http://www.telegraph.co.uk/news/main.jhtml?xml=/news/2003/02/16/ndemo116.xml] [accessed 21 June 2007].

[13] Stoker, conference paper, *Remoralizing Britain?* p. 15.

[14] Ibid. p. 13.

[15] Furedi, 'Foreword', p. xii.

[16] Stoker, *Why Politics Matters*, pp. 47–51.

[17] Ibid. p. 102.

[18] Ibid. pp. 101–2.

19 Peter Burnham, 'New Labour and the politics of depoliticisation', *British Journal of Politics and International Relations*, vol. 3, no. 2, June 2001 (pp. 127–49) p. 128.

20 Burnham's argument goes something like this: Blair's approach to regaining confidence in its economic ability while maintaining a traditional left-of-centre electoral base has translated into an 'arms-length' approach to financial regulation that surrenders certain aspects of state intervention to the markets (such as wages, working hours and other labour rights) as extrapolitical. At the same time the impression is given of retaining ultimate political control of these processes – hence economic confidence against financial crises. Depoliticization therefore represents not a separation of politics from economics but on the contrary a highly politicized strategy of statecraft. It allows government to 'off-load responsibility for unpopular policies' as no longer the realm of popular political concern. Ibid. pp. 127–49.

21 Ibid. p. 137.

22 Timothy Brewes, *Cynicism and Postmodernity* (London: Verso, 1997) pp. 69–74.

23 *The Financial Times*, 13 June 2007 [www.ft.com/cms/s/6dd34230-194b-11dc-a961-000b5df10621.html] [accessed 26 June 2007].

24 See David Michie, *The Invisible Persuaders: How Britain's Spin Doctors Manipulate the Media* (London: Bantam Press, 1998).

25 Stoker, *Why Politics Matters*, p. 59.

26 Colin Crouch, *Post-Democracy* (London: Polity, 2004) p. 4.

27 Quoted by Simon Hoggart, 'A sprinkle of stardust on our John and Paul', *The Guardian*, 30 September 2004 [http://politics.guardian.co.uk/labour2004/comment/0,,1316054,00.html] [accessed 12 July 2007].

28 Stoker, conference paper, *Remoralizing Britain?* p. 17.

29 Stuart Hodkinson, 'Inside the murky world of the UK's Make Poverty History Campaign', *Spinwatch*, 27 June 2005.

30 Mark Tran, 'Geldof hits out at "G8 farce"', *The Guardian*, 8 June 2007 [http://politics.guardian.co.uk/development/story/0,,2098835,00.html#article_continue] [accessed 14 June 2007].

31 MPH was also the occasion for a wake-up call about Oxfam's (the biggest player in MPH from development agencies) close ties with New Labour and the World Bank. Following the New Statesman's report on numerous Oxfam board members going on to serve as New Labour advisers, such as Justin Forsyth, now Blair's special adviser on international development, some suggested at the time that Oxfam had become a 'feeder school for government special advisers and World Bank Officials' (Hodkinson, 'Inside the murky world', p. 2). With £40 million of their annual income coming directly from government, it is hardly surprising that scrutiny has crept into the ability for an organization like Oxfam's ability to distance itself from the government's own economic policies.

32 Bruce Whitehead, quoted by John Pilger, 'The ghost at Gleneagles' in *The New Statesman*, 11 July 2005 [www.newstatesman.com/200507110004] [accessed 14 June 2007].

33 Kofi Maluwi Klu, quoted by Hodkinson, 'Inside the murky world'.

34 *The Making of an Impoverished History: The politics of Live 8, G8 and the UK Media from an African British Perspective*, August 2000, Ligali organisation.

35 George Monbiot, 'Bards of the Powerful', *The Guardian*, 21 June 2005 [http://arts.guardian.co.uk/print/0,,5220235-116859,00.html] [accessed 14 June 2007].

36 Hodkinson, 'Inside the murky world'.

37 Ibid.

38 Quoted by John Pilger, 'From Iraq to the G8: The Polite Crushing of Dissent and Truth', www.pilger.com [accessed 13 June 2007].

39 Michel Chossudovsky, 'Live 8: Corporate Media Bonanza' *ALAI, América Latina en Moviento* [www.alainet.org/active/8627&lang=es] [accessed 14 June 2007].

40 Ann Talbot, 'Live 8: Who Organised the PR Campaign for Blair and Bush?', *World Socialist Website* [www.wsws.org/articles/2005/jul2005/live-j11.shtml] [accessed 14 June 2007].

41 Both Matthew Freud and Elisabeth Murdoch sit on various government committees. Ten Alps is also closely tied to the government, producing through Teachers' TV, programmes for the Department of Education and Skills. Ann Talbot, 'Live 8'.

42 Hodkinson, 'Inside the murky world'.

43 Condoleeza Rice, quoted by Thomas Riggins, 'The immoral clarity of Natan Sharansky' *PoliticalAffairs* [www.politicalaffairs.net/article/articleview/672/1/77] [accessed 22 June 2007].

44 Both the G8 and World Bank represent to most serious development campaigners the principal source of that poverty they purport to 'make history'. At a parallel meeting of the 'Group of 77' world leaders, representing 80% of the world's countries, the Prime Minister of Belize, Said Musa, once put it this way: the economic policies of the G8, representing the interests of the minority richest, represented not, as they argued, the stabilization of economies, but the stabilization of poverty – Roger Burbach, *Globalization and Post-modern Politics: From Zapatistas to High-Tech Robber Barons* (London: Pluto Press, 2001) p. 148. The G8 meeting fulfilled successive previous meetings in the economic conditions it attached to new aid packages. Most significant of these are the demands for greater privatization of natural resources, or 'elimination of impediments to private investment, both domestic and foreign' – deals that will secure business for European firms keen to get a foothold in the 'new scramble for Africa' – David Miller, 'Was the G8 Gr8?' *Spinwatch*, 11 July 2005 [www.spinwatch.org/content/view/3691/8/] [accessed 12 July 2007].

45 Nigel Morris, 'Blair's "frenzied law making": a new offence for every day spent in office', *The Independent*, 16 August 2006 [http://news.independent.co.uk/uk/politics/article1219484.ece] [accessed 22 June 2007].

46 *The Terrorism Act 2000* (London: Crown Copyright, 2000) p. 25.

47 George Monbiot, 'A threat to democracy', *The Guardian*, 3 August 2004 [www.guardian.co.uk/comment/story/0,3604,1274676,00.html] [accessed 22 June 2007].

48 Ibid.

49 See Michel Foucault, *Discipline and Punish: Birth of the Prison*, trans. Alan Sheridan (London: Penguin, 1991).

50 Chris Atkins, Sarah Bee and Fiona Button, *Taking Liberties* (London: Revolver Books, 2007) p. 35.

51 Nigel Farndale, 'Try saluting, Mr Straw, it's a lot safer', *The Daily Telegraph*, 3 November 2004 [www.telegraph.co.uk/opinion/main.jhtml?xml=/opinion/2004/10/03/do0308.xml] [accessed 25 June 2007].

52 Polly Toynbee, 'In the Name of God', *The Guardian*, 22 July, 2005 [http://www.guardian.co.uk/comment/story/0,,1533942,00.html] [accessed 12 July 2007].

53 Russell T. McCutcheon, *Religion and the Domestication of Dissent* (London: Equinox, 2005).

54 In the months that followed 11 September bookshops stocked up on a new wave of 'introductions' to Islam and experienced a huge increase in sales of the Koran. As a best-selling post-11September book, *Islam: A Short Introduction* by Karen Armstrong puts it, '(Islam's) power struggles are not what religion is really all about, but an unworthy distraction from the *life of the spirit*, which is conducted far from the madding crowd, unseen, silent, and unobstructive.' – quoted in Ibid. p. 63. Or again, from Salman Rushdie: 'The restoration of religion to the sphere of the personal, its depoliticization . . . is the nettle that all Muslim societies must grasp in order to become modern . . .' – Ibid. p. 59. McCutcheon argues that these attempts to 'understand' and stand in solidarity with 'true' Islam fell into a fundamental illusion that religions deposit a unifying, enduring truth over time that we can all grasp through a guided reading of its central tenets and appreciate on the 'spiritual' level.

55 Ibid. p. 37; emphasis in original.

56 Ibid. p. 92.

57 Stoker, *Why Politics Matters*, p. 127.

Chapter 4

New Labour and a Liberal Labour Tradition

Will Hutton

Introduction

The enduring importance of Tony Blair for British politics – and perhaps European and North American politics as well – is going to be the establishment of what I call a 'liberal Labour tradition', which I see as almost a mirror image of the liberal conservative tradition. This 'liberal Labour tradition' will join Methodism, Marxism and trade unionism as one of the traditions that make up the Labour Party. In terms of British politics, it is setting up some very interesting dynamics in the Labour Party. It will be very interesting indeed to see whether Gordon Brown actually understands himself in these terms, or whether he's just going to revert to a kind of modernist version of Labourism. It will also force social democrats and liberal conservatives to rethink their understanding of the plural nature of our society. I am hoping that this is going to be illuminating in terms of the preoccupations of this book, concerned as it is with, among other things, the moral foundations of Blairism. As I go through, I'll try to point out where I think there are moral implications for what I'm saying.

Critiques of capitalism and the formation of the British Left

For me, the foundation of a Leftist position is an economic critique of capitalism. And essentially there are two: the Keynesian critique and the Marxist critique. Broadly, from the mid-1870s to the late-1940s, it was difficult to mount a liberal critique – a Keynesian critique – of capitalism. Marxism was dominant because it seemed like capitalism was conforming to Marx's precepts – the instabilities, the recessions, the immiseration of the working class by 1914 more than justified Marx's predictions. Then there was the communist revolution in Russia, then China, and by 1950, most of the Eurasian land mass was run by communist parties. They were building on the notion that there *was* class war, which emanated from class structures which themselves were based on the possession of private property, that the instabilities in capitalism require a mass response, and that the response should be through the state, which the party should run. British Labourism was a diluted version of this Marxist critique.

The other option was the Keynesian tradition – Keynes was a liberal – whose view was that markets may have instabilities, they may throw up inequities and there may be monopolies, but actually the state can proactively manage them, and the good things about markets, such as their pluralism and their capacity for wealth generation mustn't become the baby thrown out with the bathwater. The British left, from its inception, from Keir Hardie to the first Labour government of Ramsay MacDonald, then the Attlee 1945–51 government, were more informed by a Marxist view than by a Keynesian view. And I think that the battle's been on within not just the British left but the European left, to reinvent a left position, as it has become obvious from the 1950s onward that two things are true. First of all, the kind of response that the left proposed to capitalism doesn't work; and secondly, that the kind of Keynesian interventions, coupled with the construction of welfare state, health and education, does create a compromise, if you like, which works *better* than conventional socialist blueprints. And it doesn't matter whether it's Pierre Safra[1] *or* the various kinds of Marxist left scholars – all of them have been intellectually proven wrong. And that's created a genuine crisis on the Left.

The most obvious place where Marxism is shown to be wrong is in the reactions of the Chinese Communist Party. In my *The Writing on the Wall,* I note Deng Xiaoping's view that it does not matter whether the cat is black or white, as long as it catches mice.[2] When in deposition and exile under the Cultural Revolution, Deng Xiaoping spent from 1967 to 1974 working in a tractor factory outside Shanghai. Deng was a great listener to the BBC World Service. And, when he took power in 1978/9, it was actually hearing the story of what was happening in South Korea, Hong Kong, Taiwan and the Philippines, that convinced him the position he'd taken in the early 1960s was correct. Subsequently, it was the determination of Deng Xiaoping to liberate China from state planning that meant he was the father of the Chinese boom.

Compared to what's taken place in the past 25 years, there is no denying that the economic performance of China under a communist way of looking at the world from 1948 to 1976 is transparently different. So much so that you can't find any intellectual of the left based in China who believes in Marxist precepts. That's now formally been incorporated, of course, into the constitution of China: the Chinese Constitution was changed in February 2002. The People's Republic of China is now committed to constructing a socialist *market* economy – the doctrine that Hu represents – and the Chinese Communist Party has repudiated class war, and has also repudiated the notion that it is spreading international communism. Now this is really very important for the

European left. This is why I have become in the past ten years more Keynesian, more liberal in the sense that Keynes understood it. And it has helped me better to understand the significance of Tony Blair for the renewal of the Left.

Three things have happened. First, intellectually, you cannot make a Marxist case about capitalism. You can certainly say that capitalism throws up inequality, you can certainly argue that capitalism throws up private monopoly, you can certainly argue that capitalism throws up class, you can certainly make an argument that capitalism throws up instability. I make all those arguments, which is why I am a critic of capitalism. What you cannot say is that there is an embedded dynamic within capitalism that will bring its own demise. And what you cannot say is that the response to capitalism should be widespread public ownership and planning. So that kind of intellectual critique of capitalism has gone, and it's meant the left has lost its foundation, and this is why the British Labour Party does not now have a coherent story; it can't find a position to cohere around.

Second, there has been 'proof positive' about the operation of capitalism. Take the arguments that people like John Kay[3] make about capitalism – that the point about capitalism and markets is not price mechanism and private property and decentralized decision-making (the kind of Adam Smith argument), but rather that the point about markets is a pluralist one. They permit endless experimentation, and the system doesn't have to bet on one monopoly thinker and one monopoly producer. It can insure itself against the notion that if it backs one horse it might be wrong by having *plural* runners and riders at any one time to back. And this affects the notion of how to run an organization and of what kind of technology to back.

Third, of course, it has been warranted by people's lived experience, which in turn has supported a change in the social basis of Labourism. In the British private sector, less than 12% of the labour force is unionized. In the private service sector it is less than 8%. If you try to organize in a bank or insurance company or retailer (unless you follow the model of USDAW, which has been a very interesting and dynamic union that talks entirely about partnering companies and partnering in a way that is absolute against the ideology of other parts of the labour movement), you can't make a pitch; you can't persuade workers to sign up.

Three pillars of liberalism and the Blairite response

So there you are – it's 1994, and you're Tony Blair taking up the post of leader of the Labour Party: the social base has altered for the Labour Party, the intellectual argument has been eviscerated, and the lived experience is that markets work. But it is also true that there is inequality, monopoly, declining social mobility, decline of opportunity. Blair actually said in the 1995 Labour Party conference, 'I am my brother's keeper; I will not pass by on the other side.' Blair has told me that what took him into politics, at university and immediately after university, was not being upset about the condition of the working class in Britain, but actually about the condition of the less-developed world. Certainly it's a kind of 'Kiplingesque' desire to engage with the poverty of others outside these islands, which was inspired by religious belief. And he has also acknowledged the importance of religious belief to him in that he comes to the left from *values*, and then he tries to build a political position on values, but always trying to align those values with the centre-left.

And that's how he saw the only way for Labour to win in 1994. That led to my own reflections about liberalism. In the middle chapters of *The Writing on the Wall*, I try to develop a framework for thinking about liberal precepts, whether it be drawn from J. S. Mill, John Rawls, Amartya Sen or Charles Taylor. What I've tried to do is distil the essence of these great liberal thinkers, and come up with what I think their precepts are. I was actually doing this to critique Jiang Zemin's document of the Three Represents, and to show how shallow I thought the ideological revisions were in the Chinese Communist Party. But the more I did it, the more illuminating I found it about political revisions closer to home, and it led me to conclude that there are three pillars on which liberal thought is constructed.

The first is pluralism: an absolute hostility to notions of monopoly in both the public and the private sector, and thus not only traditional liberal suspicions of the overmighty state, but also liberal concerns in the American tradition about 'trust bust', and the need to take on private monopoly very aggressively. This constitutes a recognition that the virtue of markets is less profit-motive and respect for private property, although clearly that *is* a precondition for successful markets.

The second pillar found in the great liberal thinkers, is a desire to enhance, invest in and sustain individual capacities through public action. This isn't – and this is important – in the first place a *redistributional* agenda; it's actually about, in Rawlsian terms, providing minimum education, minimum living standards, minimum safeguards, minimum right to participate in civil society. Amartya Sen takes the same line. And so this extends the 'night watchman' idea of Hayek, who is a minimalist for whom all you do is promote property rights and provide a legal framework for effective policing of contract, defence of the realm, and security of law and order. Of course, Rawls and Sen extend that and say you have to broaden your conception of capacities well beyond that, through cradle to grave welfare. Because if you're going to have a pluralist system, it's got to be peopled by articulate, self-confident actors, and there needs to be public investment to make sure that they are forthcoming.

And then the third pillar of liberal society is justification and accountability processes. I began to see how a public realm in which you can operate not only checks-and-balance government, but also a free press, independent court system, independent audit, independent provision of statistics, independent competition authorities, trade unions – the whole paraphernalia of corporate governance – all of that is a process of mutual holding-to-account which again in China does not take place. It became obvious to me as I studied it that actually being held to account in these complex ways by shareholders and unions is an important *driver* of managerial productivity – and that's quite apart from the moral case for the justification of accountability processes.

Now those three pillars are emergent in Britain in the seventeenth and eighteenth century; they underpin the great Whig tradition in Britain. Of course, the Tories up until the middle of the nineteenth century were broadly opposed to that: opposed to any form of pluralism against aristocratic government. They were certainly against any justification or accountability processes because that denied either the crown or the church the scope it had for discretion – it might challenge the traditional bases of order. The Tory or 'country' view of England was opposed to these three liberal precepts. It was the Whigs that carried them. And it was Disraeli, in his invention of one nation Toryism, who led the Tory party to the beginnings of the embrace of these three pillars of liberalism.

Then came the rise of Marx and Marxism, the arrival of the Labour Party, which was building a political base in the era of universal franchise, and then of course the crisis in Whig England or liberal England after the First World War, when between 50 and 100 liberal members of parliament literally stood down in favour of conservatives. This was when Winston Churchill crossed over to the Conservative Party and created the Whig liberal tradition *within* the Conservative Party. And we all know 'Whig Tories'; I think the classic Whig Tory is Ian Gilmore, and under Mrs Thatcher they were the Tory 'wets'. In some respects, I think that David Cameron is a pale version of a Whig Tory; he has put his name to 'liberal conservatism' in a couple of foreign policy speeches he has given. It was a great tradition in British politics – it was a winning card. It was the *appropriation* by the Tories of the liberal tradition; the precepts of pluralism, individual capacities and justification were the underpinning of Conservative one nation policy. It was actually the foundation of winning successive elections, except for 1945 and 1966, which were the only elections that the Labour Party won 'big' until 1997.

How I understand Tony Blair is having invented a *liberal Labour tradition* as a counterweight to the liberal conservative tradition. When I put this to him, he said, 'precisely'. Think about what he's tried to do since 1994, such as the totemic and important announcement that he wanted the abolition of Clause 4. Rejecting this commitment to abolish private property and establish public ownership was much more than just saying 'I repudiate that tradition'. It was overt embrace of pluralism in the private sector. Actually, I think that it's also distinctive how Blair has wanted to *use* the state from 1997–2007: he was trying to use public institutions and devise public institutions that contain within them social democratic, and in his terms Christian, values – but to construct these as 'intermediate institutions', residing between the State and civil society.

There are three or four examples of these institutions. The 'City Academy' is a classic example of an independent public institution, governed independently by boards of governors of whom the majority are appointed by the private sector or the charity for the City Academy. This can only go on in school because the constitutional architecture is set up in a number of Education Acts which only permit a limited amount of selection or banding and insists upon that kind of universalist or comprehensive tradition. As Blair would put it, they are schools which are independently founded around a social democratic notion. And the City Academies I've been round have actually rather impressed me. A second example: my wife chairs a mental health trust, in the 'gap' between the State and civil society (an 'intermediate' kind of position if you like). I think these have been rather effective drivers for improvement in British healthcare. Third, I think the sector skills councils have been effective intermediate institutions. And that is how I understand Blair's attempt to develop a pluralist tradition, but on the Left.

On the question of capacities, Blair and Brown are not redistributionalist in the sense of going for high marginal rates of tax and the construction of a financial welfare state. What they do is they justify investing in education, investing in training, investment in housing, by describing it as about 'building up' the capacities of individuals. In particular, that's why they focus so much of their effort and rhetoric around 'investing in children'.

And then lastly, on the matter of justification and accountability is where Blair has been weakest. But in his first term in office he did incorporate the European Convention on Human Rights into British Law, devolved government, established a mayor for London and there has been the Freedom of Information Act. He would argue that that's the way he's trying to advance the last of these three liberal pillars.

Conclusion

This liberal Labourism is also not above a bit of liberal populism. When it comes to Anti-Social Behaviour Orders (ASBOs) and asylum seekers, Blair would argue that the Labour Party needs to demonstrate that it's engaging with real fears on housing estates. And there's a great paper been done by Nicola Gavron for the Young Foundation looking at housing in the East End, revisiting Wilmot and Young's great study.[4] What's fascinating is that the first wave of Bangladeshi immigrants, who came in the 1960s, 70s and 80s, are really anxious to move away from *needs*-based housing to *entitlement*-based housing. In other words, being virtuous should entitle you to a flat or a house, and you should be able to move up the ladder, rather than see, as some Bangladeshis said in interviews with Nicola Gavron and others, the latest asylum seekers off the plane 'getting over' others on the housing ladder because of their housing need. You get a kind of 'intra-tension' between ethnic minorities. The Blairites would say, 'what would you expect?' That is, as a moral proposition, earning your place in housing is a kind of liberal populist notion.

So I do think that we have on the one hand a Tony Blair who himself says, 'I've tried to reinvent the liberal Labour tradition'. In this chapter I've tried to indicate the ways in which he's done it: that is, around these notions of pluralism, investment in capacities and justification. On the other hand, he has stayed away from being resdistributionalist. He's been far too willing to let the private sector in, which threatens to lead to the development of 'turbo-capitalism'. I find the financial engineering, and what's taking place in our great companies at the moment very destructive. Yet all this is happening on Labour's watch. However, I have to acknowledge that this liberal Labour tradition has won three general elections, and it's going to make an indelible imprint on left-centre politics.

The most important reason that Gordon Brown had to wait for three more years to take office is that Brown himself has migrated, importantly, in that time, and Blair had been watching this process taking place. In Brown's Mais Lecture, an important paper he gave to the Social Market Foundation,[5] Brown was differentiating himself importantly from Blair, saying that there were some institutions that must remain unambiguously in the public domain, and run by the public sector. He was very resistant to the notion that you could construct intermediate institutions of the type that Blair has done. He didn't like Foundation Hospitals, and he didn't like City Academies. But I now think that Gordon Brown will keep Andrew Adonis on at the DfES and *promote* the City Academies. He has himself migrated to a much more liberal Labour position than he would have held three years ago. He hasn't migrated enough for Blair, but more than Brown would have considered previously.

I think a Presbyterian 'Roundhead' running a united Labour Party around a liberal Labour programme is going to be quite tough for the Conservative Party to beat in 2009/2010 if Brown can meet that billing – quite an 'ask'. Given the historic inability of the Left to get themselves together, we can see just what an achievement Blair has pulled off. But putting that to one side, I think we can, when talking about the domestic record of Blair, see the construction of this liberal Labour tradition, and the clear understanding of it persisting. David Miliband talks, as we know, about 'liberal Labour'; so does Alan Johnson; so does Tessa Jowell; so does Blair himself. If this 'liberal Labour tradition' becomes one of the traditions which actually make up the Labour Party, as I suggested at the beginning, this will make it a much tougher political force for the Tories to beat. Moreover, it will provide for ambitious young men and women who want to run a left-of-centre government in Britain a role model and an approach they can borrow in future. I am much more confident that Labour will be a genuine contender for power in the next 50 years, unlike the past 50.

Notes

1 Cambridge economist writing in the 1920s, who tried to develop a Ricardian system – the production of commodities by commodities.
2 Will Hutton, 2007, *The Writing on the Wall: China and the West in the 21st Century* (London: Little & Brown).
3 John Kay, 2004, *The Truth about Markets* (London: Penguin).
4 Wilmot and Young, 'Family Life in Bethnal Green'.
5 18 May 2004 Speech by the Chancellor of the Exchequer to the Social Market Foundation.

Chapter 5

Gordon Brown and His Presbyterian Moral Compass

Doug Gay

The reformation of New Labour, if not its denomination, predates the Blair–Brown project. If Neil Kinnock's leadership is hailed as having stopped the rot, it was under John Smith that Labour finally began to rebuild its electoral credibility. A key part of this renewal involved restoring Labour's battered reputation for economic competence. Smith, seen to combine 'the earnest goodwill of a Kirk elder with the solid trustworthiness of an Edinburgh bank manager',[1] was well placed to begin this task. It is significant therefore that even before Gordon Brown's final rise to power, restoration of the 'trust factor' had already been given a Scots-Presbyterian assist.

Following his early death, John Smith was buried on the island of Iona, like a Scottish king of old; reflecting both his love of the island and his increasing affinity with the Iona Community.[2] The *realpolitik* attached to such passings meant that grief and shock were swiftly mingled with jockeying for position in the race to succeed him. The Blair–Brown compact was twisted into its now classic shape and Brown finally took the Scots-Presbyterian mantle into No. 11 rather than No. 10. The calculation cruelly forced upon Brown by, first among others, Peter Mandelson, was that he simply would not win against Tony. The Kirk elder/bank manager gravitas functioned best it was reckoned, to *reassure* middle England, rather than to inspire it.

Within New Labour's religious devotion to image and media presentation, there was an awareness, dating from the Smith years, that the Scots-Presbyterian *aura*, positioned rightly, could enhance Labour's electoral appeal. Despite his bitterness about missing out on the top job, since he was the prudent housekeeper rather than the visionary leader, Brown could expect this image/ethos cluster to work in his favour. He could afford to remain relatively relaxed about the more negative hues it contained, since even a reputation for thriftiness and dourness were seen at least initially as potent allies in combating old Labour tax and spend stereotypes. It certainly provided colour for journalists creating profiles and features on Brown, who splashed it relentlessly with little concern to do justice to either the cultural or theological implications of their references.

In terms of boosting Labour's 'ethical capital',[3] what the aura signalled above all was that Brown could be trusted. To the watching public he might not (as the elder or bank manager might not) pass the George W. 'barbecue' test[4] with flying colours, but there was a sense that their money/the economy might be safe in his hands. This was enormously valuable to Labour, particularly in their first post-1997 term, but ultimately right through Brown's time as Chancellor. In fact, as New Labour's decade in power progressed, Brown's 'Presbyterian' origins and associations came to be increasingly valued as a positive identifier by his own advisers, speech-writers and media managers.

The narrative is now well-known, because it is well-spun and often repeated in public, but it deserves some greater exposition and commentary than it is often given.[5]

'Strike something, though maybe not terror'

Gordon Brown was born on 20 February 1951 in the Govan district of Glasgow. He was born not just into a Presbyterian home, but into the family of a Church of Scotland minister, his parents being Revd John and Mrs Elizabeth Brown. This fact positioned him within a particular Scottish cultural *mythos* as 'a son of the manse'.[6] One recent literary meditation on this term is found in James Robertson's *Testament of Gideon Mack*, where Gideon comments:

> You could draw up a battalion of sons of the manse and it would strike something, though maybe not terror, into the heart of anybody with an imagination: among its members would be Gordon Brown, David Steel, John Reith, John Buchan, John Logie Baird and William Kidd. I wonder what elements of such an upbringing conspired to produce a Lord Reith or a Captain Kidd, a Chancellor Brown or a Governor-General Buchan.[7]

To be a son of the manse[8] was to occupy a distinctive niche within Scottish society. In class terms, the minister's family was unmistakably middle class, but the relatively low level of ministerial stipends[9] meant that the status conferred by a prominent social position and a large house was in most cases, not accompanied by any great personal wealth. This relative lack of wealth, combined with the specifically religious role of the minister, meant that the manse family had a certain 'outsider' status within middle-class society. For Church of Scotland ministers,[10] their responsibilities to the parish meant that their family home, which was owned by the church, was accessible to congregation and community in ways unlike any other middle-class residence. Gordon Brown's often-aired recollections of a steady stream of people in need coming to the front door in Kirkcaldy are therefore, entirely believable and indeed thoroughly characteristic. They also suggest something of the range of social contacts which ministers (and to a lesser extent their families) experienced as they entered the homes of both the poorest and wealthiest members of their communities in the course of their pastoral duties. The Presbyterian minister, while undeniably a middle-class Scot, is an unusual example of this class, expected to relate to rich and poor within the parish and having crossed the thresholds of a much wider range of local homes than anyone except for the local doctor or undertaker.

Lacking a Protestant tradition of state-supported religious schools and possessed of a smaller private school sector, Scottish education has had a more egalitarian cast than the more differentiated system evolved south of the border. Family incomes alone meant that most sons and daughters of the manse in postwar Scotland had little choice but to attend their local state school, but in doing this they were typical of most other middle-class children, particularly in mid-sized towns like Kirkcaldy, where the High school catered for the whole community.[11]

Brown's manse background has been an ongoing source of fascination to the media, with TV profiles regularly including shots of the manse in Kirkcaldy where he grew up and both the exterior and interior of his father's church. Brown has also been interviewed on camera inside the church by Andrew Marr of the BBC, in the days before he became Prime Minister.[12] By contrast, I don't recall ever seeing a TV shot of any of the houses in which Tony Blair lived as a child. Clearly, Brown's childhood is seen to have a powerful symbolic status within the media profiles and narratives of his life and his willingness to cooperate with the media in constructing these indicates his own judgment that these associations are positive assets. But why does he believe this and how might it relate to a broader analysis of New Labour's concern to remoralize Britain which is the theme of this volume?

The death of ideology and the rise of ethics

There were good reasons in the mid 1990s to eschew overt use of the language of morality within politics – media portrayals of the American religious right routinely pilloried the tactics of the 'moral majority' and Conservative attempts to call the nation 'back to basics' had sunk beneath accusations of sleaze and hypocrisy. However, there were broader currents running within political life, reflecting the need to redefine 'socialism' in the post 1989 world in a way which would enable the Left to appeal to the centre ground. In the face of this challenge, Tony Blair judged it essential to the New Labour project that there should be a drive to redefine socialism in what was claimed were 'ethical' rather than 'ideological' terms.[13] The most telling early example of this was to be found in Blair's speech to the Labour Party Conference in Brighton on 3 October 1995:

> I know that for some New Labour has been painful. There is no greater pain to be endured in politics than the birth of a new idea. But I believe in

it and I want to tell you why. Socialism to me was never about nationalisation or the power of the state; not just about economics, or politics even. It is a moral purpose in life; a set of values, a belief in society, in co-operation, in achieving together what we are unable to achieve alone. It is how I try to live my life.

The simple truths: I am worth no more than anyone else. I am my brother's keeper. I will not walk by on the other side. We aren't simply people set in isolation from each other, face to face with eternity, but members of the same family, the same community, the same human race. This is my socialism. And the irony of our long years in opposition is that those values are shared by the vast majority of the British people.[14]

The rhetoric is hyper-intentional – Blair is caring therapist – 'I know it's been painful'. Here we find public speech as intimate personal address – 'I believe and I want to tell you why. It's how I live my life' and Blair distancing himself from Thatcher by advertising his belief in society. Crucially, we see here the use of the language of morality as a way of refocusing Labour's project – zooming out the camera to create a big picture in which specific economic policies, specific divisions between the public and private sectors, specific measures of redistributive justice lose their definition and start to swim about in a soft 'ethical' focus.

In their place, the ethical vision which reframes socialism is established and thickened by deliberately religious and explicitly biblical language. Socialism, now to be pronounced 'social-ism' is being born again here: it's about 'belief', even a kind of discipleship. The truths, we are told, are simple: references to 'equal worth' and my brother's keeper evoke the Genesis creation/fall narratives; 'walking on by' invokes the parable of the Good Samaritan; add to this the cryptic mention of eternity and the preacher's rhetorical cadence evoking Blair's favourite (Scottish) philosopher John MacMurray in its invocation of the body politic in terms of a shared family. But the way the quotation continues is crucial as well – because despite this allusive thickening of the ethical vision through the Jewish and Christian tradition, it remains open enough to bid for universality – one community, one human race – and to insist that these values are shared by 'the vast majority of the British people'.

It is instructive to return to this early Blair rhetoric when reflecting on Gordon Brown's political persona, because the comparison with Blair demonstrates how this feature of the New Labour project has remained entirely constant and consistent between the two of them. Consider for example, this extract from Brown's first speech to the 2007 Labour conference as Prime Minister:

My father and my mother taught me about family and the great virtues of hard work, doing your duty and always trying to do the right thing. And I have never forgotten my father telling me to 'treat everyone equally with respect'. His optimism led him to find goodness in everyone. My father was a minister of the church, and his favourite story was the parable of the talents because he believed – and I do too – that each and everyone of us has a talent and each and everyone of us should be able to use that talent. And the values I was brought up with are not just what I learned; they are part of the fabric of the life I have led.[15]

Some of the conventions common to both speeches, such as the first person confessional-autobiographical moves, reflect in predictable ways the current repertoire of favoured techniques in political rhetoric. What is striking however, is the way in which ten years into the New Labour project, a rhetoric of 'morality', intentionally coloured by Christian and biblical metaphors is still being deployed in these high-profile (and lest we forget) meticulously crafted and redrafted speeches. This is both striking and potentially paradoxical, given the secularizing drift within public life in the UK and the way in which a leading theorist of secularization, Callum Brown, narrates this in terms of Christianity's loss of 'discursive' power.[16] A fuller analysis of the rationale for this rhetorical strategy and of its effectiveness lies beyond the scope of this chapter. However, such a study would have to consider, if this strategy was not simply mistaken and ineffective, why such a Christian-ized, neo-biblical rhetoric is still being called upon? Certainly, the work of Callum Brown, alongwith that of other revisionist theorists of secularization, such as Paul Heelas, Linda Wodhead and Grace Davie[17] is urging a more nuanced, multilayered and (at least potentially) reversible understanding of secularization as 'religious change'. Gordon Brown's strategy of continually advertising his Presbyterian roots, may be a powerful reminder of the way in which certain cultural monuments continue to act as landmarks for a secularizing electorate, who are still able (even from 'outside') to read their presence within political discourse as a signifiers for certain broad values. Brown's rhetoric may therefore be seen to function in public discourse as a set of cultural street directions, encouraging the stranger to turn left at the church on the corner.

This interpretation works better for the highly stereotyped and satirized figure of the 'Presbyterian', especially if we most often identify as 'children of' this figure rather than identifying ourselves with it more directly.[18] It may work less well as an explanation for the continuing appeal of a biblical imaginary within contemporary political rhetoric. Here, we may also have to factor in the (global) loss of discursive power experienced by 'socialism' and the whole project of the Left in the post 1989 era. Seen in this light, the Blair/Brown drive to regain traction for Labour's political discourse, involved signalling a decisive break with the past ('New') through an emphasis on the 'ethical' rather than the 'ideological'. The persistent decision for the language of morality, also suggests that many assessments of how far such discourse was contaminated by its Thatcher/Falwell appropriations were gross overreactions. While attempts to 'moralize' about personal sexual mores may well have lost credibility in the mouths of politicians, it was clearly a mistake to infer from this that a broader rhetoric of moral purpose and ethical idealism would also need to be removed from political discourse. The political rhetoric of Labour's leadership in the Blair–Brown era has consistently displayed a faith in the efficacy of appeals to the ethical and their electoral successes suggest it has not been wholly misplaced.

A final observation here might be that the continued appeal to scripture may represent a further twist in the story of secularization, in which a postmodern morality discourse needs to advertise its particularity, to insist that it has 'roots' if it is to win a hearing amid the identity politics of a crowded and pluralistic public space. The citation of Scripture takes its place as part of a discursive trajectory in which an ethical position must display both a particular genealogy and a capacity to achieve a wider 'universal' reach – it must come *from somewhere*, before it can reach out *to everyone*. The necessary shape of this trajectory accounts for the consistent but cautious way in which both Blair and Brown have added scriptural and confessional colour to their deployment of the language of morality. The rhetorical and communicative payoffs coming from this association with religious particularity can be worth the risk, if its potential for exclusiveness is as carefully managed as it always has been with New Labour. Even if the language is satirized by Iannucci, Bremner, Bird and Fortune, this is testament to its recognition factor, to its capacity to be memorable in an era when so much political discourse can seem eminently bland and forgettable. There is therefore a case to be made for the marketing value of the religious quirk in the face of the bland tendencies of secularization.[19]

While I have emphasized a common thread, the biographical differences between the two men are also relevant here. Blair says little about his early life and its influence upon his moral formation, but possesses the zeal and determination of the convert in 'confessing' his faith. Brown, by contrast, majors on his 'son of the manse' Christian formation and the 'inherited' character of his faith. Blair was famously parodied by Private Eye as the 'gushing curate' type Vicar of St Albion, but Brown's appropriation of his faith has recently attracted some sharp comment from those in the Scottish media who have followed his career. Sunday Herald columnist Ian MacWhirter reacted negatively to Brown's speech at the 2007 Labour conference:

I found it all a little scary, not least because of Gordon Brown s discovery of the Bible; his homilies, parables and references to his father's sermons. The 'moral compass' that Brown has been brandishing at every opportunity, like some holier-than-thou prig who has a hot line to the almighty. I don't remember Gordon Brown being a dedicated churchgoer – he certainly never admitted to it in his Red Paper days, or when Labour was in opposition. Perhaps he has been a closet Christian all his life, but that makes it all the more cynical, surely, to start parading your faith late in life purely for political purposes.[20]

The harshness of MacWhirter's verdict makes for good copy, but there may be a *non sequitur* in his judgment. Granted, Brown's earlier career is not marked by conspicuous Christian enthusiasm, but without crossing my self-imposed line into the inner workings of his soul, it is not implausible for me in the light of both my pastoral and personal experience, that a man in his fifties who experiences within a very few years the death of two beloved parents, marriage, fatherhood and the tragic loss of a child, might be prompted by both grief and gratitude to treat inherited faith with new seriousness. While granting that Brown's new found willingness to advertise his religious background and connections goes with the established grain of New Labour's strategy for renewal, our knowledge of his public persona gives ground for (at least) reserving judgment about whether this is merely cynical politicking. His most explicit demonstrations of theological literacy, to be found in the 2007 volume *Courage – Eight Portraits*[21] – are found in a book written we are told 'as an offer to play my part in raising money for the Jennifer Brown Research Fund'.[22] We can allow the cynic that this certainly encourages a perception of virtue, but we might also allow that there is something deeper than priggishness at work here. Even if we accept, however, that morality and calculation coexist within us all, there are still good reasons for us to keep a close eye on how they are instrumental in the public life and the public(rel)ations of our politicians.

Calculating morality: The compass and the barometer

Tony Blair, despite Alastair Campbell's fretting censures, could not resist 'doing God'. Gordon Brown, despite dropping scriptural allusions, is more circumspect about direct public professions of faith, invariably preferring the language of morality to theology. Where Blair preferred to speak about moral purpose, Brown's favoured image and metaphor for morality talk was unveiled in his speech to the 2006 Labour Party Conference in Manchester. Here, speaking still as heir apparent, we find New Labour replaced by the renewal of Labour and in place of Blair's more abstract 'purpose', we are offered the image of 'a moral compass':

And where did I learn these values? My father was a minister of the church. His motivation was not theological zeal but compassion. He told me 'you can leave your mark on the world for good or ill'. And my mother taught my brothers and me that whatever talents we had, however small, we should use them. I don't romanticise my upbringing.

But my parents were more than an influence, they were – and still are – my inspiration. The reason I am in politics. And all I believe and all I try to do comes from the values I learned from them. They believed in duty, responsibility, and respect for others. They believed in honesty and hard work, and that the things that matter had to be worked for. Most of all my parents taught me that each of us should live by a moral compass. It was a simple faith with a fundamental optimism. That each and every one of us has a talent. Each of us a duty to use that talent. And each of us should have the chance to develop that talent. And my parents thought we should use whatever talent we had to help people least able to help themselves.[23]

This is a speech which exemplifies the trajectory we set out earlier. In a move which both echoes and extends Harold Wilson's famous dismissal of arguments he disdained as 'theology', we find Brown both invoking his father's legacy and immediately distancing it from what he calls 'theological zeal'. He presents not as the zealous convert, but as the respectful son, clutching the old brass Presbyterian compass handed down by his parents and periodically using it to take his bearings.

As before, this somewhat quaint and old-fashioned image achieves a high recognition factor in part because of its incongruity. That said, it is a pointed (and pointing) image which, given its high-profile deployment, deserves comment. How far, we may ask, does Brown's record as Chancellor display the benign influence of this moral compass? For the radical and liberal Left, despite the faintly messianic hopes harboured by some that Brown would one day lead the party away from the New Labour agenda and back to a more robust form of socialism, Brown as Chancellor has often disappointed them. Two key areas where Brown was seen to have given a powerful moral lead were Labour's pledges on child poverty and the party's commitment to International Development.

Brown's achievements in tackling child poverty have proved more controversial, not so much because of suspicion about his good intentions, as because of doubts about the efficiency of a complex, poorly administered and easily defraudable Tax Credits system. The Clintonesque preference for Tax Credits as a way of helping what Brown (again in Clintonese) loves to call 'Britain's hard-working families' has of course been widely read by commentators in terms of Brown's 'Protestant work ethic'. Again, he and Labour's spinners will not protest any such association so long as it is shifting perceptions away from the wounding Thatcherite portrayals of Labour as the party which is soft on welfare scroungers. In this area at least, Brown's methods have been questioned more than his motives or morals. It might also be fair to suggest that the churches' focus on poverty within the UK has weakened since the 1980s and early 1990s, when they acted as a key site of resistance to Thatcherism, through reports like *Faith in the City* (Church of England) and *Just Sharing* (Church of Scotland).[24]

If their moral compass seemed to waver in relation to poverty at home, throughout the 1990s and into the first decade of the twenty-first century, the agenda which has grown in political salience for a broad alliance of churches has been that of Fair Trade and International Development, with the Millennium (Jubilee) Campaign for Debt Cancellation acting as a crucial platform for mobilizing awareness and support. This agenda transcended, exceeded and supplemented the normal channels of party politics in this era, to gain a support base across civil society and (through Live Aid, Comic Relief etc.) a discursive power within popular culture. International Development has been for the 1990s, what the Anti-Apartheid movement was to the 1970s and 1980s and CND was for the 1950s and 1960s: an iconic agenda, associated with the moral optimism and political idealism of a rising generation in Britain.

Gordon Brown has been widely credited as being a politician who has taken this agenda seriously, both in terms of expanding UK commitments in the area of aid and development and by giving active and distinctive leadership in international forums, such as the IMF, World Bank and G8. Here again, Brown's orientation has seemed clear and constant, even if many would have wished him to move further and faster in these directions.

Alongside and interwoven with a heightened concern for international development has been another iconic moral agenda of environmental concerns, in particular a concern to respond to climate change. Despite his key role in commissioning the influential Stern report,[25] Gordon Brown is widely perceived not to have been a Green Chancellor and New Labour's intellectual and rhetorical initiatives have been only timidly implemented at the level of domestic policy, with Brown resisting calls to use the fiscal system to create strong incentives for industry or consumers to change their behaviour. Brown's record here could again be seen as mirroring that of the UK churches, who have been relatively quiet on these issues until more recently, with green issues lacking the institutional champions of Christian Aid/Tear Fund/Catholic Agency for Overseas Development (CAFOD) which attach to broader development issues. Edinburgh based ethicist, Michael Northcott, in his recent book *A Moral Climate*[26] offers a powerful theological reading of the relationship between morality and the climate, suggesting the Joseph narratives from the book of Genesis as an example of political leadership in the face of environmental disaster. While the case can be made for Brown as Joseph figure in relation to international debt and increased aid, he has been less prescient in tackling climate change. However, it is interesting to note that his relative degrees of activism and inertia in these areas have been rather typical of the public theologies of the Church of Scotland, Church of England and the Roman Catholic Church. Arguably, Brown as disciple-politician has in this respect reflected 'the moral climate' rather than 'made the weather'.

The figure in Northcott's title, taken in its more general sense, may be a helpful metaphor to set alongside Brown's chosen one of the moral compass.

Or to keep the instrumental comparisons in line, we could opt for the image of a moral *barometer*. With its capacity to offer a clear bearing and there-fore a direction for policy, the compass is the more idealistic and utopian (Hauerwasian?)[27] metaphor. In relation to theological ethics, the barometer is perhaps a more Niebuhrian[28] device, measuring relative pressures and so predicting what activities may be most 'expedient' on any given day. Brown's compass is sufficiently antique and general a device as to not offer too great a hostage to fortune, but let us be clear that the relation between morality and politics is also calculated for New Labour with a moral barometer, which is itself closely calibrated with Peter Snow's famous 'swingometer'.[29] The well worn argument here would be that for all their theoretical powers, the cap-acity of politicians to act is both constrained and enabled by a wider moral cli-mate, which they disregard at their own electoral peril. This understanding of the political process highlights the importance of civil society organizations, including the churches, to the extent that their ideas, including their 'moral' ideas can attain a level of discursive power within civil society which may cre-ate a climate which both forces and allows politicians to move more boldly and swiftly towards the pursuit of political ideals.

The party's over? New Labour as a moral community

If societies as a whole have moral climates and civil society groups help make the moral weather, political parties such as the Labour Party are also 'moral communities'. This is reflected in the often quoted and variously attributed observation that 'the Labour Party owes more to Methodism than to Marxism', although it is more accurate to say that Labour's moral traditions owe signifi-cant debts to a wide range of religious traditions, spanning Christian (includ-ing Congregationalist, Catholic, Anglo-Catholic, Evangelical, Presbyterian and Baptist), Jewish and increasingly, Muslim sources as well as Humanist trad-itions.[30] Historically, Labour has been a moral community because of its cap-acity to function as a vehicle for the moral agency of citizens, whose variously formed moral senses, sought to transform social and economic life in the UK by working against poverty and towards greater equality. The party of com-rades, or even brothers and sisters, had from the beginning a certain church-like awareness of the need to aspire within its own life to an embodiment of the virtues it sought to promote in the wider society. While Anglo-Catholic social-ists of the Victorian era might muse on the social and political significance of the mystical inner life of the Holy Trinity, low-church Congregationalists and Methodists brought the values and protocols of the 'Church Meeting' and in Scotland Presbyterians brought those of session, presbytery and assembly into party structures. Here, Oliver O'Donovan reminds us, was one of the per-sistent (religious) roots of the Western tradition of liberal democracy, in the belief that because the Spirit might speak through any and even through the least, then all should have a right to be heard.[31]

There is a substantive issue lurking here which I believe has not always been taken as seriously as it should have been in debates about New Labour. At its root is a form of moral and political calculus, which had its origins during the long and bitter frustrations of opposition. Blair and Brown, in their role as tutors to the New Labour project, evolved a political discourse which combined a powerful mix of ethical idealism and political pragmatism. According to this calculus, one of the key lessons to be learned, was the self-defeating character of the moral purism of the Left, which had continued to saddle Labour with policies which left it unelectable. The killer argument which squared the moral circle for those lacking the political ruthlessness to support 'the project' was that the really immoral thing was to allow the Tories to continue to be in power.

The 'project' was therefore a complex and tortuous moral endeavour from the beginning, since it aimed to redeem the party from 'immoral' moralizing and to free it for 'moral' pragmatism, thus saving the party from itself and restoring it to power. Initially, the hopeful enthusiasm generated by the rise of New Labour was matched by a significant rise in party membership, as the moral community demonstrated its capacity to once again become the vehicle for a new generation of moral and political activism. Membership briefly exceeded 400,000 in the heady days of 1997, but a decade later, it had dipped below 180,000 and was continuing to fall steadily.[32] My contention here is that the disaffection at the back of this precipitous collapse in party numbers is a widespread disaffection with Labour as a moral community. This disaffection reflects serious moral qualms about policies pursued or not pursued by Labour, not least the war in Iraq, but perhaps even more significantly, it can be related to a deep dissatisfaction with the character of internal relationships within the party, above all to the bitter experience of members perceiving themselves unheard, ignored and marginalized within 'the moral community'.

To anyone joining the party in the late 1990s, it soon became clear the price of the New Labour project was to be that beyond a small elite group, party members would no longer have any significant influence on the shape of electoral manifestos or on the detailed or even strategic direction of party policy. So far as party conference was concerned, the relevant moral instrument was no longer barometer or swingometer, but the 'clapometer' beloved of 1970s TV talent shows. The standing of party members had been reduced to the point of indignity as 'reforms' systematically stripped the conference of any powers to embarrass far less influence the leadership.

Rather than representing citizen apathy and a generalized contempt for politics as is often suggested, the decision by hundreds of thousands of members to leave the Labour Party during the New Labour decade 1997–2007 can be understood as a thoroughly rational and 'moral' response to a shamelessly articulated defence of elite control as the only route to electoral success. Again, despite the forlorn hopes of some (defying the fact that Brown was one of the key strategists of the project) there are few signs that Brown has any intentions of reneging on this particular Faustian pact. The collapse in mass membership is not unique to Labour, although Labour's decline has been faster than that of the other main parties. Nonetheless, it poses troubling questions for the party under Gordon Brown's leadership. In the twenty-first century it seems that while Christian Aid and Oxfam can appeal to the idealism and activism of a younger generation – witness the latter's 'I'm In!' campaign – the same generation are giving a clear 'I'm Out!' message to Labour. Even if, in the absence of other choices, many would take Polly Toynbee's advice at the 2005 election to 'hold their noses and vote Labour'[33] they will not hold their noses and join Labour.

In this respect, Gordon Brown's moral compass also looks rather un-Presbyterian, since Presbyterian churches have tended to hold rather defiantly to a polity which both limited the power and prominence of their 'Moderators'[34] and insisted on a robust federal system of checks and balances, between centre and locality. To be sure, Presbyterians are also declining precipitously in numbers, but they have not yet used this as an excuse to sell their political souls. Unless Labour under Brown can rebuild the culture and character of their party as a moral community, they risk a future in which those whose moral vision compels them towards Labour's historic mission in UK politics, feel there is no alternative but to seek an alternative vehicle for their political agency.

Notes

[1] I have been unable to trace the original source of this telling description.

[2] Iona is an island off the West Coast of Scotland, where St Columba founded an early Christian settlement. The Iona Community is an ecumenical Christian community founded in 1938 by the late Revd George MacLeod (who became Lord MacLeod of Fuinary and took the Labour Whip in the House of Lords) a Church of Scotland minister, leading pacifist and notable broadcaster. The Community is known internationally for its commitments to justice and peace and for its distinctive traditions of worship and spirituality.

[3] The term is one of a number of variations on the theme of 'social capital', a concept normally traced to the work of Pierre Bourdieu, initially in his (1972) *Outline of a Theory of Practice.*

[4] The so-called barbecue-test reflected the judgement that despite widespread liberal derision for George W. Bush, he was someone many Americans would feel comfortable chatting to around a barbecue in their backyard.

[5] I want to note here that my interest in writing about Brown has always been a public one. I am not interested in trying to make windows into his soul or to

engage in some pseudo-psychoanalytical reading of his personality. My attention to his background is prompted by the way in which it has become part of public discourse about his political identity, both through the actions of the media and through his own self-presentation in public. He is also the most famous Presbyterian in the world and one of the most prominent Scots of his generation. My interest in how he is represented as an individual reflects my broader interest in reflecting theologically on how Presbyterianism, Calvinism and Scotland are portrayed within public discourses, which is an inversion of the more common patterns of journalistic interest.

6 The manse is the typical Presbyterian term for the minister's residence, equivalent to an Anglican vicarage or Rectory or a Catholic presbytery. Manses were traditionally large stone-built structures with at least four bedrooms and a study, many dating from the late Victorian era, usually located within the parish and in Scotland, among the more expensive house types within most areas.

7 James Robertson, *The Testament of Gideon Mack*, London, Penguin, 2006, p. 42.

8 The reference has been more common in male terms, although there have also been attempts to rework it to fit Wendy Alexander – the 'daughter of the manse' elected in 2007 as Labour's leader in Holyrood.

9 A stipend is the common term for a ministerial living or 'salary' in the Church of Scotland.

10 It should be remembered that although the Kirk is the dominant Presbyterian denomination within Scotland, it is not the only one.

11 Gordon Brown was interviewed by Andrew Marr in the High School building in Kirkcaldy on 7 Jan. 2007; transcript at: http://news.bbc.co.uk/1/hi/programmes/sunday_am/6238645.stm; on his return from the Palace to form a government 'Flanked by his wife Sarah, Brown spoke of how his schooling in Kirkcaldy, Fife, had inspired him. 'On this day I remember words that have stayed with me since my childhood and which matter a great deal to me today: my school motto, "I will try my utmost". This is my promise to all of the people of Britain', he said. 'And now let the work of change begin.' Nicholas Watt in *The Guardian* on 1 July 2007 text at http://observer.guardian.co.uk/focus/story/0,,2115798,00.html [accessed 20 Mar. 2008].

12 Panorama Special on Gordon Brown, featuring Andrew Marr interview, broadcast on 24 Sept. 2006.

13 In Blair's speech to the 2001 Labour Conference, he claims that 'ideology is dead . . . in the sense of rigid forms of economic and social theory'; *Tony Blair: In His Own Words*, ed. Paul Richards, London, Politico's, 2004, p. 223.

14 Ibid.

15 www.labour.org.uk/conference/brown_speech [accessed 3 Dec. 2007]; speech delivered 25 Sept. 2007 in Bournemouth.

16 Callum G. Brown, *The Death of Christian Britain*, London, Routledge, 2001, pp. 12–13.

17 See Heelas and Woodhead, *The Spiritual Revolution*, Oxford, Blackwell, 2005; Grace Davie, *The Sociology of Religion*, London, Sage, 2007.

18 So Brown often says 'my father was a Presbyterian', he never says 'I am a Presbyterian'.

19 This may be altogether too modest a claim – the recent work of Peter Berger, Jose Casanova, Charles Taylor, et al. asks whether there may not also be broader currents of desecularization/re-enchantment at work. The continued reach of this rhetoric may be seen in these terms as agreeing with the increasingly loud whispers within philosophy and critical theory about 'the return of religion' even in old Europe and even in the public and political spheres.

20 Ian McWhirter, Sun 30 Sept. 2007 – *Sunday Herald*; this is less the classic Scottish 'Ah ken't his faither' than a more abrupt 'Ah ken't him!'

21 *Courage*, London, Bloomsbury, 2007.

22 Ibid. p. x.

23 Text of Speech at http://politics.guardian.co.uk/labourconference2006/story/0,,1880666,00.html [accessed 26 Mar. 2008].

24 The latter though less well known was presented to Margaret Thatcher after her infamous Sermon on the Mound, when she addressed the Church of Scotland's General Assembly.

25 The full text and summaries are online at www.hm-treasury.gov.uk/independent_reviews/stern_review_economics_climate_change/sternreview_index.cfm [accessed 20 May 2008].

26 Michael Northcott, *A Moral Climate*, London, Darton, Longman & Todd, 2007.

27 The North American theologian and ethicist Stanley Hauerwas is renowned for his defence of a theological vision of virtue ethics, in which the church is called to radical non-violence and ethical distinctiveness.

28 Hauerwas' position is often contrasted (not least by him) with that of the German-American theologian Reinhold Niebuhr, whose theological ethics contrasted the personal/ecclesial and social/political realms and rejected unrealistic attempts to project the capacities or impose the values of 'moral man' upon 'immoral society'.

29 A crude device, now part of UK political mythology, used on TV to show the 'swing' from one party to another in General Elections.

30 This is an important corrective given the importance of Scotland in the beginnings of the modern Labour Party, as a country where Methodism's influence is slight and that of Catholicism and Presbyterianism very extensive.

31 Oliver O'Donovan, *The Desire of Nations*, Cambridge, CUP, 1996, pp. 269 and 281.

32 http://politics.guardian.co.uk/labour/story/0,,2101211,00.html [accessed 28 Mar. 2008].

33 www.guardian.co.uk/g2/story/0,,1479344,00.html for story and photographs of Labour voters wearing nose pegs!! [accessed 28 Mar. 2008].

34 The honorific title given to the minister or elder who chairs Kirk Session, Presbytery or General Assembly.

Part II

Justice and Community

Chapter 6

Are We Happier, Mr Brown?

John Atherton

The postwar generation, from 1950–2000, experienced a series of major changes affecting every area of life. Central to them was the consolidation and expansion of a global economy characterized by dramatic increases in world manufacturing output and in world trade. For example, the global trade in goods rose from $1.3 billion in 1977 to over $40 billions in 1990, and in services, including finance, from $3.3 billion to $325 billion.[1] Although profound inequalities continued to deeply deform that economic context, global economic growth has also contributed to major improvements in education and health, key areas of human well-being. Between 1970 and 2000, in developing economies, life expectancy improved from 55 to 65 years (1998), adult literacy from 48% to 77% (1998), infant mortality from 110 per 1,000 live births to 64 (1998) and the primary secondary enrolment rates from 50% to 72%.[2]

Yet, in this same generation, advanced economies experienced increases in ill-being, as measured by the growth of family breakdown, mental ill-health and crime, and by the corresponding decline of trust, volunteering and voluntary bodies. This Great Disruption,[3] using Fukuyama's concept, is charted across a number of disciplines, from history (Fukuyama and Himmelfarb)[4] and sociology (Putnam and Halpern)[5] to epidemiology (Wilkinson).[6]

Alongside these changes should be located the major decline, in that same historic generation, of institutional Christianity, in Europe, Canada and Australasia. There is a strong relationship between the crisis of social capital in the Great Disruption and the crisis in mainstream Christianity, not least because churches and Christians have historically and contemporarily been major sources of trust, relationships, volunteering and voluntary bodies.[7] This strongly moral dimension, wider than, though inclusive of religion, is identified as a major component in explanations of the Great Disruption in terms of social capital and its erosion.

This paradox of increasing economic growth and increasing ill-being is confirmed and elaborated by contemporary happiness research.[8] This illustrates how the growth of incomes in the West, precursor of global economic growth, no longer commensurates with the increase in happiness, not least because of the emergence of strong signs of ill-being in family and community life.

Again, the moral and religious dimensions figure strongly in the promotion or erosion of happiness.

Engaging this paradox is therefore likely to figure large in any agenda concerned with developing well-being in Britain in general, and with remoralizing Britain in particular. Addressing this necessity and limitations of political economy will invariably constitute a major contribution to that end. The previous 20 years have generated considerable agreement over the central importance for well-being of a strong market economy in terms of greater income and economic resources for health care and education, and yet its limitations as the erosion of the virtues and relationships of social capital by markets and commodification processes. The question is not whether market economies are necessary for well-being today but to what extent and in what form, including in critical interaction with other values and understandings. Engaging the paradox of economic plenty and ill-being therefore involves promoting the paradox of acknowledging the importance of political economy and of its limitations.

The recent history of British politics and its current phase both reflect and reinforce these changes and paradoxes. The period from 1960 to 2000 encompasses decisive political changes in Western economies which can be characterized as the movement from Butskellism to Blatcherism.[9] The former represents the consensus over a corporate welfare state reflected in the growing convergence between the more liberal wing of the Conservative Party led by Butler and the more conservative wing of the Labour Party led by Gaitskell. The latter suggest the major transition to a more market-oriented society based on wider individual choice, represented by Thatcher, and the acceptance by Blair and Brown of the market but seeking to reconcile it with wider social concerns, including as social justice.

It is the importance of Gordon Brown as chancellor of the exchequer and now as Prime Minister which particularly exemplifies the current phase of British politics, and which can be deployed as a modest case-study to illustrate and explore the strengths and limitations of political economy as problem and as possibility.

The significance of Gordon Brown's leadership of the treasury as chancellor is that the institution's central role in economic and political life ten years after 1997 is even more dominant. The politics of the Blair–Brown relationship before 1997, and the resulting division of labour agreed by them, gave Brown an unparalleled power base from which to develop his vision and values resourced by his intelligence, character and tradition. Of course, deep questions have been raised about his way of working, but his influence on macro- and micro-economic policy laid the basis for an impressive commitment to and delivery of economic stability and growth, including in employment. Equally importantly, this cascaded out to influence welfare reform in terms of pensions and benefits (including the important linking of benefits and taxation through the widespread use – much abused – of tax credits), but also reaching out to engage with education and health. This linking of economic to related and more socially oriented fields could provide a basis for the later proposals for the engagement of economics with wider social relationships and values, central to the happiness hypothesis. Driving this astonishing Brown agenda (not least in terms of its complexity) is a formidable intelligence deeply informed by strong ethical beliefs and commitments, especially to equity, and particularly in relation to the most vulnerable in Britain but also in the poorest economies worldwide (and including aid and debt relief). It has been an impressive exercise in what Amartya Sen has called ethical economics,[10] partly informed by Brown's Scottish Presbyterian background, and made the more impressive because of his valuing of engineering or positive economics as well as ethical economics. As Ian Steedman, Research Professor of Economics has reminded us to pursue ethical at the expense of positive economics is foolhardy.[11] What Brown has done is to begin to correct the traditional over domination of neo-classical economics by engineering economics in policy-making. It has been much more successful than New Labour's early excursion into and rapid exiting from an ethical foreign policy. I wait with interest for a careful account and analysis of these ten years because they may turn out to be of greater importance for understanding the economics of this decade but equally the politics in terms of any agenda concerned with the remoralizing of Britain, of the deeply ambiguous contribution of Mr Blair, and the shoal of government ministers notable for their inadequacies and short-termism. In May 2007, John Reid seemed to think it was an achievement to have had nine ministerial jobs in ten years!

So it is the Brown economic achievement that I want to explore briefly, first, by looking at three contextual experiences, second, by focusing on three items from happiness research, and third, by concluding with a brief reflection on the implications of such reflections for Treasury.

Given Gordon Brown's development of economics into related social arenas, and the significance of ethical as well as engineering economics in his work, I want to examine the feasibility of building on that foundation in order to engage the possibilities as well as the limitations of political economy. To do this, I will use my own journey to illustrate the growing awareness of the centrality of political economy for the promotion of human well-being, and the need now for its reformulation given our wider understanding of well-being in what Wilkinson describes as an increasingly post-scarcity age.[12] Importantly, it is a journey which parallels, at certain strategic points, the emergence of a New Labour coming to terms with political economy, particularly as market economies. The development of political economy through engagement with the happiness hypothesis[13] also connects strongly with the Labour government's use of such advisers as Layard and Halpern, the first central to the happiness hypothesis, the second to the related field of social capital.

To set my task in such a context, I will note how it emerges from three of my recent experiences.

The first experience is biographical. In the early 1980s my strong early Christian socialist convictions had focused on the redistribution of wealth in relation to the marginalized and with little regard to its production.[14] Half way through my involvement in the *Faith in the City*[15] process (1984–5), I therefore began to realize that my interest in and knowledge of the production of resources, and of wider economic processes, was lamentably deficient. In other words, I came to recognize that addressing the distribution of resources disconnected from their production was highly irresponsible. So I began to read and discuss such matters in some detail, and this led to a process of reformulating my understanding of vision and feasibilities, with a strong basis in an evolving understanding of political economy.[16] I had learned, in the words of the Revd Whately in 1830, one of the early political economists with Ricardo and Malthus, that 'Religious truth . . . appears to me to be intimately connected at the time, especially with political economy. For it seems to me that before long, political economists of some sort or other [I will add, including the Treasury] must govern the world.'[17] The journey of New Labour almost a decade later, was remarkably similar to my own reformulating of tradition.

That commitment of mine to the centrality of political economy to the contemporary agenda, and its current deep engagement with Amartya Sen's ethical as well as engineering economics, has continued to this day. Yet in the past three years that process of reformulation has continued by driving me to explore an increasingly multidisciplinary agenda around the concert for greater human well-being in its increasingly global context. It has impressed me as an astonishingly rich agenda which has led me to regard the primary ethical task as the reformulation of the relative nature and significance of political economy in relationship to and through interaction with wider agendas, disciplines and experiences.

The second experience develops from the first as I began exploring the *emerging* literatures (they are mostly post-2000) on well-being, very much initially through economics and post-1950 economic history. I will focus here on Layard's work, as professor of economics at the London School of Economics (LSE), and particularly on his *Happiness, Lessons from a New Science* – and I do so not least because of his influence on New Labour through the Welfare to Work programme, and currently through his advocacy for priority in the Autumn 2007 Comprehensive Spending Review for mental health, and education in well-being and ethics. All these strategies are profoundly focused on what I will call a more ethically adequate political economy for the early twenty-first century.

Essentially, this basic happiness hypothesis focuses on the profoundly paradoxical character of contemporary prosperity, linked as it is to economic growth and stability. So the astonishing increase in global wealth since 1945 is centrally linked to increasing well-being through better incomes, health and education (measured, for example, through the UN Development Programme's Human Development Index). Yet, most importantly, it has not resulted in increasing happiness. Of course, this in no way underestimates the foundational significance of adequate incomes for human well-being. That is reflected in the fact that, in 1998, after decades of extraordinary income growth, an astonishing 78% of Britons said no material comforts were missing from their lives.[18] Yet despite the indispensable function played by income in life satisfaction, and the Treasury's continuing focus on it, we are now increasingly aware that to increase happiness when personal income rises above a modest £11,000 then established factors beyond the economic assert their centrality to the promotion of human happiness.[19]

For Layard, all these relate to his Big Seven bases of happiness, with one to five listed in order of the importance given them by the US General Social Survey.[20] First, family relationships, including the importance of marriage and the disaster of divorce, and the lesser value of cohabitation and single-parent families. Second, the financial situation – already noted. Third, work, which provides income, but also an 'extra meaning to life' as fulfilment.[21] Unemployment is therefore a disaster, witness Layard's welfare to work commitment. Fourth, community and friends, including the importance of close friends, strong community (good neighbourliness), and the importance therefore of strong social capital, measured by, among other things, the substantial presence or absence of trust. Fifth, health, and particularly mental health, which affects so many, and is so powerfully underrecognized by the National Health Service (NHS). Layard then adds two more key factors, the sixth, being personal freedom and participation, which is linked to the nature and quality of government, and trust in it, as having a voice and as accountability including as personal, economic and political freedoms. Wilkinson develops this emphasis with reference to forms of economic democracy, as we will see later in the argument. And finally, seventh, personal values and philosophy of life, and the associated disciplining of our minds and moods, using a variety of tools including cognitive therapy, Buddhist meditation, the 12 steps of Alcoholic Anonymous and the Spiritual Exercises of St Ignatius Loyola. This is also referred to as comfort from within, with some calling its source 'divine'. So one of the robust findings of the happiness research is that 'people who believe in God are happier'.[22]

In other words, unless all these factors are addressed effectively, and at least four are not particularly economic and relate clearly to Brown's wider social agenda, then the increasing economic growth and income priorities of the Treasury will not generate increasing happiness.

The third and final experience shaping this context reflects how engagement with the happiness literature drives one beyond economics into a profoundly multidisciplinary exercise. These include economics, but also psychology, sociology, philosophy and theology. The latter involves Christian social ethics but also cascades out to embrace the contributions of other faiths and their reflections on the global economy, development economics and the environment. In these literatures the discipline of epidemiology, and the work of Wilkinson and his *The Impact of Inequality. How to Make Sick Societies Healthier* is particularly informative. Both ill-health and inequalities are powerfully located on spectrums at the opposite ends to happiness, well-being and life satisfaction. Wilkinson's initial concern is with 'the epidemiological transition'[23] which is the name given to the positive changes in health brought about by economic development as it lifted populations out of absolute material want – one of the greatest achievements of the postwar generation for an increasing proportion of the world's population. Most interestingly, he then observes 'Health in societies that have gone through the epidemiological transition ceases to be as responsive to further rises in material living standards as it had been earlier. Once you have enough of everything, it doesn't help to have much more.'[24] These limits of economic improvements are reinforced by World Bank economist, Charles Kenny, reflecting on the achievements of the Least Developed Economies (LDCs) in health and education: despite inefficiency and corruption – 'their performance is historically incredibly impressive. . . . We did not have to see huge increases in income to see very impressive gains in infant survival, life expectancy and education.' Indeed, for Kenny, 'It is the failure of income to significantly raise contentment, dignity or welfare, which makes it an irrelevance for perhaps the majority of the world's countries.'[25]

Equally importantly, Wilkinson carefully and precisely charts the profound effects of inequality on health, for example, how poor health, high rates of violence and low levels of social capital all reflect the stresses of inequality. It is confirmation of the double faceted nature of the paradox of happiness and prosperity: first, that increasing material prosperity does not generate increasing happiness; and secondly, increasing global prosperity (and New Labour's commitment to it) is associated with increasing inequalities nationally and globally, and particularly between highest and lowest incomes. These negative findings of the happiness hypothesis are strongly reflected in Wilkinson's epidemiological research, and in the use of continuums from happiness to unhappiness. And disturbingly the negative ends of the spectrums are focused particularly on that deprivation and marginalization so close to Brown's heart. For the poor are more likely to suffer from unemployment, inadequate incomes, broken or impoverished relationships, unsafe and low trust neighbourhoods, ill-health and earlier death, lower political participation and church attendance.

Given the challenge of such a spectrum and double paradox, in relation to these literatures, and the strong resonances between them, it is possible to build a profile for what I describe as a more ethically adequate political economy for the early twenty-first century in terms of detailed policy concerns.

I mention this almost in passing because I am crystal clear that any serious critique of what some in the literatures have called Selfish Capitalism,[26] has to be accompanied by an equally carefully developed feasible set of alternative programmes. For too long radical critiques politically and morally, including theologically, have been allowed to avoid Max Weber's challenge of an ethic of responsibility by generating essentially no feasible alternative policies. These emerging policy cluster areas include globalization in terms of economic growth and interdependence; global financial markets and their increasing prominence in the world economy; the nature and significance of work and income and a recognition of the company as focus of wealth creation and opportunity for developing forms of economic participation or democracy; taxation and benefits, including as means for addressing inequalities; welfare, education and health care as both support for well-being and as dyke against the harmful effects of globalization; consumers, choice and competition; engaging low-income economies in a world context, including through issues of trade, debt and aid; and finally, addressing the complex of concerns generated by the growing pressure for environmental sustainability.

In terms of the overall thinking which informs these policy areas, the guiding principle across the literatures relates to the promotion of virtuous circles of well-being essentially accompanied by the attack on vicious circles of ill-being.

What I now want to do is to select three areas for brief consideration which focus on the deeper implications of these experiences and reflections for the more effective promotion of human well-being as happiness in Britain and the wider world. Essentially, these are about moving through and also beyond economics and economic affairs because of what these realities are increasingly suggesting and requiring in themselves. The three are economic behaviour, including as the driving force of economic processes; inequalities, particularly as redistribution; and measurement systems. Although they emerge from the happiness research, they exemplify the possibilities for reformulating political economy which build on Brown's engagement with economics and also with related wider social fields.

First, there is a growing focus on economic behaviour and what it means to be human essentially contributing to a necessary expanded notion of the human. This includes addressing models of cooperation as well as competition, issues of status and positional goods, human capabilities as beyond simple equality, and the significance of character and the generation of virtues. Given the issue of remoralizing Britain, this latter is particularly worth exploring a little further. The happiness literatures, supported by much wider literatures, confirm a growing interest in communities of tradition and their role in the formation of personal character and the virtues flowing from it. There is considerable recognition that market economies are highly dependent on such virtues which are almost invariably generated outside the market remit, that market economies damage such virtuous relationships, and that the state cannot deliver them, despite its increasing attempts to do so. This is a particular temptation facing the Labour government. These problems of capitalism, state and virtue are reflected in the intriguing title of Himmelfarb's study, so relevant to the theme of remoralizing Britain, namely *The Demoralisation of Society, From Victorian Virtues to Modern Values*. At this point, it is worth pausing to explore this issue of virtue in economic behaviour a little further. For well-being literatures recognize, for example, the renewed importance of the virtues of self-control and prudence in a post-modern, postindustrial and late capitalist society given the challenge of such society to such virtue through the growing prominence of materialism in the form of increasing choice and commodification. So Offer, economic historian, notes that contemporary market economies generate greater choice for individual self-enhancement, yet individual levels of happiness, for the more marginalized in particular, do not bear this out. In his *The Challenge of Affluence, Self-Control and Well-Being in the US and Britain since 1950*,[27] he traces the inability to make rational choices conducive to well-being (so vital to economic theory) to lack of the central virtues of self-control and prudence, which in turn he strongly relates to educational attainment or lack of it. Besides challenging modern market economies, this also questions the modern consumption theory of mainstream neoclassical economics which assumes rational consumers by definition make choices for themselves that are well-informed, voluntary and prudent. The reality is that many people clearly do not. They regularly make bad myopic decisions – say over not saving for retirement, alcohol consumption, smoking and ignoring safe sex. Here, there is a most powerful link to increasing materialism and life dissatisfaction. This thesis is developed in James' *Affluenza* and its study of emotional and ill-being in elites from China to the UK, and the importance of philosophies of life and their associated ethical systems. The connection with ethics, an important dimension in Brown's approach to political economy, is particularly emphasized by the Kennys, philosopher father and economist son. Their work on well-being theory and practice includes a specific chapter on *Happiness and Morality*, with reflections on the significance of morality as community traditioning, values and codes. The latter links to the sociologist Halpern's (again a researcher for New Labour) work on social capital, and in it, the importance of sanctions in the well-being of families and communities.

What is also interesting is that out of these literatures there emerges a strong demand for a reformulated understanding of what it means to be human, for a reformulated anthropology. This stretches significantly beyond the individual-in-a-community model of Blair to a profoundly social nature of the human itself as inclusive of yet substantially beyond any form of reflexivity. This reading of the human as inextricably bound up in a series of concentric circles from person-in-community, family, neighbourhood, nation, global, environment and universe, is also profoundly rooted in the seven world religious traditions of Knitter and Muzaffar's *'Religious Perspectives on the Global Economy'*,[28] and in the eleven World Faiths views on environment as elaborated by Palmer and Finlay.[29] Equally, and for this argument particularly important, it becomes an integral part of say the economist Daly's view of a person-in-community as a reformulation of economic man, the central assumption of modern economics. As interesting, feminist economists have critically enlarged this neoclassical model into the Imperfectly Rational Somewhat Economical Person.[30] All this is an exercise with profound implications for indispensable economic processes, policies and institutions like Treasuries. For it is essentially an exercise in expanding the understanding of the characteristics belonging to economic man into a profound ethical reformulation of what it means to be human as central to the reformulation of economies and economic policy. The pursuit of well-being pushes us deep into such territories.

The second reflection relates to the issue of inequalities and the central role played in a reformulated ethical political economy by more just and egalitarian social arrangements. The happiness literatures argue that such developments are essential for human happiness and well-being in a post-scarcity era. Faced by the inexorable negative spiral of growing inequalities within many nations and particularly between nations, for Blair and Brown the task has been to focus on the opposite ends of the spectrum. On the one hand, there has been the focus on the poor, for example, the ambitious and brave pledge to abolish the scourge of child poverty in a generation. This made some early progress but slipped back again by 100,000 in 2006–7, with still over 20% of children in poverty compared with 7% in Scandinavia.[31]

On the other hand, this has been accompanied by essentially accepting the position of the richest, with no burning ambition that the Beckhams should earn less. For *The Economist*, not the most radical of publications, the conclusion is 'that each can get as rich as they like, so long as the poor are getting better off too'. Yet, despite the modest redistributive efforts of Brown, that Blatcherite consensus is increasingly lacking credibility. For the magisterial Atkinson, reflecting on data going back a century, income inequality, particularly in terms of the richest 1%, is now back at levels last seen just after 1945, 'when Britain was still a place of great estates and silver soup tureens'. And it is a position powerfully exacerbated by average incomes not rising in real terms, and those at the bottom not getting less poor.[32]

The very measurable and substantial impact of such inequalities clearly affects the well-being, life satisfaction and happiness of the poor. For them it is profoundly damaging, including as severely reduced life expectancy, essentially society's complicity in the intentional reduction of peoples lives. Yet inequality is also increasingly eroding the emotional well-being of the rich, according to James' global study, *Affluenza*. At this point, it is worth recalling the work of R. H. Tawney and his early pre-1914 research at the LSE on low pay, interestingly funded by the Rata Tata Foundation (the commercial sponsor of which ironically is now a great global Indian transnational corporation). Tawney has been particularly influential in Labour traditions, including the Christian Socialism which has informed Blair and Brown's development. He observed that the student of poverty (e.g. the government now) should 'start much higher up the stream than the point he wishes to reach; but what thoughtful rich people call the problem of poverty, thoughtful poor people call with equal justice the problem of riches'.[33] It is therefore to recognize, with Amartya Sen, that our overriding concern is with human flourishing, in which all, rich and poor, have a stake.[34] And that, quite contrary to the Blair–Brown philosophy, now involves addressing the whole of the spectrum of inequality, including both ends. And this is a judgement shared by secular and theological opinion. So, for Driver and Martell in *Blair's Britain*, 'The notion of social justice has been stripped of its radical egalitarianism and replaced with a concern for minimum levels of opportunity that will *never* challenge entrenched inequality of wealth and income'.[35] For Wilkinson, recent historian of Christian Socialism in his *From Scott Holland to Tony Blair*, 'Nearly all the government's ethical exortations seem directed towards the poor. It appears reluctant to challenge the wealthy and the powerful about their responsibilities and duties to society. There is a noticeable absence of any critique of the acquisitive society.'[36]

Yet, it is this linking of the fates of the rich and poor in terms of the paradoxes of happiness and prosperity and the central role of inequalities in both, which so powerfully emerges from the well-being literatures. Essentially this develops as a critique, among other things, of the *Acquisitive Society*, using the title of Tawney's classic tract for the times of the early post-1918 years – or to update it using a concept from current literatures, it is a judgement against Selfish Capitalism. This latter concept is additionally important because it illustrates how the literatures are agreed, like Brown, over the central role the market economy and mechanism plays, and must continue to play, in the indispensable promotion of economic growth in a global economy. It is a central contribution to human well-being recognized by most commentators, including the more radical New Economics Foundation, and its statement that 'There is in the current climate, no real alternative to economic growth that does not involve the risk of even greater hardships for the most vulnerable in our society.'[37] Yet all these literatures are equally agreed that without major reform of the market economy, human well-being will not be achieved, and certainly not in a sustainable way. And, such reform certainly requires, among other things, addressing economic behaviour through a reformulated understanding of the human, and inequalities through more equitable social arrangements. Indeed, for the epidemiologist Wilkinson, economic affairs lie at the heart of the problem and therefore solution by linking economic behaviour and organizational forms. In his work this interestingly focuses on developing effective participation in economic life (one of Layard's Big Seven) with particular reference to the development of employee share ownership as a basis for company reform.

This reflection recognizes the importance of developing adequate measurement systems to replace the increasingly inadequate Gross Domestic Product. The task is to address more accurately the emerging reformulation of economics and the economy including by embodying them in more appropriate forms of economic measurement. For New Labour, measuring performances has been a central part of the Treasury's overall strategies, including health and education performances. Given arguments over emerging understandings of well-being then such measurement continues to be of high importance, like economics and market economy, but only if reformulated. Now much work has been done in a variety of places on developing more adequate measurements of enlarged understandings of political economy including in Cabinet research papers, David Cameron's Genuine Progress Indicator, the New Economics Foundation and the UN Development Programme. In my *Marginalization*, an attempt is made to bring together a number of such systems in a multifaceted way, essential for addressing such a multidisciplinary phenomenon as human well-being. These systems include the UN Human Development Index, Hicks' necessary modification of it as an Inequality Adjusted Human Development Index, the UN's Gender-Related Development Index, attempts to measure political freedoms and competencies, and Cobb and Daly's environmentally sensitive Index of Sustainable Economic Welfare.[38] To these systems will now need to be added indices which engage with the emerging findings of the happiness, well-being and life-satisfaction literatures.

For Brown, as he began his chancellorship with the courageous and sound judgement to give the Bank of England independence to set interest rates in relation to government inflation targets, so as he begins his premiership, he could support greater independence for an emerging Statistical Board whose brief would include designing and implementing reformulated economic measurement systems. That would be an equally symbolic decision for this next stage of his political life, and would build on his engagement with economics and related wider social concerns.

Conclusion

These reflections on the well-being and particularly happiness literatures as they emerge out of economics and yet invariably spiral outwards to include other disciplines, have certain resonances with the Brown chancellorship. They are both concerned with stable economic growth in a global context, and a concern for the poor and the environment born out of a deep sense of equity. Both, I would argue make important contributions to the development of a tradition of ethical economics. Both are concerned, using Stiglitz's concepts, now partly Manchester University based, with *moral* growth:

> In short, the debate should not be centred on whether one is in favour of growth or against it. The question should be, are there policies that can promote what might be called moral growth – growth that is sustainable, that increases living standards not just today but for future generations as well, and that leads to a more tolerant, open society . . . to ensure that the benefits of growth are shared equitably, creating a society with more social justice and solidarity rather than one with deep rifts and cleavages.[39]

That moral growth resonates with the conclusions of *Through the Eye of a Needle. Theological Conversations over Political Economy*, and its focus on promoting a more ethically adequate political economy for the early twenty-first century. What this brief reflection has tried to do is to confirm the central role in such a task of a multidisciplinary engagement with human well-being which begins, in my case, with economics, but is increasingly driven through it and beyond it as one continuous recurring process. It is a journey which engages with the growing arguments for a more expansive understanding of human and therefore economic behaviour, the re-engagement with inequality as a societal-wide agenda, and the development of more adequate measurements of economic and wider human well-being. It is as though the message of the happiness hypothesis for economics and Treasury is that they must diminish in relative importance as other related understandings of human well-being must necessarily grow in significance.

Notes

1 J. Atherton, *Marginalization*, London, SCM Press, 2003, pp. 12–13.
2 Atherton, *Marginalization*, p. 75.
3 F. Fukuyama, *The Great Disruption. Human Nature and the Reconstitution of Social Order*, New York, Simon & Schuster, 2000.
4 G. Himmelfarb, *The De-moralization of Society. From Victorian Virtues to Modern Values*, London, IEA Health and Welfare Unit, 1995.
5 R. Putnam, *Bowling Alone. The Collapse and Revival of American Community*, New York, Simon & Schuster, 2000; D. Halpern, *Social Capital*, Cambridge, Polity Press, 2005.
6 R. Wilkinson, *The Impact of Inequality. How to Make Sick Societies Healthier*, London, Routledge, 2005.
7 Putnam, *Bowling Alone*, chapter 4.
8 R. Layard, *Happiness. Lessons from a New Science*, London, Allen Lane, 2005.

9 J. Atherton, *Public Theology for Changing Times*, London, SPCK, 2000, pp. 31–4.

10 A. Sen, *On Ethics and Economics*, Oxford, Blackwell, 1999 edition, pp. 2–7.

11 I. Steedman, 'On Not Traducing Economics', in J. Atherton and H. Skinner, eds, *Through the Eye of a Needle. Theological Conversations over Political Economy*, Peterborough, Epworth, 2007.

12 Wilkinson, *The Impact of Inequality*, pp. 8–14.

13 See J. Haidt, *The Happiness Hypothesis. Putting Ancient Wisdom and Philosophy to the Test of Modern Science*, London, Heinemann, 2006.

14 See my 'Religion and the Persistence of Poverty – a Challenge to British Social Democracy and the Churches', in M. Taylor, ed., *Christians and the Future of Social Democracy*, Ormskirk, Lancs, Hesketh, 1982.

15 *Faith in the City: A Call for Action by Church and Nation*, London, Church House Publishing, 1985.

16 For the early fruits of this development, see J. Atherton, *Faith in the Nation. A Christian Vision for Britain*, London, SPCK, 1988.

17 B. Hilton, *The Age of Atonement. The Influence of Evangelicalism on Social and Economic Thought*, Oxford, Oxford University Press, 1988, p. 46.

18 'The Paradox of Prosperity' in *Prosperity with a Purpose. Exploring the Ethics of Affluence*, London, CTBI, 2005, p. 32.

19 J. Atherton, 'Exploring the Paradox of Prosperity: Developing Agendas for Christian Social Ethics and Political Economy', in Atherton and Skinner, p. 87.

20 Layard, *Happiness*, pp. 63–73.

21 Ibid. p. 67.

22 Ibid. p. 72.

23 Wilkinson, *The Impact of Inequality*, pp. 8–14.

24 Ibid. p. 10.

25 A. and C. Kenny, *Life, Liberty and the Pursuit of Utility. Happiness in Philosophical and Economic Thought*, Exeter, Imprint Academic, 2006, pp. 198, 191.

26 O. James, *Affluenza* (æFlu'enza) *How to be Successful and Stay Sane*, London, Vermillion, 2007, p. 11.

27 A. Offer, *The Challenge of Affluence. Self-Control and Well-Being in the United States and Britain*, Oxford, Oxford University Press, 2006.

28 P. Knitter and C. Muzaffar, *Subverting Greed, Religious Perspectives on the Global Economy*, Maryknoll, NY, Orbis Books, 2002.

29 M. Palmer with V. Finlay, *Faith in Conservation. New Approaches to Religions and the Environment*, Washington, DC, The World Bank, 2003.

30 Atherton, *Marginalization*, pp. 155–6.

31 *The Financial Times*, 30 August 2006.

32 *The Economist*, 31 March–6 April 2007.

33 R. H. Tawney, 'Poverty as an Industrial Problem', in J. Atherton, ed., *The Scandal of Poverty*, London, Mowbray, 1983, p. 48.

34 A. Sen, *Development as Freedom*, Oxford, Oxford University Press, 2001.

35 S. Driver and L. Martell, *Blair's Britain*, London, Polity Press, 2002, p. 183.

36 A. Wilkinson, *Christian Socialism. Scott Holland to Tony Blair*, London, SCM Press, 1998, p. 242.

37 New Economics Foundation, 'Chasing Progress Beyond Measuring Economic Growth', at www.neweconomics.org, 2004 [accessed 15 Apr. 2007].

38 Atherton, *Marginalization*, pp. 161–6.

39 J. Stiglitz, 'The Ethical Economist', in *Foreign Affairs*, November–December, 2005.

Chapter 7

Social Justice, Social Control or the Pursuit of Happiness? The Goals and Values of the Regeneration Industry

Jess Steele

This chapter will consider the definitions and perceptions of regeneration, together with its driving purposes (explicit and implicit). I will tell two 'real-life' stories that show what happens when different players lack shared values and give an example of a regeneration programme built on explicitly agreed values. We will then take a tour through changes in regeneration over the past ten years and what they tell us about 'remoralized Britain'. I will offer some thoughts on how we can better understand and apply a values-based approach to regeneration, and finish with some suggestions for regeneration practice in the next ten years.

Our best ally?

On 1 May 1997 the election of a Labour government with its enormous majority offered both hope and fear to those of us interested in regeneration. The detailed research and better understanding of the causes of deprivation that followed, the focus on neighbourhoods and the feeling that government was willing not just to listen to community groups but to put them in charge of their own local futures – all this was exhilarating. Meanwhile great leadership in some of England's core cities transformed the city centres of Manchester, Leeds, Newcastle and Sheffield, challenging old perceptions of 'the grim north'.

However, not all was well in the world of regeneration. While it is difficult to pin these trends to dates, this chapter will outline a series of curves in which understanding and support for holistic community-based regeneration grew steadily up to and just beyond the millennium and then, under pressure from a variety of political, economic and social forces, declined. As the 'respect agenda' came to the fore, the environmental focus on *clean, green and safe* became personalized onto 'ASBO youth',[1] problem families and hostile mutterings about immigration. Although there were moments in the Blair years when top-down looked like it might actually support bottom-up, when communities were given leadership roles, such as the Bradford organization Royds which directly delivered a substantial regeneration programme, and the 39 New Deal for Communities programmes. Yet the authoritarian streak in social policy was increasingly legitimized, culminating in Blair's speech to the Joseph Rowntree Foundation in autumn 2006, abandoning area-based regeneration to home in on individual 'problem families' instead.

Despite all the well-intentioned hand wringing, however, the bottom rung was never quite brought within reach, though some of us jumped onto it nonetheless. While city centres became fabulous, the outer estates remained dire. The government continued to fail to help ex-offenders leaving prison or children leaving care, to understand the benefits trap, to reform the civil service, to control the housing market and build affordable housing, or to provide basic youth facilities. Moreover, as reshuffles piled up over the years, new ministers wanted new announcements to make, ignoring and then abolishing the core units that had made so much progress since 1997 (Social Exclusion Unit (SEU), Neighbourhood Renewal Unit (NRU), No. 10 Strategy Unit). The creation of the Department for Communities and Local Government in May 2006 made explicit the unresolved tensions between communities and local authorities. The municipalists[2] achieved a coup in the form of Area Based Grant and the principle that funds should all go through local authorities, guided by the Local Area Agreement and with no ring-fencing. This effectively abolished the community programmes that had aimed to support community involvement in regeneration at strategic and neighbourhood levels.[3]

What is regeneration?

Peter Roberts, chair of the Academy of the Sustainable Communities, has called regeneration 'the retro-fitting of sustainability into failed neighbourhoods'.[4] It is the process of refurbishment (social and economic as well as physical) of areas that have not had access to (or used wisely) the necessary ongoing investment in maintenance that all places need. The idea of refurbishment, of making places work again, is important but it does not do justice to the passionate drive for rejuvenation, renewal and renaissance – in other words, transformational change that is at the heart of regeneration ambition and is increasingly referred to as 'place-making'.

Another thread of the regeneration story focuses more strongly on social justice. In this version regeneration is a collection of interventions to raise the Quality of Life of poor neighbourhoods up to and beyond the average. The ground-breaking National Strategy for Neighbourhood Renewal (2001) aimed to 'close the gap' between poor neighbourhoods and the rest by focusing on 'floor targets' (minimums rather than averages). It also took the brave step of spotlighting the links between health, education, employment, crime, housing and environment – these became the 'themes' of hundreds of strategies and programmes.

Who is it for?

In the title, I have offered three underpinning concepts – social justice, social control and the pursuit of happiness. I have not mentioned money, but we will come to that. A piece of graffiti appearing in Deptford in 1992 – 'RESIST THE YUPPIE INVASION' – illustrated serious questions about who regeneration was for. The recent emphasis on creating 'mixed income' neighbourhoods raises this question again, along with concerns about 'social engineering'.

Many regeneration approaches, either deliberately or by implication, involve the dilution of statistical need, both through the displacement of poor people and, more commonly now, through the importing of affluence into previously poor neighbourhoods. While the gathering of small-area data has been one of the triumphs of turn-of-the-millennia regeneration, there are many problems with the metrics used to measure deprivation and change. Clearly, you can dilute statistical need by importing the affluent without actually solving the problems of any real individuals or families. Equally, you can displace people, either forcibly through decant and demolition or by providing them opportunities to leave and no reason to stay (that phenomenon is known as 'the revolving door' because they are quickly replaced in the cheap housing by new poor). The very ways in which we measure regeneration success reflect the tension between the desire to improve poor places (e.g. land improved as open space) and the desire to improve poor lives (e.g. qualifications gained). These metrics also illustrate the direction of 'leakage' into other policy areas at a given time. For example, City Challenge outputs (1992–1997) included kilometres of road improved and local authority dwellings demolished. Childcare places turned up as measures during Round 6 of the Single Regeneration Budget (2000). A few years later New Deal for Communities programmes began to aim for reducing the incidence of coronary heart disease.

Who does regeneration?

I have been watching regeneration for a long time, and have been actively engaged in it since 1996. Over the last decade, I have seen it move from an obscure and haphazard branch of public policy to a multibillion-pound industry, a charitable objective in its own right, and a much-discussed evidence-based approach to a multitude of interconnected problems. Done well, regeneration involves weaving a complex web of economic, physical, social and cultural interventions. It requires sophisticated partnerships and change-agents who are skilled at straddling silos both horizontally (between agencies and departments) and vertically (between authorities and communities). Very rarely is it done as well as it could be.

Throughout the 1990s, I was a community activist in Deptford, South East London, where I lived, worked and breathed the place. As my interest in the theory and practice of regeneration grew, I taught 'Citizenship and Urban Change' at Goldsmiths College, worked as a Good Practice Officer for the London Regeneration Network, and was appointed to the National Community Forum, a sounding board for ministers on neighbourhood renewal. Frustrations about the ways in which other policy and practice dragged regeneration down led me to a national job for the British Urban Regeneration Association (BURA) and I now work for the Development Trusts Association where I draw on the wealth of grass-roots expertise and knowledge within the development trusts movement to provide 'consultancy with conscience' for those struggling with twenty-first-century regeneration challenges.

There are enormously varied groups of people involved in regeneration in any particular place – local residents; local authorities – both officers and councillors, those who expect to stay and those who use it as a career stepping-stone; regeneration agencies – ditto; voluntary and community sectors; faith groups; private developers; built environment professionals; social care professionals; schools; health workers; police; and many more. Do they share values? Do they agree on what they are trying to achieve? Too often, the language of transformational change is easy and loose and it hides very different perspectives. If shared values are the foundation of community, then valuing the place is glue that binds strangers to a common goal.

Two stories

These are 'real-life' stories of engagement that demonstrate clashes of values and illustrate the very diverse interests at play in the regeneration world.

Old Town – disposing of an old library

Old Town was a Carnegie library built in 1926 to house the borough of Deptford's first dedicated children's section – a pretty building constructed in a human scale dwarfed by its brutalist surroundings. Wasting away on the disposals list for years with a derelict public bathhouse next door, it suffered

1a

1b

FIGURE 1   The Old Town library was rescued and revitalized through the hard work of local people, but was then demolished to make way for a different community group (1a) Exterior (1b) Interior (1c) Children playing in the restored library

Source: Magpie Resource Library

Continued

1c

FIGURE 1—cont'd

arson, flooding, squatting and neglect. Then in 1992 local people (truly local tenants from the housing opposite) took over. With the help of the estate's community worker (a 'detached' worker who had 'escaped' from the local authority), they got a temporary licence and a small grant and undertook the refurbishment themselves, using offenders on community service. They made something truly wonderful at Old Town – a multicultural youth and community centre entirely run by volunteers.

However, the local Indo-Chinese community group was looking for premises and the Valuers (in those days one of the 'dark corners' of many local authorities) decided that this was the site. In fact they said that the Old Library was the only site (which was blatantly not true in an area at that time littered with derelict public land and underused buildings). Despite a vociferous public campaign, an oral history project and exhibition and a lot of work to identify other sites, the planning committee with its back to the public decided, literally by two votes to one, in favour of demolition.

What was at stake here? The council's values were about money for the borough as a whole (despite the fact that they would only get to keep 25% of the capital receipt), serving the needs of minorities, subduing challenge and avoiding risk. Local activist values were about saving a local asset, Do It

Yourself (DIY) self-help, whole community integration, serving diverse major-ities, challenging authority and embracing risk (since they had little left to lose). The Indo-Chinese group's values were about DIY self-help, achieving sta-bility and profile, serving their own constituents, and managing risk (to their funding and hard work).

Each player was trying to get what he or she wanted because they believed it was right. Of course, as always, those with power were able to play out their values in the real world while those without power became angry and disengaged. Unlike many regeneration stories, there was no obvious profit motive but, though the council was vendor, surveyor, negotiator, funder and planning authority, they did not even see that they had a conflict of interest. The local regeneration agency, Deptford City Challenge (run by the now-famous Joe Montgomery) failed to mediate or take a strategic view.

Aragon Tower – flogging a tower block

The locally notorious Pepys Estate was built in the early 1960s by the GLC on the Thames-side site of the old naval victualling yard (where Captain James Cook loaded up with limes and saved the lives of generations of sailors). There are three towers (I used to live in one of them). Aragon was the one where the money from Estate Action ran out so the council chose to leave it undone and sell it on the private market. A cutting-edge report in 2003 urging trans-fer of a number of flats in the block to the nascent local development trust was buried – the conversion of Lewisham's chief executive Barry Quirk to the advantages of asset transfer was still some years off.[5]

What was at stake here? The council's values were about getting £11 mil-lion into the coffers for the borough as a whole including the pet Lewisham Gateway scheme, achieving a better mix of overall housing tenure/income, keeping control, avoiding risk and subduing challenge. Community activist values were about getting something back in compensation for the loss of social housing and disruption to individuals and the estate, achieving some-thing worthwhile from this major disposal and avoiding 'them and us' div-isions on the estate. The developer's values were about making best possible profit, maintaining good relations with the council, creating something spe-cial out of old council housing on the riverside (a precedent) and achieving profile in the industry.

The registered social landlord's values, judging from the images on their hoardings, were about changing the demographic perception and perhaps, eventually, the reality of the estate from 60-year-old white working class and 16-year-old black hoodies to 30-year-old cappuccino couples (although why this should be the case still baffles me).

2a

2b

FIGURE 2   Aragon Tower was left out of Estate Action and sold to a private developer for £11 million. The story of its renovation has been told in the BBC documentary 'The Tower'. The faces are a mixture of historical figures and contemporary Pepys Estate residents made as part of a community-led 'Art on the Waterfront' project. (2a) Tower before refurbishment by Berkeley Group (2b) Faces on Aragon

Source: Magpie Resource Library

Building shared values

What guides action when the objectives and approaches are so varied? Given the unnerving unpredictability of interventions, regeneration relies heavily on good faith (integrity) and vigilant evaluation (open-mindedness). The biggest problem for regeneration is that only some of the players have a strong focus on the benefits for the neighbourhood. People want to 'make a difference' but that phrase can hide a multitude of vague and mutually exclusive intentions. What could be achieved, then, if all those involved approached regeneration from a position of strong, explicit and mutually agreed values?

For me, a set of 'principles' have emerged over time: some are tenets of the trade, others are more personal observations. According to the strap-line of the NRU 'no-one should be disadvantaged by where they live', but they are – massively. Multiple aspects of deprivation are mutually reinforcing. Places experience spirals of decline or success – vicious or virtuous circles – and regeneration must intervene to change the direction. Local people are best placed to understand their own areas but they also need to see beyond the horizon, to know about what has worked elsewhere. We need to protect the genius of place – local distinctiveness – and encourage renewal without destruction. God won't fix it however hard you pray, but people who see their local work as a mission (either for God or for some other value-based driving force) are an asset to be channelled. Money alone won't fix it however much of it is poured in (although Housing Action Trust area where life expectancy has increased by seven years after a £300 million spend are impressive). Regeneration must involve the building of social capital.[6] In the end, the human resource is key to all change, but you have to get it to stay.

One example of a programme based entirely on a principled approach to regeneration is the Get Set for Citizenship programme (Deptford and New Cross, 2000–3). This was a community-led bid in an area that had already seen 18 different regeneration programmes spending over £200 million with almost no impact on the area's deprivation ranking.

We were proud that our bid for Single Regeneration Programme funding looked quite different from a standard application (Figure 3). It was authored from the ground up during an 18-month process of outreach and community engagement. The inside was just as unusual in that it was explicit about our moral commitments as well as our grasp of regeneration programme procedure. Get Set was a values-based programme, led by the local community sector in a partnership of choice not convenience. The back cover blurb reads: 'A community-led programme to end the cycle of regeneration failure, "Get Set for Citizenship" will change hearts and minds, find creative solutions to "impossible" problems, and prepare for a new millennium of active local citizenship.'

FIGURE 3   The cover of the 'Get Set for Citizenship' bid for regeneration funding for a programme based on shared values

Source: Magpie Resource Library

There were nine principles written into the bid document.

1. Learning from the past – heed warnings, find inspiration from history.
2. Informed decision-making – find out what is there before destroying it, overcome impossibilities through specialist but inclusive investigations.
3. Local knowledge is key – invest in local experts, and in ways for them to share their knowledge.
4. Recognition and protection of 'the genius of place' – understand the differences between neighbourhoods. Don't streamline out the distinctiveness. However exciting any vision for renewal, it has to be balanced against the negatives of destroying what is already good about the area.
5. Citizenship is rooted in the area – many of the people who make community are those whose lives are lived most locally, the most parochial are often the most passionate.
6. A collection of neighbourhoods can create a sustainable 'town' – the broad social mix, mix of zones, assets, opportunities already exists. We need good physical links and good strategic thinking about those things that are best done at a hub level.

7. Inclusive, constant process of outreach – be imaginative, be ambitious, be open.
8. Participation is a valuable learning process for everyone involved – never stop learning.
9. Community and citizenship development is integral to regeneration process and long-term neighbourhood-level management. Local pride, neighbourhood identity and social networks are key to sustainable regeneration. Only in this way can we encourage people to stay in the area even when they could afford to leave.

We were clear that we wanted regeneration that improved both the lives of local people AND the quality of the place, and that established a virtuous circle that Bruce Katz calls 'neighbourhoods of choice and connection'.[7]

Get Set had the wind of government behind it at the time, but the local authority was able to sit it out and, by just nodding and waiting, they more or less nullified its successes. Get Set's money ran out, the Local Strategic Partnership (LSP) came along, controlled by the council but distributing regeneration funding on behalf of government. Then came the Local Area Agreement, funnelled entirely through the council. From this local community perspective the ten years of Blair rule is a Bell curve of support where the high point was the millennial cusp (1999–2001). The following section explores this curve from the perspective of national policy to complement the local experience.

A decade of change

The changes in regeneration policy and practice at the national level during the past decade have been very mixed: some are fine in theory, some worked all right in the end, some are just wrong-headed and others were abused by political players on the ground. The party that pledged to abolish the 'beauty contest'[8] has overseen ten years in which the regeneration industry has got older and a great deal bigger, and occasionally a little bit wiser. Since everyone involved is learning at a different pace, and policy and practice take time to influence each other, the aim is to indicate the key trends rather than pin precise dates to them.

Change 1: Targeting the money

How you obtained regeneration money changed. Rather than being awarded regeneration funds on the merits of *a good plan* plus *a good partnership* and clarity about opportunities to generate high volumes of '*outputs*', you got it through the display of proven need in a statistical format. Originally the language of 'outcomes' – the less measurable but more important goals of intervention – was a dissident voice scorning the bean-counting output-focus. Later, 'outcomes' were themselves bureaucratized and are now in theory at the heart of public procurement.

Meanwhile, with land values in deprived neighbourhoods rocketing (especially but not exclusively within London and the greater South East), private funds began to search out these projected opportunities and the house-builders joined the list of those seeking 'transformational change'. St James, for example, boasted how they were transforming 'once-grim Deptford' through their luxury accommodation at Deal's Gateway. Half a century earlier, the site was a metropolitan public park blooming with the flowers of 150,000 Deptford Pinks.

Change 2: Understanding the problem

How we understood deprivation changed. You would think it would be the other way round but in fact Labour had decided to change the way they targeted the money even before getting into government.[9] Then they set about working out what the problem was.

The SEU was like having a well-resourced think-tank at the heart of government. Having scoured the country for evidence, visited projects and spoken to hundreds of people, the SEU produced a series of Policy Action Team (PAT) reports that identified the core issues for deprived neighbourhoods: crime, poor health, worklessness and low educational attainment. Increasingly recognized was the impact of concentrations of multiple deprivation. The core ideas that underpinned the National Strategy for Neighbourhood Renewal (2001) were spot-on: the notion of 'bending the mainstream' – both budgets and traditional practice – to achieve change for poor neighbourhoods; closing the gap through attention to floor targets rather than national averages; understanding the mutually reinforcing links between health, education, employment, crime, housing and environment; the importance of the *neighbourhood* as the key unit of local life; and the need for sustained, joined-up management at neighbourhood level that actively engaged local people in making choices and delivering or 'co-producing' their own better futures. With the intense focus on worklessness, the Brown government appears to be taking this narrowing of focus to its logical but unhelpful conclusion: losing the holistic approach before it had proper time to bed down.

Change 3: Language

The language of regeneration is a clue to the ideological 'baggage' (values) behind public policy. As one would expect from an incoming Labour government, the language changed. The concept of 'social exclusion' was a clear break from the more pathological discourses around an 'underclass'. In theory at least, exclusion was something that happened to you, rather than something you were; it could be 'addressed' through the actions of the well intended. It was a matter of social justice. This was important, but there were other aspects of the National Strategy that read differently, and were forewarnings of what was to come. The Strategy aimed to 'restore order; bear down on antisocial behaviour; and stave off the threats that loom over deprived communities'.[10] This was about battening down the hatches, keeping the lid on. This is pre-9/11, and before the shock of home-grown terrorism. For all the trendy new language, we were still facing the basic Victorian Social Question – how poor are the poor? How many of them are there? What will happen if we don't do something (riot and rebellion and possibly revolution)? The ASBO Agenda was on its way, couched in the essential decency of 'respect'.

The language of 'rights and responsibilities' was initially easy to swallow but in one policy round-table the man engaged in crafting housing benefit policy talked about how if only the poor would manage their money properly things would be much better. Between his designer spectacles and his expensive hair-cut, this was a man for whom managing money might mean setting up a direct debit to the wine club, rather than the real experience of making ends meet.

Regeneration did not escape the government's oft-noted tendency to turn everything into sound bites, but they did not always translate well. 'Bending the mainstream', for example, was used by one JobCentre Plus manager to say 'the government is going to get rid of you lot', meaning the weird and wonderful third sector. With the shift to the verb 'mainstreaming', her words became prophetic, though I believe this was not the government's original intention. Similar disconnections between the rhetoric and its interpretation on the ground have been seen in relation to the ideas of 'choice and voice', of 'double devolution' and of local area agreements.

My current work involves supporting community asset transfer in the context of a national empowerment strategy. Sometimes it feels like we are just moving the words around, but at least I know they are the right words. Building on the findings of the Quirk Review,[11] our demonstration programme helps local authorities to transfer assets (land and buildings) to community organizations. It has focused explicitly on culture change – political will, officer imagination and business sense in local communities – because we know that 'culture eats strategy for breakfast'!

Change 4: The bigger picture

There was a realization that mainstream spend: (1) dwarfs the 'funny money',[12] and (2) is skewed to the continuing disadvantage of poor neighbourhoods (through bad service design, lacklustre delivery and the lack of political clout to challenge it). There was a rapidly increasing understanding of how main-stream public spend plays out at local level, exposing the need for the famous 'joined-up thinking' that people have been struggling with ever since, not least because government departments are themselves so notoriously bad at it.

This led to support for the idea of Local Strategic Partnerships (LSPs) – those areas to receive Neighbourhood Renewal Fund would have to have one, the others were encouraged to do so. The LSPs are now part of the furniture for regeneration and many other service-areas. It is worth remembering that it was a major shock to return to a local authority-wide programming for regeneration – the approach had last been seen with Urban Programme before the riots of the early 1980s. Moreover, the original idea of bringing together strategic decision-makers aimed to provide an effective route for frontline staff to resolve problems they faced on the ground in particular neighbourhoods. A 180-degree rotation in the thinking repositioned LSPs as the source of top-down instruction rather than the beneficiaries of bottom-up intelligence.

The pace of growth in understanding of poor neighbourhoods was not only a feature of the early years. The SEU (and the Prime Minister's Strategy Unit) were still doing important work in 2005 when SEU revisited 'Jobs and Enterprise in Deprived Areas' (the theme of PAT1) to consider 'those left behind' and No. 10 took an overview on how 'concentrations of deprivation' are sustained in misery.[13] Both of these resonated in the regeneration world, but the media-conditioned 'real world' had moved firmly into its hoodies and terrorists era, and Blair's attention was permanently elsewhere (Iraq, foundation hospitals, city academies). So while people on the ground were saying – 'it's the same old issue: *nothing for young people to do*' – people in Whitehall were busy news managing and coming up with the next sound bites.

Meanwhile, in another corridor of government Prescott's Office of the Deputy Prime Minister had generated, hyped and then more or less abandoned the concept of 'sustainable communities'. The two most important civil servants in this field were Joe Montgomery (NRU) and Richard McCarthy (Sustainable Communities Unit). You never saw them together; they were too busy out on the road preaching the importance of joining up our thinking.

Change 5: 'Community'

In the early 1990s, the very survival of the word 'community' was in doubt.[14] A decade later, it was a prefix for a string of activities – *consultation, engagement, participation, empowerment* – that began to be taken seriously in some hard-nosed places – from the House of Commons to the house-builders' boardrooms. For a brief period in the early stages of the New Deal for Communities (NDC) programme the pendulum swung so far towards 'communities at the helm' that local people were more or less left alone to get on with planning £50 million spend programmes.

Those of us who had remained committed to the concept throughout, or had discovered its true worth directly through our own local community activity, could only rejoice in the rediscovery of ideas and techniques around empowerment. Their move towards the centre of Government has been astonishing, though somewhat bumpy. The words found a place in Eland House first through initiatives like the National Community Forum, the Community Empowerment Networks and Statements of Community Involvement. With Hazel Blears as Communities Secretary since June 2007, a more practical approach is emerging through the exotic import of participatory budgeting methods from Brazil (partially rebranded as 'community kitties'), the push towards community asset transfer and the promised support for community anchors.[15] All this is part of the forthcoming Community Empowerment White Paper that might finally kill off the term by narrowing its focus too tightly to one measure – the degree to which people feel they can influence decisions about their locality.

Perhaps inevitably – when everyone talks about empowerment but no-one lets go – the concept has become ever harder to pin down or believe in. Unfortunately, what central government has never seemed to understand is that, on the way down to the ground, these wonderful ideas go through a filtration process governed by local power plays that can make them look quite different once they land. This is by no means a problem everywhere. There are many strong partnerships and capable communities, and they make good use of the investment. However, in many places the 'cultural barriers' of local politics (now a multi-agency game) stop the investment getting to the right places, or coming at all.

Despite huge successes in bringing the concept of community, laden as it is with values, into the regeneration debate, the wider context, both political and economic, is looking increasingly ill-favoured for actual communities. With recent focus on the failures of multiculturalism, the targeting of particular communities of interest has been thrown into question, yet the 'cohesion' field remains relatively underdeveloped and too often disengaged from fundamental questions of equality and discrimination. Tightened local government belts and generally lower public spending, the credit crunch, a declining and uncertain housing market despite continuing demand, and maybe a full-blown recession, all add to the threats facing community action. Meanwhile other government moves illustrate a different, potentially hostile, change. The ring-fenced funding for Community Empowerment Networks to help people engage with strategic decisions, and Community Chests to generate the fizz of grass-roots activity, have gone. The Local Area Agreement is negotiated by and fed through the local authorities. The £1.5 billion Working Neighbourhoods Fund (WNF) announced in 2007 is focused on worklessness and appears to move away from the holistic focus on the neighbourhood (place) and community (people) that was a mark of Neighbourhood Renewal. With every month that goes by the political landscape shifts again.

Generally, 'the community sector' is hostile to this latest shift of focus, but I believe we can bring together the focus on worklessness with the fabulous resource of the community sector: through the Community Allowance that would let community organizations pay local people to do work that strengthens their neighbourhood without it affecting their benefits status.[16] The CREATE Consortium welcomes the long overdue collaboration between CLG and Department for Work and Pensions (DWP) and is now working with both departments to pilot the Community Allowance over the next few years.

Change 6: The power of well-being

The whole idea of well-being and its inclusion as a 'general power' of local authorities in the Local Government Act 2000 opened up a different world. Alongside the imperative to create sustainable, thriving communities, it led quickly to what has been called 'The Happiness Agenda'. People in regeneration who once felt guilty about being 'in the poverty business' can now say we're in the 'happiness sector'. It is easy to be cynical about this very millennial policy thrust, which has been somewhat overshadowed by the announcement of the tight focus on tackling worklessness in the WNF. Yet it was a crucial moment in the development of holistic approaches to regeneration, widening once again the vision of what must be addressed in order to make good places and improve real lives.

Change 7: The big boys arrive

At BURA I met a different kind of regenerator altogether. I already had some experience of developers at Deptford Creek and of Berkeley Group specifically with Aragon Tower. I had seen how the local authorities were taken by surprise by development interest, having long viewed Deptford as a place no-one would ever choose for investment, and how this attitude short-changed the place through low expectations around design quality and planning gain.

Now I came to see the challenges from the developers' perspective. There was a huge range on the sincerity score but growing numbers of private developers in all fields began to brand themselves as regenerators and stress their concern with place-making. The best examples would include Berkeley Group with their award-winning development at Gunwharf Quays, Portsmouth, Urban Splash who both saved and regenerated Manchester's historic but run-down canalside, and Argent who were responsible for Brindley Place, Birmingham and are now leading the redevelopment of Kings Cross.

Just as in the 1890s with the Housing of the Working Classes Act that enabled 'philanthropy at 5%', it was policy change that allowed regeneration to become profitable a century later. The impact and added value of the enormous subsidy directed by the Office of the Deputy Prime Minister (1999–2005) and regeneration agency English Partnerships towards the private sector to achieve regeneration and growth in this period would merit further exploration.

There is no reason why private developers should not be involved in regeneration – indeed, they are essential to create large-scale physical change. However, we need to engage with them on questions of values and move away from the 'sit up and beg' approach often displayed in the public sector.

Change 8: Profit for reinvestment

In the Blair decade, there was a shift in understanding and attitudes towards enterprise and wealth creation. Despite the New Labour ease with big business, the Government was slow to understand the importance of SMEs (small and medium sized enterprises) in regeneration. Having lost the Thatcher idea of the 'nation of shopkeepers', it was not until 2004 that a mini revolution in the NRU brought enterprise to the forefront and led to the Local Enterprise Growth Initiative (LEGI) programme. This useful and important programme has been one of the casualties of the Brown Government before it had much chance to get going. It was a sign of great change that so many of the LEGI bids submitted in 2006 and 2007 included a focus on social enterprise.

Social enterprise, a term invented in the 1870s to describe the 'villages of cooperation' created by followers of Robert Owen, has been resurrected in the last decade with astonishing success. Embracing everything from the Big Issue magazine to the Eden Project, from Café Direct to Coin Street Community Builders, the concept of social enterprise found favour with those determined to subject public services to 'contestability' and to wean voluntary and community organizations from grant dependency. It also appealed to those within the community sector, including development trusts, social firms and community cooperatives, who realized that stale community development practice could be revitalized by the can-do problem-solving culture that flows from combining business skills with social mission.

Within government, the social enterprise virus first appeared in a small enclave within the Department of Trade and Industry, and has progressively infected many other parts of government. The Office of the Deputy Prime Minister under John Prescott proved particularly resistant. That is, until David Miliband, given a year as minister of state for Communities and Local Government and tasked with tackling the failures of command and control regeneration, realized that community-led social enterprise and community asset ownership could be a useful vehicle for his double devolution agenda. His brother Ed Miliband has continued to promote the cause as minister in the Cabinet Office, and so have Cameron's Conservatives as evidence of their born-again social responsibility politics.

Analysis by the New Economics Foundation of local money flows,[17] and by Stephen Thake of the impacts of multi-purpose 'community anchor' organizations, provided the intellectual capital for a strand of regeneration driven not by local authorities or developers but by independent community enterprises.

New investment vehicles such as the Yorkshire Key Fund and the Adventure Capital Fund were set up, and their combination of patient capital (mixing grants and loans) with business development support, has been gradually influencing the practice of other funders.

At first, the rhetoric outstripped the practice, though by 2007 development trusts held more than £400 million of assets in community ownership and were earning £100 million a year through their trading activities, generating surpluses and reinvesting them to create social value. This approach of 'creating wealth in communities and keeping it there' requires a genuine shift in the public and community sectors to see land and property assets as core units of community regeneration, on a par with funding programmes. In East Leeds, for example, officers are well aware that they must use the public asset base as leverage. The Advancing Assets demonstration programme has been working with local authorities and their community partners in 50 areas across England to broker 'fair and effective transfers' from councils to independent local community organizations. Development trusts (and their subset community land trusts) are much in the spotlight, especially since the prospectus for the new 'eco-towns' laid out the need for investment in a community trust, 'a delivery organisation to manage the town and its development and provide support for people, businesses and community services'.[18]

Change 9: The way that you do it

Sir John Egan's review of skills for sustainable communities (2004)[19] highlighted for the first time the fundamental importance of behaviour and attitudes (ways of acting and ways of thinking) in achieving positive regeneration. Rather than just making a list, Egan asked the radical question 'what is a sustainable community?' and tried to come up with an answer (and it's the best one we've got so far – see Figure 4). Then he said, well you don't make one of those with technical skills: it's all about the generic skills and the ways of thinking and ways of acting. This was the first time someone official had said that behaviour matters.

To those of us on the receiving end of arrogant, uncommunicative, suspicious and generally unpleasant regeneration managers and council officers this had been obvious for a long time. If you have power, you can get away with being nasty and you will be moved on before your failure to make any positive impact is realized. If you have no power and you are not planning an exit strategy (in other words the local community) then you *have to* use communication, trust building, brokerage, inclusive visioning, negotiation, humility, etc. to get anywhere at all. Egan also drew attention to the crucial importance of leadership in regeneration – the quality rather than the

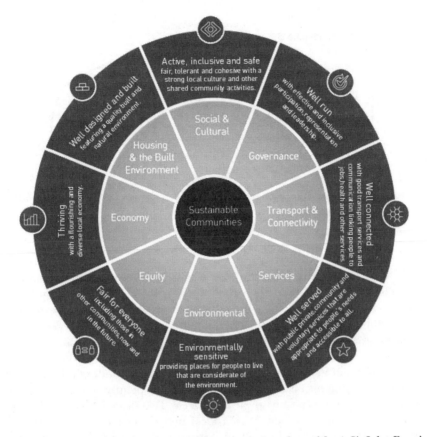

FIGURE 4 Components of a sustainable community, adapted from Sir John Egan's Review, 2004. Source: South East Excellence

qualifications of people, including strategic thinking, breakthrough thinking and collaboration.

Sadly, the government then off-loaded this whole agenda by granting £11 million to establish the Academy for Sustainable Communities which set about establishing qualifications! Instead, I believe they should have absorbed it into the very heart of the civil service as part of a major reform programme which would link every civil servant with at least one outsider 'buddy'; encourage public management values (including openness); give them opportunities to specialize while maintaining their generalism; and overhaul the obscure and time-wasting Whitehall and town hall 'etiquettes'. John Egan complained recently in *Regeneration & Renewal*[20] that he had not been listened to by ministers or asked to return to evaluate progress since his review.

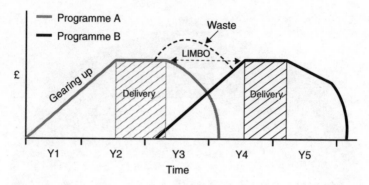

FIGURE 5 Professor Peter Roberts sketches this diagram to show how much local people lose out because of the short-term, 'jumpy' approach to regeneration

Change 10: Continuity

In 1996, facing the end of the five-year City Challenge programme I wrote a report for Deptford Community Forum called 'Who's Leaving? Who's Staying?' This was a pithy title at the time because 'exit strategies' were in vogue and the local community sector was getting frustrated at so many different regeneration agencies, spending so much money with no clear thread from one to the next.

Peter Roberts draws a shocking diagram by which he describes the impact of 'initiativitus' and the stop-start nature of regeneration funding (Figure 5). It demonstrates graphically the vast wastefulness of repetitive short-term regeneration programmes in any given local area. The shaded 'delivery' blocks represent the fractional benefit that local people get out of this stop-start programming. Not least of the many impacts is that a whole industry sector workforce has grown up with this peripatetic culture, so regenerators tend to be, and indeed need to be, grasshoppers. This has implications for the kinds of people who are able to make it to the top in the field – many women, for example, refuse to leave their families behind or uproot their children every few years in order to join the regeneration circuit.

At last, now the need for an effective succession rather than the hope of a smooth exit is finally being taken seriously. The NDC programmes are in the best position to create succession vehicles and many are moving towards the development trust model. Even without such explicit instructions, there is far more talk of sustainability so another of regeneration's core values – laying down the best possible future – can now be prioritized.

Learning or doing?

Some say there is too much navel-gazing in regeneration and it is what you can see on the ground that matters – delivery, delivery, delivery. I disagree; in fact

I would say the field has been characterized by a scarcity of reflective thinking, an appalling lack of archives and shared learning (despite lots of expensive evaluations), and not enough properly facilitated cross-project visiting. On the other hand, regenerators can only truly learn through 'doing'. Like Collingwood's 'historical imagination', there is a 'regeneration imagination' that is developed through practice. This helps a practitioner to see what might make sense in the complex, dynamic environment of a *very particular* deprived neighbourhood. The experience of groping towards solutions on the ground is scary, difficult, uncertain and rewarding all at the same time.

So, how should we be doing it?

I welcome the moves over the Blair decade and beyond, tentative though some have been, towards values-based regeneration. I would like to see more explicit discussion and negotiation around values, along with further progress in several areas. We need to continue to work towards independent sustainability for the community sector, and learn to capture the benefits of community DIY more effectively. We need strong leadership from within all sectors, by people willing to challenge and take challenge. They need to be capable of engaging across sector-boundaries. We must return to a strong, sustained focus on neighbourhoods by retrenching the right and duty to ring-fence resources for specific localities. At all levels from neighbourhood to nation, we need a more mature understanding of different agendas – how they can help each other, or might conflict. We need a clearer understanding of assets, including land and buildings, people and culture, services and organizations, as core potential units of community regeneration.

Regeneration requires risk, and has become obsessed by managing it out, yet most regenerators are still unclear on how to assess risk, or even how to feel about it. I believe we have to treat change as a development opportunity and failure as a development cost – if you learn from it then it is the price of the next success. Nothing has stayed still while I've been writing this chapter and now we're seeing the horizon of the new Labour project, wondering what it will be like on the other side of it. Regenerators are all too familiar with uncertainty and short-term swings, but with a strong set of values to guide practice we will continue to try to make a difference for the better.

Abbreviations

BURA – British Urban Regeneration Association
CENs – Community Empowerment Networks
CLG – Department for Communities and Local Government
DTA – Development Trusts Association

LSPs – Local Strategic Partnerships
NRF – Neighbourhood Renewal Fund
NRU – Neighbourhood Renewal Unit
PAT   – Policy Action Team
SCU – Sustainable Communities Unit
SEU – Social Exclusion Unit
SRB – Single Regeneration Budget
WNF – Working Neighbourhoods Fund

Policy reports

PAT Reports x 14, 2000–1
National Strategy for Neighbourhood Renewal, 2001
Sustainable Communities Plan, 2003
Jobs and Enterprise in Deprived Areas, 2004
Taking Stock, 2004
Policy reports available at http://www.neighbourhood.gov.uk/page.asp?id=737

Notes

[1] ASBO = Anti-Social Behaviour Order. See www.crimereduction.homeoffice.
gov.uk/asbos/asbos9.htm [accessed 28 Oct. 2008].
[2] Supporters of local government power in all things.
[3] Urban Forum recently found that empowerment networks had lost 40% of their
funding (New Start, 18 April 2008). The original research by Urban Forum is at
http://www.urbanforum.org.uk/pdf_files/community%20empowerment%20
network%20cen%20research%20report%202008%2004%20.pdf
[4] Peter Roberts, Renaisi lecture, 'Regeneration – Retrofitting sustainable communities', London, July 2006.
[5] Quirk Review: Making Assets Work, May 2007.
[6] Social capital is the glue the binds communities – Robert D. Putnam, *Bowling
alone: the collapse and revival of American community* (New York: Simon & Schuster,
2000).
[7] Bruce Katz, 'Neighbourhoods of choice and connection: The evolution of
American neighbourhood policy and what it means for the United Kingdom'
(Joseph Rowntree Foundation, 2004. Available in electronic format only from
http://www.jrf.org.uk/bookshop/details.asp?pubid=616).
[8] Frank Dobson MP and Keith Vaz MP at a Labour Party briefing on regeneration, 1996.
[9] Ibid.
[10] National Strategy for Neighbourhood Renewal, 2001.
[11] 'Making Making assets work', Quirk Review transfer window', the Government's. The Review is available at http://www.communities.gov.uk/publications/

communities/makingassetswork/ and the Response at http://www.communities. gov.uk/publications/communities/openingtransfer.

[12] 'Funny money' is a term I have often used and heard used to describe special regeneration funding (i.e. non-mainstream public budgets).

[13] 'Jobs & Enterprise in Deprived Areas', SEU, September 2004; 'Improving the prospects of people living in areas of multiple deprivation in England', Prime Minister's Strategy Unit, January 2005. These reports are available at http:// www.cabinetoffice.gov.uk/media/cabinetoffice/social_exclusion_task_force/ assets/publications_1997_to_2006/jobs_deprived_full_report.pdf and http:// www.cabinetoffice.gov.uk/media/cabinetoffice/strategy/assets/deprived_ areas.pdf

[14] 'Networks & Boundaries: Race, Gender & Poverty in the Construction and Reconstruction of Community in Deptford, 1930–1990', Jess Steele, 1991, unpublished dissertation.

[15] 'Community Anchors are independent community-led organisations. They are multi-purpose and provide holistic solutions to local problems and challenges, bringing out the best in people and agencies. They are there for the long term, not just the quick fix. Community anchors are often the driving force in community renewal' – Community Alliance publicity leaflet 'Transformation through community anchors' 2007. See www.comm-alliance.org/ [accessed 28 Oct. 2008].

[16] CREATE: A Community Allowance. Jess Steele and Aaron Barbour, 2007.

[17] LM3 is the tool invented by new economics foundation to measure local economic multipliers. See www.lm3online.org [accessed 28 Oct. 2008].

[18] Eco-towns Prospectus, CLG, July 2007. Available at http://www.communities. gov.uk/publications/housing/ecotownsprospectus

[19] www.communities.gov.uk/publications/communities/eganreview [accessed 28 Oct. 2008].

[20] *Regeneration & Renewal*, 2 May 2008, p. 2.

Chapter 8

But What is a Community? The Continuing Development of a New Labour Concept

Mark D. Chapman

A few years ago I spent a fair bit of time looking at how the word 'community' was used in the rhetoric and policy initiatives of New Labour and the subsequent Labour Government. This was an interest that eventually found its way into a little book which I published just before the last British General Election in 2005, called *Blair's Britain: A Christian Critique*.[1] As well as discussing the British scene I also took account of how similar 'Third Way' thinking had been used in Government policy in both South Africa and Germany. On a careful reading it turned out that community was a very vague term which, although frequently used, was short on content. The basic gist of the rhetoric was that communities were good things, and provided a far better structure for human society than simply lots of isolated individuals, and they were therefore to be encouraged. Now since I published *Blair's Britain* in early 2005 things have moved relatively quickly. Most important in relation to the concept of community is the mutation, on 5 May 2006, of the Office of the Deputy Prime Minister into the new Department for Communities and Local Government, headed up by Ruth Kelly, and in the latest reshuffle, by Hazel Blears. The departmental brief seems laudable. The vision of the first secretary of state, which Kelly gave shortly after the Department was set up, was to create a department which is on the

> side of people who want to make a difference, where everyone has the opportunity to fulfil their potential and to build a stake in society for them and their families. We want strong, cohesive communities in which people feel comfortable and proud to live, with a vibrant civic culture and strong local economy.[2]

Here there is strategic use of the terms 'community' and 'society' along with the idea of 'cohesion'. 'Society' is a social unit in which people who want to make a difference build a stake, and 'community' is a social group which should be strong and cohesive and where people feel proud to live. The core of the departmental ethos is thus founded on the virtues of wanting to make a difference and pride in place.

Community cohesion

Through the Department for Communities, the British Government clearly sees itself as having a role in the promotion of cohesive communities, principally through partnership with other agencies or what it imprecisely calls 'community organisations and communities themselves'.[3] These goals have recently been spelt out at length in the White Paper, *Strong and Prosperous Communities*, published in October 2006,[4] which claimed to be 'on the side of individuals and families who want to make a difference, both to their own lives and to the communities in which they live.' This process, it claimed, required 'revitalised local authorities', and at the same time, a reduction in 'the amount of top-down control from central government'. People, we are told, 'want choice over the services they receive, influence over those who provide them, and higher service standards'. People were to be able to 'demand an answer to their questions through a new Community Call for Action'. And there were to be measures to promote increased community ownership and management of local facilities and assets. The White Paper also calls for the creation of what are called 'Quality Parish Councils', where councillors will speak out on local issues and be champions of their 'local communities'. Greater power is to be devolved to cities and regions and stronger local leadership will be promoted. Communities, it goes on, will need 'strategic leadership', and as part of the centrally directed decentralization, local authorities will be required to set up a 'Sustainable Community Strategy' with about 35 (nationally set) priorities tailored to local needs and depending on 'about 200 outcome-based indicators covering important national priorities'. In turn there will also be a delivery plan known as a 'Local Area Agreement', which has to be ratified with central government. Finally, the goal of the White Paper is to ensure that 'stronger local leadership, greater resident participation in decisions and an enhanced role for community groups, can all help local areas to promote community cohesion.' The policy delivery Quango, the Commission on Integration and Cohesion would set up 'detailed plans on how to deliver a step change in promoting cohesion'.

This ambitious and wide-ranging set of policy objectives forms an aspect of a broader set of community cohesion policies across the Government: the role of the state is understood as promoting a form of social engineering to ensure that people live in cohesive communities. Such communities become agents of certain socially desirable goals, among them crime reduction and delivery of services. Indeed, the idea of community cohesion has been adopted across all governments departments, especially in education.[5]

This set of ideas seems to be based on the idea of what has been called 'social capital'. Many commentators have spoken of the decline in 'social capital', some in rather more apocalyptic ways than others. In a recent and rather overstated essay, for instance, the cultural theorist, Zygmunt Bauman has written

that 'every single measure of the Thatcher/Blair programme [has contrib-
uted] to the *progressive decomposition and crumbling of social bonds and communal
cohesion*'.[6] Policies to overcome what he calls 'wilting solidarity' become crucial
for the good functioning of democracy and society, as people are encouraged
to participate as actors in the 'social state'.[7] Commentators on both left and
right see the central importance of community cohesion, which is understood
to function as a normative goal to which social policy is to be directed. The
recent *Faithful Cities* report commissioned by the Church of England and the
Methodist Church has similarly sought to promote a specific form of social
capital, which it calls 'faithful capital', based on shared values underpinned by
religious practice and beliefs.[8]

In all this, Robert Putnam's popular characterization of the problem which
community cohesion is meant to address has proved influential. The basic
thesis presented in his rather long book, *Bowling Alone* is straightforward.
Writing about American society, he claims that whereas earlier in the twentieth
century there was a deep engagement in the life of communities, over the
past 30 years,

> silently, without warning – that tide reversed and we were overtaken by
> a treacherous rip current. Without at first noticing, we have been pulled
> apart from one another and from our communities over the last third of the
> century.[9]

According to Putnam, there has been a decline in participation in social activities[10] and consequently huge shifts in the levels of 'social capital', a term which
he understands to refer to what he calls 'connections among individuals'. He
sees these connections in terms of the

> social networks and the norms of reciprocity and trustworthiness that arise
> from them. In that sense, social capital is closely related to what some have
> called 'civic virtue.' The difference is that 'social capital' calls attention to
> the fact that civic virtue is most powerful when embedded in a dense net-
> work of reciprocal social relations. A society of many virtuous but isolated
> individuals is not necessarily rich in social capital.[11]

In what he regards as something of a vicious circle, Putnam regards the decline
of social capital as both the cause and effect of contemporary social problems.[12] He concludes with a plea for what he calls

> an era of civic inventiveness to create a renewed set of institutions and chan-
> nels for a reinvigorated civic life that will fit the way we have come to live.
> Our challenge now is to reinvent the twenty-first century equivalent of the
> Boy Scouts or the settlement house or the playground.[13]

Community cohesion policies can be understood as part of this 'civic invent-iveness' in the investment in social capital.

The background to the explicit adoption of community cohesion policies in Britain lies in the responses to perceived social dismemberment and conflict, exemplified by what were classified by the press as 'riots' in Oldham, Burnley and Bradford in 2001.[14] Five major reports were produced in the early years of the present century in response to these events.[15] The term 'community cohesion' itself was used in the reports chaired by John Denham and Ted Cantle. The theory behind the various solutions to the perceived breakdown of community in these two reports is again based, at least implicitly, on the idea of a decline in social capital. The promotion of cohesive communities offers a remedy to social unrest based on greater exchange and interchange between the different groups and ethnicities who often live cheek by jowl in British cities. Indeed rather than understanding the chief causes of unrest to lie in the failures of economic redistribution and inequality of income, the conflicts between communities were seen as caused by the breakdown of social relations. Ted Cantle, who was appointed chair of the 'Community Cohesion Review Team' in August 2001, makes this clear, differentiating between 'social cohesion', which focuses on economic and structural solutions, and 'community cohesion' which is more explicitly concerned with relations between different ethnic, religious and cultural groups.[16] As he wrote in the 2001 Report:

> There is evidence to suggest that a considerable amount of volunteering takes place within minority ethnic communities, usually through schools and religious activities. The problem, however, is that these activities tend to be for the benefit of others from the same ethnic group/community.[17]

In passing, one might ask why this form of self-help activity should necessarily be a problem at all.

There now exist a number of Quangos aimed at the promotion of this form of community cohesion. These include the 'Commission on Integration and Cohesion' chaired by Darra Singh, launched in August 2006, and the 'Race, Cohesion and Faiths Directorate', which is more explicitly concerned with policy delivery in the area of equal rights legislation. At the same time the Directorate exists to promote community cohesion, which it defines simply in terms of a 'shared sense of belonging'. In a list of bullet points it goes on to clarify in more detail the characteristics of a cohesive community:

- there is a common vision and a sense of belonging for all communities;
- the diversity of people's different backgrounds and circumstances is appreciated and positively valued;
- those from different backgrounds have similar life opportunities;

- strong and positive relationships are being developed between people from different backgrounds in the workplace, in schools and within neighbourhoods.

Here there is an explicit mention of the increase in social capital (i.e. 'strong and positive relationships') between people from different backgrounds. Although much of the work of the Department for Communities and Local Government involves the related and central activities of planning and promoting equal opportunities and equal access for all, it is this aspect – the promotion of community cohesion (sometimes simply called the promotion of 'community') – that I want to dwell on in the remainder of this chapter.

Some historical myths

Historically at least, the goal and tasks of the Department for Communities and Local Government resemble those of sociology in the early years of its existence as a discipline. Sociology was about amelioration and social engineering and the promotion of community – at its beginning most sociology was a long way from being a value-neutral discipline undertaken by social scientists (whatever the claims made by some who regarded it as a positive science). It was instead concerned with what it understood to be the improvement of society. This task required a set of myths, which frequently centred on the overarching historical myth of a form of social order called 'community' and usually associated with villages,[18] which could be glimpsed in a purer form in the pre-modern past but which needed to be recreated in the present in order for society to function peacefully. What was important was that community was something which depended on face-to-face contact as was found in the small-scale life of medieval society. Community was measured in terms of the density and necessity of human contact.

Here the influence of one of the first German sociologists, Ferdinand Tönnies, cannot be underestimated. Tönnies differentiated between two key forms of social organization, loosely translated as 'community' (*Gemeinschaft*) and 'society' (*Gesellschaft*). 'Being together', he wrote,

is the vegetative heart and soul of Community (*Gemeinschaft*) – the very existence of *Gemeinschaft* rests in the consciousness of belonging together and the affirmation of the condition of mutual dependence which is posed by that affirmation. Living together may be called the animal soul of *Gemeinschaft*; for it is the condition of its active life, of a shared feeling of pleasure and pain, of a shared enjoyment of the commonly possessed goods, by which one is surrounded, and by the cooperation in teamwork as well as in divided labour. Working together may be conceived of as the rational or human soul of *Gemeinschaft*. It is a higher, more conscious cooperation in the unity of spirit and purpose, including, therefore, a striving for common or shared ideals, as invisible goods that are knowable only to thought. Regarding being together it is descent (blood), regarding living together it is soil (land), regarding working together it is occupation (*Beruf*) that is the substance, as it were, by which the wills of men, which otherwise are far apart from and even antagonistic to each other, are essentially united.[19]

The concept of community, as this reveals, is deeply rooted in the historical myths of kinship as well as blood and soil.

It is not implausible to read the history of the relationship between sociology and politics as one of exchange and replacement. Thus, perhaps ironically, as sociology became less involved with amelioration and social reconstruction and more concerned with social analysis, so the role of government expanded to embrace these ameliorative tasks of sociology. Politics adopted many of the same myths of the 'common vision' of the nation which had once guided both sociologists and historians. For instance, waxing lyrical about the origins of English freedom, the great constitutional historian, Edward Freeman wrote of its survival in its purest form only in Switzerland: 'Year by year, on certain spots among the dales and mountainsides of Switzerland [one can look] face to face on freedom in its purest and most ancient form.'[20] Here there is inevitably a romanticism and an element of wishful thinking, and yet there are also some lessons to be learnt for contemporary policy debates. One should never underestimate the impact of Tuscan urban life, with its strong sense of local identity, on the politics of New Labour.[21]

But what precisely is a community?

It may even be the case that the clamour for community cohesion amounts to an unconscious recreation of national myth, something like a new version of the old myth of the free village community of Anglo-Saxon times upholding the ancient Teutonic freedoms.[22] It is not a long journey from Freeman and other great Victorian historians like William Stubbs to Ruth Kelly's version of the national myth based on what she called 'building up a shared sense of purpose and belonging' in a speech to the Commission for Racial Equality in November 2006.[23] In the same speech she explicitly notes the work of Ted Cantle, whose 2001 report on *Community Cohesion* spoke of 'inter-cultural collaboration rather than recognising merely specific demands'. For Cantle, and for many others, the concept of community seems to be identified with a homogeneous ethnic or religious group, which is to be encouraged to talk to and work with other groups rather than focus in on itself. It must be said, however, the use of the word 'community' in such contexts is frequently unnuanced and a product of the imagination rather than anything based on empirical evidence, and lacks an awareness of the fluctuating and complex nature of ethnic and cultural identity.[24] Communities can even be regarded as fixed entities given by ethnic origin rather than through complex interaction with context.[25] For instance, in a piece of apocalyptic rhetoric, Trevor Phillips spoke of 'marooned communities' which would 'steadily drift away from the rest of us' into 'crime, no-go areas and chronic conflict'.[26] Participation and interaction between these cultural and ethnic communities become key to the solution, but what is most obvious from the literature is that there is little clarity about what precisely it is that people are supposed to participate in and with whom they are meant to interact.

This problem points to a larger issue. What is left unspoken in most of the discussions and the government literature on community cohesion is any concrete evidence for or even discussion about what precisely constitutes a community or how people identify themselves. Amartya Sen has noted that there is a tendency to pigeonhole and to categorize people – to see them as products of their ethnic or religious origins. Consequently a country like Britain now has a group called 'Muslims' who are understood as principally determined by their religion. And yet it is also clear that there is a huge diversity among Muslims – there will be multiple rather than singular identities. Bangladeshis, for instance, will identify themselves quite differently from Pakistanis in relation to their language and the particularity of their culture. As Sen writes: 'It is, of course, not surprising at all that the champions of Islamic fundamentalism would like to suppress all other identities of Muslims in favour of being only Islamic.'[27] But what seems to me to be important is that for much of the time there is not one community through which identity is defined, but a whole range made up of local, national and international ways of identifying oneself. Such identities might be based, for instance, on language, food, or even musical and aesthetic taste. Identity is not simply conferred by face-to-face contact (along the Putnam model) but is something far more complex and multifaceted, and it may even be something that is chosen.[28]

A recent visit to Sri Lanka reinforced this sense of multifaceted identity. I was speaking to the clergy of the Anglican diocese of Colombo. They were Christian priests in a predominantly Buddhist society with a significant number of Hindus and Muslims. Christians form about 7% of the population, and Anglicans only about 1%. But the identity of the clergy could not be accounted for solely in Christian terms. Ethnically, the clergy comprised Sinhalese, Tamils, and a few Burghers; a few had their first language as English; most spoke Sinhala, although there was a large minority of Tamils, most of whom found Sinhala difficult. The conference had to be conducted in English, a language that had been deliberately suppressed in the earlier period of Sri Lankan independence. Christian identity makes sense only in the context of the history of oppression, particularly of Tamils, which has led to significant levels of civil unrest. Furthermore, even the Christian identity was complex: while most clergy were identifiably Anglo-Catholic, some were more Evangelical, depending partly on the legacy of the different Anglican missionary societies. To complicate matters still further the Church of Ceylon (as it is still known) is associated with the Church of the former colonizer, and it still controls some of the most elite schools in Sri Lanka. Identities are contested and emerge through interaction and self-definitions, as well as definitions constructed by outsiders. Other shared identities – for instance, love of cricket – displayed something of the way in which cultures or identities are far from static but emerge from dialogue and interaction.[29]

Cultural identities combine with histories and myths and narratives, sometimes of liberation from a perceived oppressor, and sometimes in terms of the demonization of another group. Sometimes the two aspects can combine (as with the Spanish narratives of expulsion of the Moors). Another example comes from the US. In Boston in Massachusetts I followed a red line around the city centre marking what is called the 'Freedom Trail', celebrating liberation from the British Crown. For a Church of England priest, who has sworn allegiance to that Crown, this raised some interesting questions about the nature of American freedom and identity. Identities are complex and often ambiguous.

The complexity of identity and multiculturalism becomes especially pressing since, more often than not, the word 'community' is used to mean something other than faith-based or ethnic communities – according to some of the British Government rhetoric, community is something in which members of *different* ethnic and faith groups are meant to cohere. Indeed the word 'community' most frequently points to something which is larger than these smaller ethnic communities, and in that sense it moves a long way from the sort of face-to-face community founded on blood and soil envisaged by Tönnies. It is often far closer to his concept of society. Just one recent example is sufficient to show the vagueness of the use of the word: despite using the word 'community' 134 times throughout the document, the Government's lengthy Sustainable Communities five-year plan nowhere offers a definition of community beyond a geographical place. The closest it comes to any clarity is where it differentiates communities from neighbourhoods ('the areas which people identify with most').[30] In the new White Paper there is an interesting section on naming the new 'Parish Councils'. These will be called either parish, town or city councils, but also community, village or neighbourhood councils as well.

A highly instructive example of the employment of the term 'community' is that used by the 'Belonging to Blackburn with Darwen' Local Strategic Partnership (LSP) campaign, which features as one of the flagship examples of community cohesion planning in the Local Government Association *Community Cohesion Action Guide*.[31] The Blackburn with Darwen LSP has focused on the 'many lives . . . many faces . . . all belonging to Blackburn with Darwen'.

It featured 'local people saying why they are proud to belong to the borough'. All these citizens had signed up to what was called a 'charter of belonging'. It was noted in the document that, 'This formal charter was signed by the members of the LSP, and a shorter summary was distributed across the borough so that the spirit of the charter is available to all.'[32] In this example, the community is something to which one subscribes through some sort of explicit declaration of shared values. It would appear to be coterminous with a geographical and government entity of relatively recent origin, namely the Borough of Blackburn with Darwen.

However, little is said about those who choose not to avail themselves of this spirit of belonging, or who do not wish to sign the charter. It is hard to know what room is made for those who simply do not wish to become members of a cohesive community identified with a local government area. (It would be equally hard for me to understand how I might belong to South Oxfordshire, another recent entity, whose offices are in what is, at least historically, Berkshire). The rhetoric of community is underpinned by constitutional (and occasionally historical) myths of belonging to a particular place, as with many examples in the Local Government Association *Action Guide*. Yet within the very same *Guide* there is also much use of the word 'community' in relation to the different ethnic and religious groups that make up the larger 'community'. At other times the official documents discuss the physical surroundings which make the very existence of community possible – in the five-year plan, for instance, there is a moving story about Constantine Blake, the first park ranger in St Agnes Park, Bristol, who talks about 'creating space for a community': 'I made [the park] a space the community could use – it's their decision on how they want to use it.' Clearing away drug litter made space for the possibility of social interaction and community cohesion.[33]

It is in this context that there has been some reflection on the idea of Britishness. In the final speeches of the previous Prime Minister there was further slippage in the use of the term 'community'. In a lecture given to the Runnymede Trust on 1 December 2006, entitled 'The Duty to Integrate: Shared British Values',[34] Blair spoke of integration not into local communities but 'integrating at the point of shared, common unifying values'. Following in the pattern of many earlier speeches, he speaks of these values in terms of 'belief in democracy, rule of law, tolerance' as well as 'respect for this country and its shared heritage'. This means that the *national* rather than the local community functions as the locus for integration, primarily through government-sponsored plans for community cohesion. In this speech he emphasized the national curriculum on citizenship and the importance of interreligious dialogue (although it is not clear from the speech that the Government promotion of faith-based schools assists in this project – the only point noted was that there would be an encouragement of links with schools of another faith, and the rather bold statement that 'religious bigotry is inconsistent with most true religion').[35] Echoing the White Paper, Blair noted that grants would be awarded to local groups against a test 'of promoting community cohesion and integration'. The national community would also require proficiency in English as a common language. At the end of the speech he slips explicitly into the language of national community:

> If you come here lawfully, we welcome you. If you are permitted to stay here permanently, you become an equal member of our community and become one of us. Then you, and all of us, who want to, can worship God in our own way, take pride in our different cultures after our own fashion, respect our distinctive histories according to our own traditions; but do so within a shared space of shared values in which we take no less pride and show no less respect. The right to be different. The duty to integrate. That is what being British means. And neither racists nor extremists should be allowed to destroy it.

Or, as David Blunkett, the former Home Secretary, put it at the end of 2001:

> The UK has had a relatively weak sense of what political citizenship should entail. Our values of individual freedom, the protection of liberty and respect for difference, have not been accompanied by a strong, shared understanding of the civic realm. This has to change.[36]

Being British is about the duty to integrate into a strong civic realm – and that is a duty promoted and sponsored by government. Nothing is said about those who do not wish to avail themselves of the duty to participate, or who have little stake in the political process.

Conclusion

By way of a very brief conclusion to this survey let me simply point to some of the obvious problems in the British language of community and multiculturalism, which I think apply to other societies equally well. First, all local authorities are required to have a community cohesion policy, and are encouraged to measure and quantify their practices in accord with explicit criteria. There is already a substantial body of literature in this area. But what is completely lacking is a clear definition of what a community might be, in which case there can be no adequate criteria for success. Indeed, as some commentators from the Old Left have noted, the community agenda, based on the social capital model, may serve to mask some of the other social inequalities and conflicts in the quest for what might be regarded as perhaps premature harmony. There is much that is laudable and impressive in the community cohesion policy, but the rhetoric and ethics of community can perhaps sometimes be a distraction from the more material causes of deprivation and equality.[37]

Second is another related issue. There is much in the policy statements that speaks of devolution and a decentralization of power away from the centre to the local. There is also a recognition of the importance of participation in local structures of government. And yet the central regulative framework is as tight as ever. It seems to me that a complete rethink of the relationship between the centre and the local is crucial – the decline of voter participation, especially in local politics, is hardly surprising when local government is simply a deliverer of centrally set and regulated targets. There is little in the White Paper to suggest that this will change. 'Post-democracy', as Colin Crouch calls it, is a situation that needs to be addressed through the creation of more flexible and responsive institutions entrusted with far greater responsibility for setting policy objectives and delivery.[38] Similarly, as Tom Bentley writes:

> There is little sign that the new infrastructure of regulation, procurement and implementation is able to offer the forms of responsiveness or local legitimacy that such approaches have been seeking, even when their political champions are passionately committed to creating them.[39]

Nevertheless there are some grounds for hope: in his 2004 speech for the 70th anniversary of the British Council, Gordon Brown, like the Prime Minister before him, enunciated the British virtues of liberty, duty, fair play and decency, but also thought that there was a need 'to restore and enhance local initiative and mutual responsibility' by strengthening local government. He went on:

> Rather than asking more people to look upwards to Whitehall to solve all their problems, the British way is surely to encourage more and more people, from their own localities, to take more charge of decisions that affect their lives . . . a reinvigorated local democracy can, I believe, emerge to empower people in their own neighbourhoods to deal with the challenges they face.[40]

Whether the recent regime change will lead to a rethink of local democracy and the 'letting-go' by the centre is an open question, but there are early signs that constitutional change is at least on the agenda.[41] But there is a long way to go. Treating citizens not as consumers (i.e. passive users) of education, health and other public services with centrally imposed objectives, which has been the focus of Blair's third term, but as participating agents and decision-makers in policy-creation and delivery, would amount to a complete reversal of government policy. Without this reversal, however, there seems little hope of the reinvigoration of democracy (and communities) either at a local or national level. As *Faithful Cities* notes, it is easy for churches and other voluntary organizations to become deliverers of a centrally set policy to consumers of services with little sense of participation in the formulation of that policy (or indeed possibility of critique of those policies).[42] It may well be that less time and expense should be devoted by churches to policy delivery, and more energy should be put into reinvigorating the witness of Christians in the democratic process and in voluntary organizations: that, after all, tends to be where Christians have traditionally made the greatest impact. This would mean that the role of the church is more about inspiring its members with Gospel values to live and work in the power of the spirit in the world rather than as another agency or pressure group.

Finally, and this is my most important point, it may simply be impossible, except in a very vague and ultimately pointless way, to find any mutually shared universal values. After all, most religious communities have enough problems trying to do this themselves – conflict has been the normal condition of churches throughout most of Christian history, and the recent history of my own Anglican Communion is a good case-study. And yet, if identities are complex, and if the understanding of culture (like religion and ethnicity) is bitterly contested, then the idea of a federation of different religious (or ethnic) communities is both implausible and possibly dangerous – who, after all, will ultimately decide on which categories people will fall under? This is one of the reasons why some critics of multiculturalism, including Trevor Phillips, have used such powerful rhetoric.[43]

The alternative vision of strong national communities based on historical myths, however, seems to me to be far worse and could rapidly homogenize society and deny the vitality of minorities (as has happened at times in polarized societies like that of Sri Lanka). Here I think there is much of interest in Anthony Giddens's idea of 'sophisticated' as opposed to 'naïve' multiculturalism which resists simple categorization of ethnic and religious identity, but which allows for a plurality of identities to coexist on the basis of government-sanctioned mutual respect.[44] Similarly, as Amartya Sen writes:

> There is a real need to rethink the understanding of multiculturalism both to avoid conceptual disarray about social identity and also to resist the purposeful exploitation of the divisiveness that this conceptual disarray allows and even, to some extent, encourages. What has to be particularly avoided . . . is the confusion between multiculturalism with cultural liberty, on the one side, and plural monoculturalism with faith-based separatism on the other. A nation can hardly be seen as a collection of sequestered segments, with citizens being assigned fixed places in predetermined segments. Nor can Britain be seen, explicitly or by implication, as an imagined federation of religious ethnicities.[45]

Working out the necessary pragmatic principles for such a society to function seems to me to be a key role for government. The principal issue is less that of finding shared values than that of having to learn to live with people who are in some ways different and also in some ways the same. This is what might be referred to as a form of patriotism which amounts to a commitment to respect one another and to work together despite differences.[46] At times this might lead to government action to restrain those who clamour for singular identity at the expense of others (including fundamentalists). Going much further, however, and providing too many positive values (of, say, Britishness) seems both pointless and unnecessarily conflictual, especially for those whose historical identity is based on not being 'British' in that way. Few people like to be told what values they should adopt by central government, or indeed that they have a duty to integrate at all. What Giddens imagines instead is what he calls 'acceptance of a common overall identity as members of a national community, as a "community of fate" – that is, being bound by laws and collective decisions that affect everyone'.[47] That may well be what citizenship (another recent concept in British politics) is really about. Britain (and any other country for that matter) is where people happen to live and it is best for them if they learn to live together with one another in relative peace and tranquillity.

A degree of value pluralism is inevitable, in which case it might be better to return to tolerant multiculturalism rather than to impose a centrally determined idea of what counts as a good community. Rather than sponsoring 'community cohesion' the British government (and the same could be said of other governments) might be well advised to expend energy on working out the limits of pluralism through promoting the language of rights and equality, without worrying too much about corresponding responsibilities and duties or the promotion of community. Contemporary identities might simply be too confusing for governments to understand – and popular politics, with its tendency to simplification, can easily create forms of exclusive identities with violent repercussions. Ultimately equality before the law, and equality of access and opportunity for all people, whatever their identities, may be far more important than community cohesion. And we can leave community cohesion to what has been called the 'weak social capital' of democratic governance based on coming together to make decisions in a whole range of groups underpinned by strong local government.[48] But strong executives tend not to like to lose control, and they often enjoy dictating what we should think.

Notes

[1] Mark D. Chapman, *Blair's Britain* (London: DLT, 2005), chapter three. See also Alex Callinicos, *Against the Third Way* (Cambridge: Polity Press, 2001), esp. pp. 55–67.

[2] Ruth Kelly, July 2006 from Departmental website at: www.communities.gov.uk/index.asp?id=1501559 (accessed 28 Aug. 2007).

3 Departmental website at: www.communities.gov.uk/index.asp?id=1500185 (accessed 28 Aug. 2007).

4 Posted at: www.communities.gov.uk/pub/98/StrongandProsperousCommunities theLocalGovernmentWhitePaperVol1_id1504098.pdf (accessed 21 Apr. 2007). Summary at: www.communities.gov.uk/pub/100/StrongandProsperousCommunities theLocalGovernmentWhitePaperSummary_id1504100.pdf (accessed 21 Apr. 2007).

5 See, for instance, Community Cohesion Standards for Schools posted at: www. standards.dfes.gov.uk/pdf/commcohesion.pdf (accessed 21 Apr. 2007).

6 Zygmunt Bauman, 'Britain after Blair, or Thatcherism Consolidated' in Gerry Hassan (ed.), *After Blair: Politics after the New Labour Decade* (London: Lawrence and Wishart, 2007), pp. 60–74, here p. 61, emphasis in original.

7 Bauman, 'Britain after Blair', p. 65.

8 The Report from the Commission on Urban Life and Faith, *Faithful Cities: A Call for Celebration, Vision and Justice* (London: Church House Publishing and Peterborough: Methodist Publishing House, 2006), §§1.11–1.16.

9 Robert D. Putnam, *Bowling Alone: The Collapse and Revival of American Community* (New York: Simon & Schuster, 2000), p. 27. For a detailed critique of social capital in relation to community cohesion, see Derek McGhee, 'Moving to "our" common ground – a critical examination of community cohesion discourse in twenty-first century Britain' in *The Sociological Review* 51 (2003), pp. 376–404.

10 Putnam, *Bowling Alone*, p. 63.

11 Ibid. p. 19.

12 Ibid. pp. 294–5.

13 Ibid. p. 401.

14 On the history of this term in relation to the 'riots' of 2001, see Paul Bagguley and Yasmin Hussain, 'Conflict and Cohesion: constructions of "community" around the 2001 "riots"' (lecture to 2003 Communities Conference) at: www. leeds.ac.uk/sociology/people/pbdocs/Conflict%20and%20Cohesion%204% 20conference.doc (accessed 18 Jan. 2007).

15 On Bradford, Herman Ouseley, *Community Pride, Not Prejudice: Making Diversity Work in Practice* (Bradford: Bradford Vision, 2001); on Burnley, Anthony Clarke, *Burnley Task Force Report* (Burnley: Burnley Task Force, 2001); on Oldham, David Ritchie *Oldham Independent Review Panel Report* (Manchester: Government Office for the North-west, 2001); John Denham, *Building Cohesive Communities: A Report of the Ministerial Group on Public Order and Community Cohesion* (London: Home Office, 2001); and Ted Cantle, *Community Cohesion: A Report of the Independent Review Team Chaired by Ted Cantle* (London: Home Office, 2001) at: http://image. guardian.co.uk/sys-files/Guardian/documents/2001/12/11/communitycohesion report.pdf (accessed 6 Nov. 2008).

16 See Ted Cantle, *Community Cohesion: A New Framework for Race and Diversity* (Basingstoke: Palgrave, 2005), p. 52.

17 Cantle, *Community Cohesion*, p. 72.

18 See J. W. Burrow, 'The Village Community' in Neil McKendrick (ed.), *Historical Perspectives: Studies in English Thought and Society* (London: Europa, 1974), pp. 255–84. Tönnies was strongly influenced by Sir Henry Maine, *Village Communities in the East and West* (London: John Murray, 1890).

19 Ferdinand Tönnies, 'The Concept of Gemeinschaft', in Werner J. Cahnman and Rudolf Heberle (eds), *Ferdinand Tönnies on Sociology: Pure, Applied and Empirical. Selected Writings* (Chicago: University of Chicago Press, 1971), pp. 62–72, here p. 69. See also the new translation of Tönnies' classic work, *Gemeinschaft und Gesellschaft* by José Harris and M. Hollis: *Community and Civil Society*, translated (Cambridge: Cambridge University Press, 2001).

20 Edward A. Freeman, *The Growth of the Constitution* (London: Macmillan, third edition, 1876), p. 1.

21 On the idea of Englishness and identity, see Robert Colls' wide-ranging survey in *Identity of England* (Oxford: Oxford University Press, 2002).

22 See Christopher Parker, *The English Historical Tradition since 1850* (Edinburgh: John Donald, 1990), pp. 44–8; and Peter Hinchliff, *God and History* (Oxford: Clarendon, 1992), chapter 1.

23 Speech given on 27 November 2006 at: http://comunities.gov.uk/index.asp?id= 1504751 (accessed 18 Jan. 2007).

24 See Michael Keith, *Riots, Race and Policing: Lore and Disorder in a Multi-Racial Society* (London: UCL Press, 1993).

25 See Hannah Jones, 'Faith in Community' *eSharp* issue 7, pp. 11–13 at: www. sharp.arts.gla.ac.uk/issue7/Jones.pdf (accessed 6 Nov. 2008).

26 Trevor Phillips, 'After 7/7: Sleepwalking to Segregation' (Speech given at Manchester Town Hall, 22 Sept. 2005) at: www.cre.gov.uk/Default.aspx.LocID-0hgnew07r. RefLocID-0hg00900c001001.Lang-EN.htm (accessed 18 Jan. 2007).

27 Amartya Sen, *Identity and Violence* (London: Allen Lane, 2006), p. 14.

28 Sen, *Identity and Violence*, p. 4.

29 On this, see Nira Wickramasinghe, *Sri Lanka in the Modern Age: A History of Contested Identities* (Colombo: Vijitha Yapa Publications, 2006), esp. Part 1.

30 Office of the Deputy Prime Minister, *Sustainable Communities: People, Places and Prosperity. A Five Year Plan from the office of the Deputy Prime Minister* (London: HMSO, 2005), p. 18 at: www.communities.gov.uk/pub/490/SustainableCommunities PeoplePlacesandProsperity_id1500490.pdf (accessed 18 Jan. 2007).

31 *Community Cohesion: An Action Guide* (London: Local Government Association, 2004).

32 Ibid. p. 10.

33 Office of the Deputy Prime Minister, *Sustainable Communities*, p. 24.

34 Tony Blair, 'The Duty to Integrate: Shared British Values' (speech given at Downing Street to an event hosted by the Runnymede Trust) at: www.number10. gov.uk/output/Page10563.asp (accessed 18 Jan. 2007).

35 Amartya Sen offers a vigorous critique of faith-based education: 'In Britain a confounded view of what a multiethnic society must do has led to encouraging the development of state-financed Muslim schools, Hindu schools, Sikh schools, etc., to supplement preexisting state-supported Christian schools, and young children are powerfully placed in the domain of singular affiliations well before they have the ability to reason about different systems of identification that may compete for their attention' (*Identity and Violence*, p. 13). But see also Anthony Giddens, *Over to You, Mr Brown* (Cambridge: Polity, 2007), p. 160.

36 'Blunkett Calls for Honest and Open Debate on Citizenship and Community' (17 Dec. 2001) 10 Downing Street Newsroom at: www.number-10.gov.uk/news. asp?newsID=3255 (accessed 18 Jan. 2007).

[37] Derek McGhee, 'Moving to "our" common ground', p. 400.

[38] Colin Crouch, *Post-democracy* (Cambridge: Polity, 2004).

[39] See Tom Bentley, 'Learning to let go: The potential of a self-creating society' in Hassan, *After Blair*, pp. 94–106, here p. 100.

[40] Gordon Brown, 'Britishness' (7 July 2004) in *Moving Britain Forward: Selected Speeches 1997–2006* (London: Bloomsbury, 2006), pp. 1–26, here p. 21.

[41] See Bentley, 'Learning to let go', p. 101.

[42] *Faithful Cities*, §§7.62–7.68.

[43] See Giddens, *Over to You, Mr Brown*, p. 155.

[44] Giddens, *Over to You, Mr Brown*, chapter 7. See also, Sen, *Identity and Violence*, pp. 158–65.

[45] Sen, *Identity and Violence*, p. 165.

[46] On this, see Charles Taylor, *Multiculturalism: Examining the Politics of Recognition* (Princeton: Princeton University Press, 1994).

[47] Giddens, *Over to You, Mr Brown*, p. 156.

[48] Sue Goss, 'Re-imagining the public realm' in Hassan (ed.), *After Blair*, pp. 107–19, esp. pp. 114–15.

Chapter 9

Constructing Christian Right Enemies and Allies: US, UK and Eastern Europe

Cynthia Burack and Angelia R. Wilson

Casting political opponents as enemies of God, race, culture or nation is a common form of political discourse.[1] No less common is casting ideological adversaries as political enemies through discourse that translates shared cultural fears and convictions into political principles and policy recommendations. A number of theorists have provided tools for explicating these kinds of processes. Norman Fairclough, for example, identifies such discourse as one version of 'synthetic personalisation' and highlights the way narratives about 'the other' explicitly or implicitly construct narratives about 'us' creating 'perceptions of constituency' and 'perceptions of enemies'.[2]

In this chapter, we examine one case of the translation of an ideological enemy – a foe conceptualized in moral/theological terms – into political discourses in the US, UK and Eastern Europe. For the US and UK, we provide a brief genealogy of the construction of homosexuals as enemies since the 1970s. We then turn to recent events involving political rhetoric about same-sex sexuality in Poland and Latvia in which the US Christian Right has fuelled backlash against Western European social values. In all these contexts, 'the homosexual' has functioned as an ideological, as well as a political, enemy, though the cultural and institutional circumstances vary in important respects. Also crucial in the process of constructing internal enemies and allies are the ways in which the concept of 'enemy' is a flexible concept, one that often embraces not only the ideological other but also those political actors who are perceived to tolerate and facilitate the depredations of the other. These 'allies' of the enemy are frequently indicted by the Christian Right, the socio-political movement that is at the forefront of national and transnational activism against gay rights.

Identifying homosexuals as 'other' serves moral as well as political purposes. Published in 1968, Mary McIntosh's essay, 'The Homosexual Role' highlighted 'homosexuals as a social category, rather than a medical or psychiatric one' and challenged sociologists to 'ask the right questions about the specific content of the homosexual role and about the organization and functions of homosexual groups'.[3] McIntosh's work captures the spirit of modern political discourse in which 'the creation of a specialized, despised, and punished role of homosexual keeps the bulk of society pure in rather the same way that the similar treatment of some kinds of criminals helps keep the rest of society law-abiding'.[4] Labelling homosexuals as deviants is a mechanism of social control which 'helps to provide a clear-cut, publicized, and recognizable threshold between permissible and impermissible behavior'.[5]

Since the 1970s, in both the US and the UK, the conservative Christian Right has developed and operationalized its antigay ideology in order to perpetuate or challenge relations and institutions of power.[6] Conservative Christian politics are usually associated with the US, but Revd Kenneth Leech's *The Social God* documents the rise of UK moral right in the 1970s as a 'kind of creeping fascism'.[7] 'A distinctive "new Christian Right" has emerged', writes Leech, with a 'marked trend towards authoritarian rule'.[8] Describing as 'bigoted intolerance' the ideology of these new Christian Right actors and groups, he notes the 'disturbing growth of irrationalism and intolerance' among movement followers and warns that this new movement could lead to 'a crude fundamentalist theology . . . and a leadership marked by intolerance, irrational polemic and absolute conviction that they are right'.[9]

Leech's analysis is a general description of ideology in the formative years of a movement. Since the 1970s the transnational Christian Right has become a more mature and sophisticated movement with national and international organizations, interchurch and interdenominational cooperation, inclusion in political institutions and media outlets that communicate with conservative Christian activists. In this movement, Christian Right leaders craft macro-level antigay rhetoric; when it comes to the construction of homosexuals as enemies, a variety of conservative Christian leaders engage in instruction, preaching and induction into political activity that reaches down from national antigay projects through middle-level church institutions to individual believers.[10] At least since the 1980s, political analysts have predicted that the Christian Right movement has run its course and lost cultural and political influence.[11] To the contrary, the movement and its leaders display remarkable adaptability to a variety of political contexts, including outreach and mobilization of Christian conservatives around the world.[12]

The Christian Right in the US

From the 1970s onward, the mobilization of the New Christian Right was spurred on by a disparate set of influences, including: backlash to the African American Civil Rights movement as well as the anti-Vietnam War, Women's, and Gay Liberation movements; Supreme Court decisions that were perceived to abet the secular drift of America; and a general loosening of sexual norms.[13] Conservative Christian leaders were crucial to this mobilization because they refuted earlier narratives of Christian separation from an immoral secular order.[14] In place of Godly separation, movement leaders substituted a Christian responsibility to reform American culture, society and politics. In this new dispensation, homosexuals came to the fore as a special case of immorality in a way that was unprecedented in US history. It was no accident that this new concentration on the homosexual as the enemy of God, Christianity, and America coincided with greater social visibility of lesbians and gay men and the existence of a gay rights movement.

In the US, the term 'Christian Right' designates a loose identification that is not bound to a single institutional affiliation. Although no denomination defines the boundaries of conservative Christianity, a core constituency is made up of Southern Baptists, Pentecostals, conservative Catholics, members of independent conservative churches and a more amorphous group of conservative evangelicals. As students of the movement often point out, this term does not denote a single theological perspective; however, especially since the 1990s the movement has used ecumenism and the doctrine of co-belligerency to shape and maintain a political agenda, lobby and elect political leaders, influence public policy, educate the public on matters of social and political interest to conservative Christians, and create and direct grass-roots movements to achieve conservative Christian political goals.[15]

Prominent among the political issues of interest to Christian Right leaders and organizations today is the issue of sexual minority rights, an issue that is often framed for conservative Christian adherents as the 'gay agenda'. To lesbians and gay men and to those who understand homosexuals merely as fellow citizens, support for this 'agenda' includes relationship recognition and human rights policies that prohibit discrimination in employment and public accommodations. On the Christian Right, these goals are reframed as the destruction of marriage, the sexual or ideological seduction of children, the undermining of religious freedom, and the ultimate delivery of communities and nations to godless secular humanism. A key foundation for Christian Right antigay ideology is the refusal to distinguish between the civil rights/citizenship status of homosexuals and their status as moral enemies. For this movement, moral enemies are and must be political enemies; the stakes of this equation are the survival of the nation and, indeed, Christianity itself.

In considering the contemporary relationship between conservative Christianity and sexual minorities in the US, it is necessary to look to the social change of the 1970s. After ten years of growing gay discontent and public visibility, gay civil rights organizations sponsored the first mass rally for gay and lesbian civil rights in Washington, DC in 1979. That same year the Revd Jerry Falwell and other conservative Christian leaders founded the Moral Majority. The 1980 election, in which conservative Protestants would play a new kind of mobilizing and proselytizing role, was around the corner. The contemporary construction of homosexuals as the enemy was well underway. As Didi Herman points out, by the late 1970s, the prominent conservative evangelical publication *Christianity Today* had gone from representing homosexuals as 'pathetic' to representing them as an active 'counter-evangelistic', 'anti-Christian force'.[16] This kind of transformation of rhetoric sets the stage for constructing lesbians and gay men as cultural-ideological enemies and as political opponents whose defeat was essential to a Christian nation.

On 3 July 1981, shortly after the beginning of the Reagan era in US politics, the *New York Times* announced a 'rare cancer' that was initially named GRID, for 'gay-related immunodeficiency'.[17] Although the disease was later renamed Acquired Immune Deficiency Syndrome, or AIDS, the stigma attached by the medical community stuck. Before long, those who suffered from AIDS or had tested positive for the virus that causes the disease were subjected to social stigma, but neither ignorance about the disease nor the stigma associated with it alone constructed people with AIDS as political enemies. This enemy construction was accomplished by political rhetoric, one example of which was an AIDS stump speech delivered by the Revd Jerry Falwell:

> There is hardly a press conference in which someone doesn't ask me, 'Do you believe AIDS is God's judgment against homosexuals'? I always say, 'No, I don't believe that. I believe it is God's judgment against America, for endorsing immorality, even embracing it.' I believe it is God's judgment against the whole society.[18]

In comments such as this, Falwell and many other Christian conservatives explicitly endorsed the idea of the homosexual as enemy, situating the verdict in the context of conservative Christian doctrine regarding God's judgment on national sins.[19]

A significant event for both sexual minorities and the Christian Right occurred in June, 2003 when, in the case of *Lawrence v. Texas*,[20] the US Supreme Court nullified existing state sodomy laws and established the right of US citizens to engage in private same-sex sexual conduct. It appeared to many supporters and critics alike that the opinion prepared the legal path for challenges to the exclusion of same-sex couples from the right to civil marriage. The majority decision was read across the political spectrum as a blow to conservative Christian political attempts to contain or reverse gay legal and political victories. However, far from signalling the loss of homosexuals as an enemy, the Court decision incited Christian conservatives to support a Constitutional Amendment banning same-sex marriage in the US. In addition to passing state statutes and ratifying state constitutional amendments to ban same-sex marriage, the Christian Right continues to campaign against laws to prohibit discrimination and to campaign for a federal marriage amendment to the US Constitution. And the movement continues to mobilize its followers with enemy rhetoric that reinforces the intrinsic evil of homosexuality and the malign designs of homosexuals.

Thatcher and the homosexual enemy

Jeffrey Weeks writes of 'two major, interrelated but separable', reasons why sexuality became a central issue on the 1980s UK political agenda.[21] The first was a change in political culture associated with the government of Margaret Thatcher and the rise of the New Right, a shift also associated with the Reagan administration in the US. The second reason was 'the emergence during the course of the decade of a major, and potentially catastrophic, health crisis associated with the spread of AIDS (the acquired immune deficiency syndrome) and of HIV (the human immuno-deficiency virus) infection'.[22] As Weeks suggests, the growth of conservative Christianity by the 1980s was in large measure a backlash against the sexual revolution, including the Sexual Offences Act 1967,[23] and its perceived consequences.

The backlash against the 'permissive society' can be traced through the work of the Moral Re-armament, the Conservative Family Campaign, Society for the Protection of Unborn Children, and the National Viewers and Listeners Association. The link between these conservative Christian groups and the Tory Party was strengthened significantly in 1974 when Sir Keith Joseph addressed 'matters which concern the nation' such as the decline of 'family values' and the 'rise of sexual offences' threatening the nation with 'destruction from the enemy within'.[24] His answer to these 'dilemmas inherent in remoralizing public life' drew clear distinctions between enemies and 'people like you and me'. While the UK Moral Right was never synonymous with the Tory Party, with the election of Thatcher conservative Christians gained significant access to political power. Durham's history of the Thatcher era clarifies that while the UK pro-life movement had ideologically varied supporters, the powerful concept of 'a moral right' movement in Britain 'does capture something important about "pro-family" organizations', particularly on issues of sex education and homosexuality.[25]

Leo Abse, supporter of decriminalization in 1967, blamed the backlash on the 'shrill and new-paranoic extreme gay liberation lobbies . . . the new freedom to come out has meant only that they have freaked out: their exhibitionism arouses resentment and indeed, in those lacking certainty in their own heterosexuality, it arouses fears which can only be warded off by regressive legislation'.[26] Anna Marie Smith notes that during the Thatcher years the backlash against gays effectively distinguished between the 'good homosexual' and the 'dangerous queer'.[27] While there was limited toleration during the period for a 'good homosexual' who is 'self-limiting, closeted, desexualized, and invisible', the 'dangerous queer' was an 'incorrigible pervert who pursues the socio-political infection of the general population at every opportunity'.[28]

It was in this charged political context that HIV/AIDS was first diagnosed. The magazine *Doctor* informed the medical community on 17 December 1981, 'The common usage of that pretty little adjective "gay" as a euphemism has now become the sad name for a mysterious virus that turns harmless germs into killers. . . . Perhaps there should be a Government health warning: Gays can kill.'[29] The press depicted the disease as the Gay Plague. And soon a large part of socio-political discourse claimed the disease as 'God's answer to the new Sodom and Gomorrah'.[30] The reporting of the *Times* linked sexuality with a threat to the foundations of social and political life:

> This disease is capable not only of physical harm but also of dissolving the trust on which social life is built, the trust which allows us to separate and tolerate private conduct, even of an immoral and exotic kind, from the public business of society.[31]

The *Guardian* quoted Chief Constable of Manchester James Anderton, 'People at risk are swirling around in a cesspit of their own making.'[32]

The lack of response by the government to the crisis left care and education in the hands of the gay community. Weeks observed that 'AIDS came to represent for many the inevitable end-product of permissiveness and of rapid social dislocation, and thus fed into the wider political and moral agenda'.[33] In explaining how AIDS was perceived to constitute a homosexual threat to stable, normal society, Weeks alludes to the course of moral panics, a course that includes a 'definition of a threat', the 'stereotyping of the main characters', the 'escalation of the perceived threat', the 'emergence of an imaginary solution' and a 'subsidence of the anxiety', a conclusion that establishes a new status quo with which victims of the panic must now contend.[34]

In the UK, the impact of AIDS, in conjunction with increased 'positive images' of the gay and lesbian community, pushed the limits of toleration. During the 1987 election Conservatives promised a ban on 'sexual propaganda' from the classroom.[35] Tory back-bencher Geoffrey Dickens argued that, due to AIDS, homosexuality should be recriminalized:

> What we should be saying is: 'Look, I'm afraid this sort of behaviour is totally unacceptable. You're putting your nation at risk by your behaviour. We're not going to have this in the future.' And that's why we're legislating to make this a crime once again.[36]

Thatcher's assault on the gay community served her political strategy and defined the political agenda. Linking normative sexuality to the well-being of the nation, Thatcher claimed that moral values must be reasserted to salvage the nation's future. Notably, the threat of lesbianism began to be articulated in the custody cases where judges determined lesbians as unfit mothers. In one case which reached the House of Lords, Lord Wilberforce argued that 'whatever new attitudes Parliament or public opinion might have chosen to take with regard to the behaviour of consenting adults over 21, these should not entitle the courts to relax in any degree the vigilance and severity with which they should regard the risk to children at critical ages' to be exposed to the threats associated with lesbianism.[37]

Thatcher built on such fears, arguing that 'children who need to be taught to respect traditional values are being taught that they have an inalienable right to be gay'.[38] A few months later, in the final committee stage of the Local Government Bill, an amendment was added. A local authority should not 'promote homosexuality or publish material for the promotion of homosexuality' or 'promote the teaching in any maintained school of the acceptability of homosexuality as a pretended family relationship'.[39] In a lamentable tactical error, Labour's failure to challenge the amendment at committee stage led to the largest public debate on homosexuality since the 1950s, including a march of thousands of lesbians and gay men through the streets of London. Politicians, church leaders and academics publicly petitioned for Parliament to show restraint. Despite many public protests, it appeared that Kenneth Leech's predictions about the consequences of the rise of conservative Christianity had been borne out. In the wake of AIDS and contemporary morality politics, homosexuals were constructed as a threat to society and as a political enemy.

Leech noted that the Tory Party of the 1970s was characterized by 'authoritarian populism' that targeted 'welfare scroungers', as well as 'homosexuals, liberals, trade unionists, Marxists'.[40] The constructions of conservative 'perceptions of constituencies' and 'perceptions of enemies' were clearly economically and morally motivated with the homosexual enemy, a cultural and now physical threat to the nation, at centre stage throughout the 1980s. However, by the late 1990s and with significant reframing of perceptions of New Labour constituencies, lesbian and gay citizens became political allies of Tony Blair, and a new 'good gay' emerged.

The importance of political allies

A key element of any tableau of political enemies is the extent to which popular conceptions of the enemy are certified and institutionalized by political elites. In the US, the Democratic Party is widely associated with the interests of such identity groups as women, African Americans and homosexuals. In spite of this association, however, the Democratic Party has been careful about championing the gay equality agenda, especially with regard to such issues as same-sex marriage, which a majority of the US electorate opposes. The Republican Party, on the other hand, is explicitly aligned with an antigay agenda, even if secular politicians leave it to the Christian Right to name lesbians and gay men as enemies in their in-group political rhetoric.

In fact, Christian conservatives occupy a 'privileged position' in the Republican coalition that involves collaboration between party elites and Christian Right representatives and even party deference to the goals of the movement.[41] A past President of the National Association of Evangelicals (NAE), Robert Dugan, describes the relationship between the Republican Party and Christian conservatives in this way:

> I am often asked: why do evangelicals align themselves so much with the Republican party? The reverse may be even more the case. Republicans have been actively cultivating evangelicals, and the Republican party was a natural place for them to end up.[42]

In 2006, Christian conservative voters made up more than one-third of Republican voters, and 'the party's political fortunes depend, in large part, on retaining the solid support of the evangelical community'.[43] In US politics, the Christian Right is not an outsider to political power. And one of the most important goals for the movement is to cultivate a conception of lesbians and gay men as enemies. To accomplish this goal, national Christian Right leaders are willing to link homosexuals with terrorism, a linkage that uses fear to perform political work.[44]

In the UK, Section 28 embodied the reconstruction of the homosexual as a threat to society in the era of HIV/AIDS, but from its conception it also aroused opposition. The fledgling lesbian and gay political movement solidified into substantial, professional activists groups. These groups, most notably Stonewall, kept discrimination on the political agenda and privately provided information and motivation for politicians to fight for equality. New Labour openly courted the lesbian and gay vote, including fielding openly gay candidates, and their election in 1997 marked a significant shift in official attitudes towards the 'Equality Agenda'.[45] The Labour campaign called for the repeal of Section 28,[46] and while that goal was only realized in their second term, a raft of other legislation solidified their commitment to equality: The Sexual offences Amendment Act 2000 equalized the age of consent; The Civil Partnership Act 2004 recognized same-sex relationships; The Adoption and Children Act 2002, implemented in December 2005, enabled same-sex couples to adopt jointly; The Learning and Skills Act 2000 and Sex and Relationship Education Guidance 2000 targeted homophobia in schools; and The Equality Act (Sexual Orientation) Regulations 2007 criminalized discrimination against lesbians and gay men in the delivery of public goods and services.

The cultural and political difference between 1987 and 2007 testifies to the fluidity of the construction of homosexuals as enemies and allies. In addition, it reinforces Smith's analysis regarding the political strategy of that construction and reconstruction. In 2007 different sides of political discourse might still see 'good homosexuals' and 'dangerous queers', but New Labour defined and championed 'good gays' as economically active, civilly partnered, parentally responsible, civically engaged gays.

The orchestration of inclusion was carefully crafted by New Labour. For example, during the debate over the Adoption and Children Act, the Prime Minister's Official Spokesperson was compelled to clarify that this was 'not about gay adoptions' but about 'giving better life chances to children in care and increasing the pool of potential adopters'.[47] Nevertheless, the underpinning of social justice established a discursive commitment to an outcome of equal opportunities and non-discrimination. The Institute for Public Policy Research (IPPR) and the former Commission on Social Justice, both left-centre think-tanks, outlined basic motivating principles including 'the equal worth of all citizens' and 'the right to self-respect and personal autonomy' needing 'the widest possible spread of opportunities'.[48] In *Third Way* and *Transformation of Intimacy*, sociologist Anthony Giddens articulates a New Labour approach to governance; his compelling analysis of shifting family structure, commitments and sexuality placed Labour economic, welfare and family policy at the cutting edge of social science research and capitalist development. Giddens argues that 'pure relationships' 'ha[ve] no specific connection to heterosexuality'.[49] With these interpretations of liberalism at its foundation, it is little surprise that New Labour found allies among lesbian and gay citizens.

As the keynote speaker at a recent Stonewall Equality dinner, former Prime Minister Tony Blair reflected upon his time in office, the legal changes regarding issues facing lesbian and gay citizens, and greater tolerance of same-sex sexuality:

> [T]he change in the culture and the civilising effect of it has gone far greater than the gay and lesbian community . . . [B]y taking a stand on this issue and by removing a piece of prejudice and discrimination, and by enabling people to stand proud as what they are, it has had an impact that I think profoundly affects the way the country thinks about itself . . . [A]ny country that will succeed in the future . . . [must] make the most of the talents and abilities of your people, and if you allow discrimination to fester, that is the complete rejection of that modernising and civilising notion.[50]

It is worth noting the way commentators have contextualized the alliance between Labour and lesbians and gay men by calling into question the ideological heritage of both Giddens and Blair. Biographer John Rentoul describes Blair's education history at a conservative boys boarding school as 'hardly a crucible of liberal tolerance, but he was a persistent rebel and identified with the liberalism of the Sixties because that was what the school authorities were against'.[51] Rentoul adds that, given 1967 decriminalization of homosexuality, by 1971 Blair was 'a member of the first post-Wolfenden cohort' and as such, as Blair himself states, at the time and among his friends, homosexuality 'wasn't a problem . . . wasn't an issue'.[52] Conservative Stanley Kurtz worries about the influence of 'radical' Giddens on Blair:

> Giddens's views about marriage and homosexuality closely resemble the ideas of radical 'queer theorists'. Giddens spent 1968 teaching in America, at UCLA, and it was during that dramatic year that Giddens added sexual radicalism to an already left-leaning political agenda. Yet Giddens is an utterly mainstream figure. Director of the influential London School of Economics, Giddens has been famously dubbed Tony Blair's 'guru'. In 2000, for example, Giddens played a key role in convincing Blair to withdraw backing for a policy that would have supported marriage as 'the best model' for British family life. . . . Viewpoints that are mainstream in Europe, where Giddens advises Britain's Prime Minister, are the province of far-left academics in the United States.[53]

For Kurtz, Giddens and Blair inhaled the values of a radical generation. As a result their views about the role of homosexuality are warped and threaten conservative values of family stability and appropriate sexuality. Various commentators from the US and UK have reflected on the number of New Labour gay MPs and government officials and questioned whether there was a 'gay mafia' in Whitehall.[54] More recently, Foust frets in the Baptist Press that the new Prime Minister, Gordon Brown, 'appears to be on the same page as his predecessor on so-called "gay rights", and that's bad news for pro-family citizens in the country'.[55] He implies that the safety of heterosexuals in other countries are threatened by Brown's commitment to 'an international strategy to promote rights overseas, which includes Britain's commitment to the universal decriminalization of homosexuality' and the government's willingness to 'work with foreign partners and domestic organizations to protect the human rights of gay and lesbian people throughout the world'.[56]

However, this global interconnectedness works in a variety of ways with overt political links now between US and UK conservative political groups. The Centre for Social Justice (CSJ), founded by former Tory-leader Ian Duncan-Smith, offers a clear articulation of conservative support for 'traditional, marriage-based families' that should receive more 'legal recognition' than alternative family forms, for example, through taxation.[57] In addition the CSJ worries about 'disordered families' where 'a woman's partner is not the natural father of her child(ren)'.[58] The organization's website on families offers direct links to the Bush administration's initiative on Healthy Marriages.[59] Of course, the current Tory leader, David Cameron, is a 'kinder gentler' conservative with apparently progressive views on same-sex sexuality.[60] This worries Tim Montgomerie, a new breed of UK conservative blogger fashioned and trained by US Republican pundits. He points out that Cameron's support does not run deep; for example, regarding his support of the Equality Act 2007, Montgomerie writes that only 25% 'are in line with David Cameron on this right'.[61]

Appeals to the middle ground of traditional marriage, family and Christianity continues to stake a claim to the future political agenda. The title of Ian Duncan-Smith's *Daily Mail* article in late 2007 challenged new legislation to make IVF available on the NHS to lesbians by clearly establishing lesbians, and their political friends, as enemies of tradition, family and fatherhood: 'Now they want to abolish fatherhood . . . changes in IVF laws could erase the need for Dads'.[62] Duncan-Smith argues that the 'liberal elite' is confusing the definition of parenthood: 'The traditional meanings of fatherhood and motherhood are being redefined by our culture and our legal system. . . . We have enshrined adults' freedom to live their lives however they please. Any suggestion that a particular family form is better for a child is treated as an affront on that unassailable liberty.'[63] Interestingly, both of these stories target the family structure, particularly the centrality of genetic fatherhood, and in doing so may offer some indication that in contemporary conservative discourse lesbian mothers occupy an important rhetorical niche.

Undoubtedly, much social conservative discourse constructs the liberal elite as allies of cultural enemies such as homosexuals against the 'us' who believe in family, tradition and the moral nation. In the US, these cultural elites include the media, the culture industry and academia. Here we see the underlying questioning of alliances and influences but also a worry about the spread of these political influences, and the use of this anxiety for political purposes. In both the US and nations of the former Soviet bloc, the anxiety is of secular, leftist and European influence supporting a gay agenda. For social conservatives to win the culture war, it is necessary to continue to draw attention to ideological enemies and how the allies of these enemies help to constitute the political agenda of Western democracies.

Beyond the US and UK

Legal changes to the status of lesbians and gay men in the UK must be seen in a larger context, in particular that of an EU push towards equality. For example, in 1999 the European Court of Human Rights denounced the UK ban of gays in the military as unlawful. The 1997 Treaty of Amsterdam Article 13 committed member states to combating discrimination based on sexual orientation and led to the 2000 Directive requiring EU member states to ban such discrimination. New Labour complied with this directive five years later with the Employment Equality (Sexual Orientation) Regulation 2003.[64] However, EU integration has had quite different effects in different national contexts, ranging from the expansion of rights to cultural and political backlash. The recent experience of both Poland and Latvia illustrate the flexibility of antigay politics and the emergence of a 'new form of transnational Christian fundamentalism' that attests to the influence of the US Christian Right in constructing homosexuals as enemies around the world.[65]

In the summer of 2005, Gay Pride marches were planned for the capital cities of Poland and Latvia. In spite of pressure from the EU and international organizations, the Polish event was cancelled by the Mayor of Warsaw, who was a leader in the conservative Law and Justice Party and the future president of Poland. The march in Riga went forward but was marred by antigay threats and violence mobilized by a variety of groups, including nationalist and evangelical Christian groups. Both events became notable for the threats and antigay political mobilization associated with them, and the political response in both cases – which included the failure of Latvian police to protect a small group of marchers from a larger contingent of protesters – violated both international and European law.[66]

The 2005 Gay Pride march in Riga, Latvia has received close scrutiny from scholars because the political reaction to the march exposed a contrast with modes of political mobilization during the Cold War and in the immediate aftermath of the fall of the Soviet Union. In particular, antigay rhetoric and activism in Latvia demonstrates a deliberate shift from ethnic xenophobia and mobilization to an antigay strategy that is ethnically tolerant and multicultural.[67] Since the early 1990s, US conservative Christian churches and organizations have responded to the end of communist rule in Russia and Eastern Europe by evangelizing on behalf of free market reform and 'natural family'/'family values' politics. One outcome of US Christian Right influence on Latvian and Polish nationalists like politicians of Latvia's 'Preacher's Party' is the transformation of lesbians and gay men from objects of moral repugnance to political enemies. As the nationalist Latvian organization commented on opposition to Gay Pride: 'This time Russians and Latvians are standing shoulder-to-shoulder . . . [and] everyone is standing up against a common enemy.'[68]

In May 2007, over 3,000 people from 75 different countries attended the fourth World Congress of Families conference in Warsaw. The World Congress of Families (WCF) is an international network of pro-family organizations, scholars and leaders that seek to restore the natural family as the fundamental social unit and the 'seedbed' of civil society.[69] The network was founded in 1997 by Allan C. Carlson, president of the Howard Center for Family, Religion, and Society, located in Illinois. Given its recent morality politics, Poland was an appropriate venue for the World Congress of Families. According to conservatives, Poland faces a 'demographic winter' perpetuated by an attack on the family from the European Parliament. The general secretary of the European Forum for Human Rights and Family, Catherine Vierling, announced: 'We are at war. Which kind of war? The European Union was built for peace but today Europe is struggling for survival because Europe has no babies. Europe has no families.'[70] In his role as WCF international secretary, Allan Carlson explained that 'Their [European] agenda [on the family] leads to social dissolution, demographic decline, a failure to socialize the young and a lack of hope in the future.'[71] Ex-President and WCF patron Lech Kaczynki linked European family policies and practices with same-sex sexuality at the conference: 'If [the homosexual] approach to sexual life were to be promoted on a grand scale, the human race would disappear.'[72]

The discursive construction of same-sex sexuality and gay identity as a threat to national identity and the Polish nation is accompanied by the construction of Europe – the ally of homosexuals – as the enemy. O'Dwyer and Schwartz argue that virulent antigay politics in Poland and Latvia can be explained by 'Europeanization blowback' as illiberal populist leaders capitalize on widespread 'hard euroscepticism' that conflates the EU with 'an anti-church agenda of gay rights, abortion, and euthanasia'.[73] Countries where political changes were forced quickly in order to reap the economic benefits of EU membership, but where social attitudes/values do not resonate with those expressed in EU commitments to non-discrimination, are particularly receptive to the theo-political messages of the Christian Right. The WCF's Carlson sums up this convergence of interests:

[I]f Europe succumbs to the modern, post-family, secular worldview completely, it's like losing a great ally in a global contest. The ramifications will be direct and indirect for the US, so we need to be there – we need to support pro-family movements and people and governments that exist in Europe right now.[74]

Carlson confirms the stakes of US Christian Right influence on the WCF, and by extension, on global morality politics.[75]

Conclusion

The morality and collective consequences of same-sex sexuality are persistent issues in the politics of many nations. As sexual minorities have become increasingly visible in many societies, the Christian Right has responded with appeals to scriptural transparency and authority on the subject of sexuality, activism for laws and public policies, and cultural campaigns to stigmatize same-sex sexuality. Of course, this agenda of constructing homosexuals as political enemies requires the refutation of alternative readings of scripture and alternative Christian doctrines on sexuality, to say nothing of secular democratic defences of constitutional equality. What Christian Right activism against homosexuals and their political allies demonstrates is the continuing existence and utility of labelling the 'other' as a political enemy.

Shane Phelan argues that the status of LGBT people in US society is that of 'sexual strangers'. By this she means that sexual minorities are neither entirely 'other'/outsider nor friend/insider but that they occupy an ambiguous liminal socio-political status. They are partial strangers to US citizenship, lacking many political rights and forms of respect and inclusion that other citizens enjoy. However, the Christian Right pursues a politics that is restigmatizing and remoralizing – one that seeks to reverse trends of increasing tolerance and cement the status of homosexuals as 'other'. To Christian conservatives, a nation that would move towards acceptance of same-sex sexuality, even slowly and unevenly, is a nation that has lost its soul. There are many differences between the political cultures and institutions of the US and the more recent democracies of Eastern Europe, but there are also deep connections, including pervasive discourse that labels lesbians and gay men as potent ideological and political enemies and situates them within a broader group of their presumed allies: educated cultural elites, political parties, and Western European values and institutions. Poland and Latvia have proven to be fertile soil for embedding US based Christian Right antigay ideology.

In as much as conspiracy theories hinge upon close connections of political actors with similar intentions, we are not proposing a global homogeneous Christian Right informing all of conservative politics in the US, UK and Eastern Europe. What is clear, however, is that US and UK conservative Christians have mobilized politically since the 1970s and in doing so have employed antigay rhetoric to distinguish between moral, and therefore political, enemies and allies. More recently, and across old and new Western democracies, Christian Right activists share political strategies, deploying antigay theologies and communicating in a rhetorical style that deliberately constructs perceptions of constituency and perceptions of enemies. While there is some diversity of actors within the Christian Right in each of these different political contexts, the most obvious and maligned common enemy remains the homosexual. Mary McIntosh's words of 40 years ago continue to resonate: 'the creation of a specialized, despised and punished role of homosexual keeps the bulk of society pure . . . [and] . . . helps to provide a clear-cut, publicized and recognizable threshold between permissible and impermissible behaviour'.[76]

Notes

1 Volkan, *The Need to Have Enemies and Allies.*
2 Fairclough, *Language and Power,* p. 52.
3 McIntosh, 'The Homosexual Role', p. 192.
4 Ibid. pp. 183–4.

[5] Ibid. p. 183.
[6] van Dijk, *Elite Discourse and Racism* 1993; van Dijk, 'Principles of Critical Discourse Analysis' 2001.
[7] Leech, *The Social God*, p. 115; Hedges, *American Fascists*.
[8] Leech, *The Social God*, pp. 109–10.
[9] Ibid. pp. 113–14.
[10] Burack, *Sin, Sex, and Democracy: Antigay Rhetoric and the Christian Right*.
[11] See Kirkpatrick, 'The Evangelical Crackup'; Sharlet, '*New York Times* Declares Religious Right Dead. Again'.
[12] Jenkins, *The Next Christendom: The Coming of Global Christianity*.
[13] Diamond, *Spiritual Warfare: The Politics of the Christian Right*; Martin, *With God On Our Side: The Rise of the Religious Right in America*; and McGirr, *Suburban Warriors: The Origins of the New American Right*.
[14] Harding, *The Book of Jerry Falwell: Fundamentalist Language and Politics*.
[15] Schaeffer, *Plan for Action: An Action Alternative Handbook for 'Whatever Happened to the Human Race?'*
[16] Herman, *The Antigay Agenda*, p. 50.
[17] Altman, 'Rare Cancer Seen in 41 Homosexuals'.
[18] Falwell quoted in Harding, *The Book of Jerry Falwell: Fundamentalist Language and Politics*, p. 160.
[19] Burack, 'Getting What "We" Deserve: Terrorism, Tolerance, Sexuality, and the Christian Right'.
[20] 539 U.S. 558.
[21] Weeks, *Sex, Politics and Society: The Regulation of Sexuality Since 1800*, p. 294.
[22] Ibid.
[23] Decriminalization of private sex acts between civilian men over 21.
[24] 'Speech at Edgbaston'.
[25] Durham, *Sex & Politics*, pp. 177–8.
[26] Ibid. p. 126.
[27] Smith, 'The Good Homosexual and the Dangerous Queer' and 'Centering of Right-Wing Extremism'.
[28] Ibid. p. 121.
[29] Jeffery-Poulter, *Peers, Queers and Commons*, p. 177.
[30] Kitzinger, *The Social Construction of Lesbianism*, p. 3.
[31] 19 February 1985, in Jeffery-Poulter, *Peers, Queers and Commons*, p. 184.
[32] 12 December 1986, ibid. p. 196.
[33] Weeks, *Sex, Politics and Society*, p. 310.
[34] Weeks, *Sexuality and Its Discontents: Meanings, Myths and Modern Sexualities*, p. 44.
[35] Jeffery-Poulter, *Peers, Queers and Commons*, p. 212.
[36] Ibid. p. 213.
[37] Barrett et al., *Lesbian Mothers' Legal Handbook*, pp. 113–14.
[38] Jeffery-Poulter, *Peers, Queers and Commons*, p. 218.
[39] Local Government Act 1988 S.28 repealed 2003.
[40] Leech, *The Social God*, p. 127.
[41] Lindblom, *Politics and Markets: The World's Political Economic Systems*, p. 175.
[42] Dugan, in Reichley, A. J. et al., 'Comment', pp. 82–3.
[43] Keeter, 'Evangelicals and the GOP: An Update'.

44 Burack, *Sin, Sex and Democracy*. For an analysis of linkages between gays and terrorists in US Christian Right rhetoric see chapter 4.
45 Wilson, 'With Friends Like These'; 'New Labour and Lesbian & Gay "Friendly" Policy'.
46 Moran, 'Childhood Sexuality and Education: The Case of Section 28'.
47 PMOS, Hansard, 31 October 2002.
48 Commission on Social Justice quoted in Franklin, *Social Policy and Social Justice*, p. 48.
49 Giddens, *The Transformation of Intimacy*, p. 63.
50 Blair, 'Speech to Stonewall Equality Ball'.
51 Rentoul, 'Tony Blair: "Within my milieu, being gay was not a problem"'.
52 Ibid.; Wolfenden Report.
53 Kurtz, 'Zombie Killers'.
54 Lyall, 'For Blair's Cabinet, These Outings are Not Picnics'.
55 Foust, 'Marriage Digest: New British P.M. says he's "proud" of record on "gay rights"'.
56 Ibid.
57 Duncan-Smith, *Breakthrough Britain: Ending the Cost of Social Breakdown*.
58 Ibid.
59 www.acf.hhs.gov/healthymarriage/ (accessed 11 Feb. 2008).
60 Montgomerie, 'Into the blue'.
61 Ibid.
62 Duncan-Smith, 'Now they want to abolish fatherhood – how changes in IVF laws could erase the need for Dads'.
63 Ibid.
64 Arguments for economic efficiency substantially buttressed those of social justice. Wilson, 'New Labour'.
65 O'Dwyer and Schwartz, 'Return to Illiberal Diversity? Anti-Gay Politics and Minority Rights after EU Enlargement', p. 31.
66 Amnesty International USA, 'Homophobia and Violence against LGBT People in Latvia'.
67 Schwartz, 'Gay Rights: United in Hostility'.
68 Quoted in ibid.
69 The WCF IV was held in Warsaw, 11–13 May, 2007 and was sponsored by American Family Association, Catholic Family and Human Rights Institute, Concerned Women for America, Family Research Council, Focus on the Family, GrasstopsUSA.com, Heritage Foundation, Watchmen on the Walls and World Family Policy Forum. Three earlier WCF Conferences took place in Prague (1997), Geneva (1999) and Mexico City (2004).
70 Vierling, speech text: www.profam.org/press/wcf.pr.070416.htm (accessed 11 Feb. 2008).
71 Carlson, 'World Congress of Families Responds to Attach by Certain Members of the European Parliament'.
72 Kaczynki, 'Polish President to open World Congress of Families IV, Serve as Honorary Patron'.
73 O'Dwyer and Schwartz, 'Europe's New Illiberals: Anti-Gay Rhetoric and Party Politics in Postcommunist Poland and Latvia', p. 33.

[74] Carlson, 'World Congress of Families Responds to Attack by Certain Members of the European Parliament'.
[75] Buss and Herman, *Globalizing Family Values*.
[76] McIntosh, 'The Homosexual Role', 183–4.

Bibliography

Altman, L. (1981) 'Rare cancer seen in 41 homosexuals'. *New York Times*. 3 July.

Amnesty International USA (2007) 'Homophobia and violence against LGBT people in Latvia'. www.amnestyusa.org/Country_Information/Latvia/page.do?id=1106572&n1=3&n2=36&n3=1040 (accessed 3 Jan. 2008).

Barrett, M. and the Rights of Women Lesbian Custody Group (1986) *Lesbian Mothers' Legal Handbook*. London: Women's Press.

Blair, T. (2007) 'Speech to Stonewall Equality Ball'. www.number10.gov.uk/output/Page11336.asp, 22 March (accessed 18 Jan. 2008).

Burack, C. (2003) 'Getting What "We" Deserve: Terrorism, Tolerance, Sexuality, and the Christian Right'. *New Political Science*, 25 (3), 329–49.

—— (2008) *Sin, Sex, and Democracy: Antigay Rhetoric and the Christian Right*. Albany, NY: SUNY Press.

Buss, D. and Herman, D. (2003) *Globalizing Family Values: Christian Right International Politics*. Minneapolis, MN: University of Minnesota Press.

Carlson, A. (2007) 'World Congress of Families responds to attack by certain members of the European Parliament'. www.profam.org/press/wcf.pr.070416.htm (accessed 18 Jan. 2008).

Diamond, S. (1989) *Spiritual Warfare: The Politics of the Christian Right*. Boston, MA: South End Press.

—— (1996) *Facing the Wrath: Confronting the Right in Dangerous Times*. Monroe, ME: Common Courage Press.

Duncan-Smith, I. (2007a) *Breakthrough Britain: Ending the Cost of Social Breakdown*. London: Social Justice Policy Group.

—— (2007b) 'Now they want to abolish fatherhood – how changes in IVF laws could erase the need for Dads'. *Daily Mail*, 17 November.

Durham, M. (1991) *Sex & Politics: The Family and Morality in the Thatcher Years*. London: Macmillan.

Elliot, H. (2007) 'Controversial gathering aims to focus Europeans on "pro-family" politics'. www.abpnews.com/2143.article (accessed 18 Jan. 2008).

Fairclough, N. (1989/2001) *Language and Power*. 1st and 2nd editions. London: Longmans.

Foust, M. 2007 'Marriage Digest: New British P.M. says he's "proud" of record on "gay rights"'. www.sbcbaptistpress.org/bpnews.asp?id=26190 (accessed 18 Jan. 2008).

Franklin, S. ed. (1998) *Social Policy and Social Justice*. Cambridge: Polity Press.

Giddens, A. (1992) *The Transformation of Intimacy*. Stanford, CA: Stanford University Press.

—— (1998) *The Third Way. The Renewal of Social Democracy*. Cambridge: Polity Press.

Harding, S. F. (2000) *The Book of Jerry Falwell: Fundamentalist Language and Politics.* Princeton, NJ: Princeton University Press.

Hedges, C. (2006) *American Fascists: The Christian Right and the War on America.* New York: Free Press.

Herman, D. (1997) *The Antigay Agenda: Orthodox Vision and the Christian Right.* Chicago: University of Chicago Press.

Hunter, J. D. (1992) *Culture Wars: The Struggle to Define America.* New York: Basic Books.

Jeffery-Poulter, A. (1991) *Peers, Queers and Commons.* London: Routledge.

Jenkins, P. (2002) *The Next Christendom: The Coming of Global Christianity.* Oxford University Press.

Joseph, K. Sir (1974) 'Speech at Edgbaston 19 October 1974', Thatcher Foundation, www.margaretthatcher.org/archive/displaydocument.asp?docid=101830 (accessed on 18 Jan. 2008).

Kaczynski, L. (2007) 'Polish President to open World Congress of Families IV, serve as Honorary Patron'. www.profam.org/press/wcf.pr.070312.htm (accessed 18 Jan. 2008).

Keeter, S. (2006) 'Evangelicals and the GOP: An update'. *Pew Research Center* http://pewresearch.org/pubs/78/evangelicals-and-the-gop-an-update (accessed 3 Jan. 2008).

Kellstedt, L. and C. Smidt (1996) 'Measuring Fundamentalism: An Analysis of Different Operational Strategies' in Green, J. C. et al., *Religion and the Culture Wars: Dispatches from the Front.* Lanham, MD: Rowman and Littlefield.

Kirkpatrick, D. D. (2007) 'The Evangelical Crackup'. *The New York Times.* 28 October. www.nytimes.com/2007/10/28/magazine/28Evangelicals-t.html?_r=1&em&ex=1193716800&en=5b6318ccb514f1c9&ei=5087%0A&oref=slogin (accessed 1 Nov. 2007).

Kitzinger, C. (1987) *The Social Construction of Lesbianism.* London: Sage.

Kurtz, S. (2006) 'Zombie Killers' *National Review Online.* 25 May. http://article.nationalreview.com/?q=MTU4NDEzNTY5ODNmOWU4M2Y1MGIwMTcyODdjZGQxOTTk=. (accessed 18 Jan. 2008).

Lakoff, G. (2002) *Moral Politics: How Liberals and Conservatives Think.* Chicago: University of Chicago Press.

Leech, K. (1981) *The Social God.* Eugene, OR: Wipf and Stock Publishers.

Lindblom, C. E. (1977) *Politics and Markets: The World's Political Economic Systems.* New York: Basic Books.

Lyall, S. (1998) 'For Blair's Cabinet, These Outings are Not Picnics'. *London Journal.* 12 November.

McGirr, L. (2001) *Suburban Warriors: The Origins of the New American Right.* Princeton: Princeton University Press.

McIntosh, M. (1968) 'The Homosexual Role'. *Social Problems,* 16 (2), 182–92.

Marsden, C. (1998) 'The Sun's anti-gay attacks on the British Labour government: A temporary fall-out between friends'. www.wsws.org/news/1998/nov1998/sun-n20.shtml. 20 November. (accessed 18 Jan. 2008).

Martin, W. (1996) *With God on Our Side: The Rise of the Religious Right in America.* New York: Broadway Books.

Montgomerie, T. (2007) 'Into the blue'. *Guardian Comment is Free*. 13 November. http://commentisfree.guardian.co.uk/tim_montgomerie/2007/11/into_the_ blue.html. (accessed 18 Jan. 2008).

Moran, J. (2001) 'Childhood Sexuality and Education: The Case of Section 28'. *Sexualities*, 4 (1), 73–89.

O'Dwyer, C. and K. Schwartz (2006) 'Europes New Illiberals: Anti-Gay Rhetoric and Party Politics in Postcommunist Poland and Latvia' (paper given at APSA conference, Philadelphia, PA: access through www.apsanet.org) (accessed 6 Feb. 2008).

O'Dwyer, C. and K. Z. S. Schwartz (2007) 'Return to Illiberal Diversity? Anti-Gay Politics and Minority Rights after EU Enlargement' (paper given at Post-Communist Politics and Economics Workshop, Davis Center, Harvard University 19 March 2007: access through www.fas.harvard.edu/~postcomm/ papers/2006-07/Odwyer2007.pdf.) (accessed 6 Feb. 2008).

Phelan, S. (2001) *Sexual Strangers: Gays, Lesbians, and Dilemmas of Citizenship*. Philadelphia: Temple University Press.

Reichley, A. J., P. Weyrich, T. Eastland, R. Reed, R. Dugan, R. D. Land and D. Wildmon (1993) 'Comments', in M. Cromartie, ed., *No Longer Exiles: The Religious New Right in American Politics*. Washington, DC: Ethics and Public Policy Center.

Rentoul, J. (2005) 'Tony Blair: "Within my milieu, being gay was not a problem"'. *Independent on Sunday*, 20 March.

Schaeffer, F. (1980) *Plan for Action: An Action Alternative Handbook for Whatever Happened to the Human Race? New York:* Flemming H. Revell.

Schwartz, K. Z. S. (2005) 'Gay Rights: United in Hostility'. *Transitions Online*. 21 September. www.clas.ufl.edu/users/bbsmith/SchwartzBB.pdf. (accessed 18 Jan. 2008).

Sharlet, J. (2007) '*New York Times* Declares the Religious Right Dead. Again'. *The Revealer: A Daily Review of Religion and the Press*. 28 October. www.therevealer. org/archives/timely_002888.php (accessed 1 Nov. 2007).

Smith, A. M. (1997a) 'The Centering of Right-Wing Extremism through the Construction of an "Inclusionary" Homophobia and Racism', in S. Phelan, ed., *Playing With Fire*. London: Routledge.

— (1997b) 'The Good Homosexual and the Dangerous Queer: Resisting the "New Homophobia"', in Lynne Segal, ed., *New Sexual Agendas: Medical, Social and Political*. London: Macmillan.

van, Dijk, T. (1993) *Elite Discourse and Racism*. London: Sage.

— (2001) 'Principles of Critical Discourse Analysis', in M. Wetherall et al., eds, *Discourse Theory and Practice*. London: Sage.

Vierling, C. (2007) Speech text. www.profam.org/press/wcf.pr.070416.htm (accessed 18 Jan. 2008).

Volkan, V. D. (1988) *The Need to Have Enemies and Allies: From Clinical Practice to International Relationships*. Northvale, NJ: Jason Aronson Inc.

Weeks, J. (1985) *Sexuality and Its Discontents: Meanings, Myths and Modern Sexualities*. London: Routledge & Kegan Paul.

— (1981/1989) *Sex, Politics and Society: The Regulation of Sexuality since 1800*. London: Longman.

Wilson, A. R. (2007a) 'New Labour and Lesbian & Gay "Friendly" Policy'. In C. Annesley et al., eds, *Women and New Labour*. Bristol: Policy Press.

— (2007b) 'With Friends Like These: The Liberalization of Queer Family Policy'. *Critical Social Policy*, 27 (1), 50–76.

Wolfenden Report (1957) *Report of the Committee on Sexual Offences and Prostitution*, CMND. 247, HMSO.

World Congress of Families IV Planning Meeting, 23–25 October 2005, Rockford, Illinois as reported on www.worldcongress.org/WCF4/wcf4.ini.htm (accessed 18 Jan. 2008).

Chapter 10

The Moral Bases of the Black Panther Party's Breakfast Program, Johnson's Head Start and Blair's Sure Start: A Critical Comparison

D. Emily Hicks

Introduction

In this chapter, I offer an analysis of three programmes, the Black Panther Party's Breakfast Program, the US program 'Head Start' and the UK programme 'Sure Start' in order to develop and clarify an argument concerning social justice. In brief, I argue that the operations of the 'nanny state' when founded upon 'moralism' do little to advance the cause of social justice. These three social programmes encompass over four decades of transformations within the welfare state and immigration law and so provide interesting case studies for my argument. I do not claim that economic behaviour is the basis of moral reformation nor that poverty can be managed through making the poor more virtuous. Rather, I argue that there is too much attention to responsibility and too little to rights in the moral bases of Head Start and Sure Start. Moreover, I argue that the Black Panther Party anticipated contemporary debates within anarchist, post-colonial and border theory by defining the ethical underpinnings of a Breakfast Program that are more conducive to an inclusive social justice agenda than the moral bases of Blairism and Lyndon B. Johnson's Head Start program as part of his Great Society.

These three programmes emerged from very different views of colonialism, the nation-state, critiques of the metropolis, attitudes towards assimilation and positions on the political compass. Head Start and the Breakfast Program of the Black Panther Party began in the 1960s. Blair's Sure Start programme was begun over three decades later in 1999. While Blair put too much emphasis on the responsibilities of the socially excluded, Johnson placed the blame for the plight of African Americans on the dysfunctionality of the black family. It was the Black Panther Party that saw capitalism in a global context as the centre of the problem of the exclusion of African Americans from mainstream America. Paying attention – first to the postnational critique of the state implicit within the Black Panther Party's commitment to the inhabitants of colonized zones within US cities, and second to their anti-colonial stance and support for Third World oppressed populations – provides progressives with the opportunity to reframe nanny state debates, whose terms have been set by conservatives.

In looking at three social programmes, Head Start, The Black Panther's Breakfast Program and Sure Start, I hope to encourage progressives to be critical of the nanny state's promises to manage poverty.[1] To advance my argument, in the remainder of this opening section I offer a brief history of each of these social programmes. In the next section, I explore the concept of the 'nanny state', and indicate why I am suspicious of the appeal to morality. The third section presents my method, which I am for convenience calling 'border machine'; I return to this method in the conclusion of the chapter. After the discussion of Method, I draw on my methodological approach to analyse these three social programmes under six headings. These headings are: Social Class, Ethnicity and Inequality; Civil Rights and Immigration; Performativity and the Role of the State; Social Cohesion, Exclusion and Social/Cultural Capital; Work and Employment (Affective Labour); and Family and Community. The chapter concludes with a second visit to the concept of the border machine.

Head Start was founded in 1965 during Johnson's presidency under the auspices of the US Department of Health and Human Services. The Equal Opportunity Act had been signed in 1964. It gave birth to programmes including Job Corps and Vista (the national form of the Peace Corps). The Black Panther Party's Breakfast Program, attributed to Huey Newton, was implemented in Oakland in January, 1969 at an Episcopal church. Earlier, in November, 1968, the Black Panther Party had begun the Breakfast Program within the context of its adoption of a 'Serve the People' programmatic focus and a continued commitment to the 'ten point' platform and program. Its demands included full employment, food, housing and education. This was a multicultural program that was intended to reach even the poor whites in Appalachia.[2] In 1968, the program's national director claimed that the program was serving between 10,000 and 15,000 children daily. The program was free for school children on welfare. A typical menu consisted of fresh orange juice, cocoa, scrambled eggs and pancakes.[3] It was intended to do what the state had not been able to do, that is, to address the basic needs of the community. Sure Start began in 1998. An outgrowth of the 1998 Comprehensive Spending Review, it was inspired by Head Start in the US. According to Norman Glass, it is 'an outstanding example of evidence based policy'.[4] The programme purports to increase the availability of childcare, improve the health and emotional development of young children and support parents both in their role as parents and in their 'aspirations' towards future employment. It is currently being implemented within the context of the Ten Year Childcare Strategy, the Work and Families Act of 2006, and the Childcare Act, passed in 2006. There are plans for 2,500 centres to be opened by 2008. The programme exists in England only, not Scotland, Wales and Northern Ireland.[5]

The nanny state

While the nanny state has been defined within many contexts, I will focus on governmental policies desiring to engage in extreme forms of social control, including the 'aspirations' of citizens. An example of the duplicity of the nanny state can be seen in Sure Start. In the Sure Start programme, there is an implied monitoring of the 'aspirations' for employment of those currently without jobs. In order to judge the success of the programme, at some point, participants will be judged as having weaker or stronger 'aspirations'. Ironically, the government is not complementing Sure Start with a commitment to full employment.

My critique of the nanny state grows out of the anarchist critique of the welfare state put forward by Noam Chomsky: 'Anarchists propose other measures to deal with these problems [poverty, healthcare, etc.], without recourse to state authority'.[6] I accept the view that social justice movements that emerge from the grass roots, and that are ethical responses to oppression, always precede actions on the part of the state; the state addresses social justice issues only when pressurized to do so by social movements. While I view support for the state as support for a 'propping up' of capitalism, that is merely a starting point; it is my desire to offer a more thorough analysis of Johnson's Great Society and Blair's policies in relation to the nanny state. I am suspicious of appeals to morality by both the supporters and the critics of the welfare state.

To associate Blairism with morality uncritically is to accept that poverty can be managed through morality and 'the creation of moral communities'. In an essay published in *Public Interest*, the journal founded by those Johnson supporters that became neo-conservative, Joel Schwartz writes:

> A hallmark of contemporary conservative thought is that poverty can be reduced most effectively or even only through character training and the creation of moral communities. Thus it is argued that poverty will be lessened only to the extent that a work ethic is inculcated among inner-city residents and stable, two-parent married families again become the norm there.[7]

I want to explore the degree to which a desire to link those deemed worthy of receiving Sure Start services to 'moral communities' is related to contemporary conservative thought, despite how this view is located in the centre of a New Labour social programme. Referring to conservative Marvin Olafy and Charles Murray's *The Tragedy of American Compassion*, Schwartz continues:

> In an important sense, this approach marks (appropriately for conservatives) a return to the past. Moral reformation or transformation was a crucial component of the antipoverty strategy of numerous deeply religious social

reformers of the nineteenth century, who attempted – putting it baldly – to make the poor less poor by making them more virtuous.[8]

The challenge for the left inside of New Labour and for religious progressives is to face the contradictory history of social reform.[9] Blair's commitment to 'social inclusion' through the nanny state, the context within which Sure Start has been developed and implemented, is undermined due to the unequal division of benefits generated by the nanny state: despite the social services provided by any particular social programme such as Sure Start and its desire to aid the poor and the excluded, the nanny state as a whole directs resources to the wealthy.

Method

In my book *Border Writing*, I privilege inhabitants in border regions and those who negotiate cultural boundaries, border subjects.[10] I agree with Avtar Brah that 'diasporic or border positionality does not in itself assure a vantage point of privileged insight'.[11] As Ramon Grosfoguel argues, of four leading figures in post-colonial discourse, Michel Foucault, Jacques Derrida, Antonio Gramsci and Rajit Guha, only the latter engages in 'decolonizing Western epistemology'.[12] Some of those positioned on cultural borders are able to think 'from the South'.[13] I put forward the model of the border machine, based on the work of Gilles Deleuze and Felix Guattari.[14] This machine included *la migra* (the immigration officer), *pollos* (border crossers), helicopters (surveillance) and those who assist the *pollos* in crossing the border (*polleros*).[15] I also discussed the *cholo* as being bicultural, that is having cultural knowledge of both sides of the border.[16] In the US–Mexico border region, *cholo* culture is associated with gang culture or the culture of the *lumpenproletariat*.

I now wish to expand the model of the border machine, in which the state actors and border crossers were represented as a machine that produced border crossings. This figure is that of the 'monitor'. The monitor can be any non-state actor who monitors human rights abuses against border crossers. Non-state actors have an important role to play within debates about immigration and the welfare state in both the US and the UK. The boundary of the colour line is crossed on a daily basis by some but not others. The Black Panther Party fought state actors, the police, with guns and law books; its members monitored the behaviour of the police. Today, inhabitants of the US and the UK who live within the Third World zones of these countries are well situated to act as monitors of rights abuses and to continue one part of the legacy left to the world community by the Black Panther Party. These zones can be seen in Bergsonian terms as 'zones of indetermination', zones discussed by Elizabeth Grosz.[17]

I will now discuss Blairism and Sure Start, Johnson and Head Start and The Black Panther Party's Breakfast Program in relation to seven zones of indetermination: (1) social class, ethnicity and inequality; (2) civil rights and immigration; (3) performativity and the role of the state; (4) social cohesion, exclusion and social/cultural capital; (5) work and employment (affective labour); (6) family and community and (7) the *cholo*, the monitor (*el monitor*) and the border machine.

Social class, ethnicity and inequality

Social class, ethnicity and inequality, including gender inequality, have been addressed in a variety of ways; feminists have addressed Marxism and feminism in a widely read collection of essays.[18] Post-colonial critics, including the Subaltern Studies Group and the Latin American Subaltern Studies Group, have attempted to discuss these issues in relation to colonialism. The Labour government's concern with 'forces and factors' that might exclude people from resources, services and opportunities is closely related to assimilation, particularly of non-Europeans, insofar as it has developed within the context of the national discussion of British identity and 'Britishness'. 'Social inclusion' has been one of the terms Blair has used to present his vision of Britain in moral terms. One result of colonialism is the return of many post-colonials to the UK. 'Social inclusion' demands attention to social class, ethnicity and gender. Social programmes that involve children will in most cases involve more women than men, and will demand familiarity with the concerns not just of white, middle-class feminists, but of women of colour as well.

Has the Third Way brought equality? While Giddens suggests that it may, Callinicos argues that it has not. Shane Hopkinson, in his review of A. Callinicos' *Against the Third Way*, describes Blair using his own words: he is calling for 'a rediscovery of our essential values – the belief in community, opportunity and responsibility'.[19] The term 'rights' does not appear in this list of beliefs. Hopkinson notes that Callinicos has found actual and worsening inequality under the Third Way.[20] He emphasizes that for Blair, equality is equality of opportunity and that community for Blairites is 'a powerful tool of exclusion'.[21] He states that for leftists, community must be linked to social justice.[22] For Callinicos, the civil rights of minorities are restricted under the guise of concern for community. Hopkinson writes: 'following neo-liberal assumptions, if supply-side settings are right, any remaining unemployment is voluntary. Thus it must be the product of individual moral failure or a "culture of poverty" '.[23]

Social class, ethnicity and inequality are addressed in a manner by Blairism that draws on several historical traditions. To make sure that parents do not follow the path of choosing not to work, emphasis is placed on 'parental aspirations' for employment and for their children's education. Given that New Labour has been more focused on the working class than on ethnic minorities, and that there has not been a Civil Rights movement in the UK like the one in the 1960s in the US, it is perhaps not surprising that Blair turned to assimilation rather than multiculturalism as a strategy, despite the growing ethnic and mixed ancestry populations in the UK. It has been reported that it is middle-class white women who are benefiting most from Sure Start.[24]

The approaches of Johnson's Great Society and the Black Panther Party to the problems of social class, ethnicity and inequality were not completely incompatible, but there were very important differences. In his essay 'What was Really Great about the Great Society, the Truth behind the Conservative Myths', Joseph A. Califano, Jr, writes: 'Great Society contributions to racial equality were not only civic and political.'[25] He cites increases in black life expectancy, job training, food stamps and increased graduation rates of blacks at both high schools and university levels. He also writes: 'Above all else, Lyndon Johnson saw The Great Society as an instrument to create social justice and eliminate poverty'.[26] Johnson saw the roots of the problem of inequality to be in the breakdown of the black family, which was itself linked to historical oppression. The Black Panther Party located inequality not in the dysfunctionality of the black family or culture poverty, but rather in the deep structural contradictions of urban capitalism and its 'colour-class-caste system', which would later be called 'the black economy'.[27]

Civil rights and immigration

Social cohesion, community and immigration, despite Blair's emphasis on assimilation, are neither neatly articulated within everyday life in the urban post-colonial UK nor well-integrated conceptually in Blairism. Zetter et al. argue that 'marginalized populations internalize social capital to fill in the chasm left by withdrawal of state support'.[28] They conclude that the 'relationship between social capital, social cohesion and immigration is one of complex and often contradictory processes'.[29]

Gordon Brown is currently struggling with the immigration issue and 'deserving immigrants' by turning to a points system. The impact of the 'deserving poor' tradition within the formation of attitudes towards the immigrant population can be negative, despite current economic data. A 2007 study by the London School of Economics researchers found that unemployment did not increase while immigration has increased in London.[30] However, the demands for public services did increase. A lukewarm enthusiasm with regard to appropriate 'parental aspirations' within immigrant communities on the part of immigrant parents may be insufficient. Now, given resentment in some quarters against providing social services to immigrants, immigrant families may have to overstate their commitment to assimilation and aspirations for employment as well as education for their children.

Johnson, like the Black Panther Party, was focused on Civil Rights, not immigration. However, he signed the 1965 Immigration Law, which changed the existing racist system, in which the Nordic, the Alpine and the Mediterranean were ranked in order of superiority, with Jews and Asians beneath these groups. In one passage of his 1965 speech, he described the bill in the following terms: 'This bill says simply that from this day forth those wishing to immigrate to America shall be admitted on the basis of their skills and their close relationship to those already here.'[31] What he did not explain was whether or not the racism of the past would distort the appreciation of skills for those immigrants wishing to live in the US.

Blairism did not deal effectively with immigration issues. Baker raises two issues that transcend national boundaries and that will confront Gordon Brown: (1) to what degree will the nanny state protect certain professions, thereby blocking international competition among, for example, doctors; (2) will conservatives control the terms of the debate regarding immigration and skills with regard to decisions about immigration? In addition to these issues, Brown is concerned with the UK's responsibilities to the EU.[32]

The Black Panther Party emerged from what Self has called the 'long' Civil Rights era.[33] While immigration was not a focus of the Black Panther Party, there were ties between the group and various Latina/o groups including the United Farmworkers and the Brown Berets. Jeffrey O. G. Ogbar writes in 'Brown Power to Brown People', that for the Berets, the lumpen element valorized by The Black Panther Party 'meant gang members and others known collectively as *vatos locos* (crazy street guys)'.[34]

Performativity and the role of the state

What can the consideration of Sure Start in relation to Head Start and the Black Panther Breakfast clarify about current debates about globalization, Empire and the state? Within Blairism, Johnson's War on Poverty and the social programmes of The Black Panther Party, the 'specific instances' of the state, to use Nikil Pal Singh's term,[35] including the police, border control agencies, the diplomatic corps, the military, public schools and state agencies are addressed differently. The performativity of the state in the US includes lynchings and slavery.[36] Sure Start is not linked to anti-colonial politics in the way that The Black Panther Party's Breakfast Program was, with their support for the North Vietnamese. Rather than espousing solidarity with the Zapatistas or other current political movements, the programme seeks to assimilate those who live the UK into Britishness.

We can ask what the impact of state actors is in the UK on ethnic minorities. It is useful to consider Sure Start in relation to The Black Panther Party's Breakfast Program when considering this question. In addition, it is important to ask if the nanny state makes the rich richer in the UK? Baker is persuasive in his critique of the nanny state in the US. Hardt and Negri's model of the multitude and its relationship to Empire is being debated in relation to colonialism, post-colonialism, the Third World and Marxism. While there may be some validity to Weldes and Laffey's view that Hardt and Negri's concept of Empire is eurocentric,[37] to which could be added that it is inadequate regarding gender issues, the book may be read in relation to the work on border cultures influenced by Deleuze and Guattari. A points system may not be adequate to make complex decisions about refugees, those without papers, and the large numbers of those who will remain outside of the EU but may wish to live in the UK. The UK will play an important role as a region characterized by multiple internal cultural borders within the context of continuing negotiations between the inside and the outside of the EU.

Johnson had a different view of the state. Joseph A. Califano claims that the shift in the role of the state at the level of the federal government occurred because the Great Society 'sensed' a mismatch between the individual and 'the nationalization of commercial power that had the potential to disadvantage the individual American consumer'.[38] As a response, the Great Society produced many consumer protection laws. In an odd way, then, the ability to see beyond the limits of the nation-state was shared by most black intellectuals and Johnson, although the Black Panther movement and the Great Society responded differently to those limits.

Social cohesion, exclusion and social/cultural capital

Kenneth Suring writes: 'In effect all capital has become social capital'.[39] The social/cultural capital within socially excluded communities, imagined as data to be commodified in an information-based society, can be mined in the sense of data-mining, through social engineering projects. The social/cultural capital that serves to maintain cohesion within excluded groups can be appropriated by the state. Excluded groups can choose to trade their autonomy and cultural uniqueness for acceptance within the mainstream.

Bagley, Ackerley and Rattray relate social exclusion and children within the New Labour project as follows: 'Social policy-making in the U.K. under the Labour government has galvanized around the issue of social exclusion, identifying young children (0–4) and their families living in areas of high social disadvantage to be particularly at risk.'[40] Jonathan S. Davies argues that in contradistinction to traditional socialist and social democratic politics,

New Labour's approach to social exclusion is contractarian, defined as offering 'conditional access to the mainstream to outsiders'.[41]

The success of the Sure Start programme, it has been argued by Bagley et al., is related to the team charged with its implementation; their approach is located, according to this view, 'within an organizational social capital framework'. This social capital framework can be examined in relation to social cohesion, defined in relation not to social policy alone, but within ethnic communities.

Johnson approached social exclusion by offering 'a hand up', not a 'hand out'.[42] In Oakland, the Black Panther Party's Breakfast Program was started in 1969 at St Augustine Episcopal Church thanks to Father Earl A. Neil, Rector of St Augustine's and to Ruth Beckford-Smith, a member of the church.[43] It was implemented throughout the country by activists. Head Start, although it was begun earlier, was built upon the success of the Panther's Breakfast Program. Head Start began as a summer project in 1965 under the auspices of the US Department of Health and Human Services. However its success is thought to have been made possible by the groundwork laid by the Black Panther's Breakfast Program. Both programmes functioned within a cultural capital framework.

Work and employment (affective labour)

Bagley et al. attribute the success of Sure Start to the teams.[44] In a more recent article, they look at the issue of the bottom-up (rather than top-down) approach of the teams, and of the attitude of team members towards parents.[45] 'Affective labour' is not only defined as 'service with a smile'.[46] It can also account for the success of the Sure Start in the subtle ways in which trust is built within and across ethnic communities. In the US–Mexico border region, immigrant caregivers provide love and affection to children and to the elderly as maids and as employees in institutions that provide care for the elderly. 'Affective labour' is a useful category for understanding the difficult-to-measure but very significant labour provided by caregivers and other service sector workers, and some of the workers who implement Sure Start. The success of the Black Panther Party's Breakfast Program and Head Start was based, in part, on the affective labour of activists with links to grass-roots organizers who chose to implement the programmes.

Johnson's Economic Opportunity Act of 1964 provided funding for programmes including the Job Corps, which helped inner-city youth to find jobs, VISTA, the domestic version of The Peace Corps and adult job training. He was concerned with providing resources for the employed as well as the unemployed. Interviews with those who worked in Great Society programs during the Johnson era reveal that there was a great deal of idealism among workers of varying backgrounds and ages.

The cultural capital that accrued within Great Society and related post-Great Society programs led to the creation of countless projects often forgotten in attacks on the program. Major alternative cultural centres in the US, including the *Centro Cultural de la Raza* in San Diego, began with the support of a post-Great Society program, CETA (Comprehensive Employment and Training Act), founded under Nixon and developed by Carter to reach low-income communities. In 1995, Idealist.org, Action without Borders, was founded in order to provide information to people seeking to work in the non-profit sector. Among the funders are the Open Society Institute and the Ford Foundation.

Family and community

In his speech on social exclusion, Blair links Heckman's analysis to the Sure Start Programme:

> The Nobel economist James Heckman famously showed that the return on human capital was very high in the early years of life and diminished rapidly thereafter. And yet the emphasis in spending in British social policy had always been the opposite. Investment was negligible in the early years. It then began to grow at just about the age that diminishing returns were setting in. If policies had been devised expressly to defy the evidence they could hardly have been better. We responded to the evidence and began to correct the anomaly.[47]

The London-based director of Sure Start in 2005, Naomi Eisenstadt, has been quoted as saying that 'the traditional approach of keeping social and economic interventions separate was ineffective and wasteful'.[48] She explains that 'Sure Start tries to integrate these and works with parents to build aspirations for employment and for their children's education.' Eisenstadt emphasizes the significance of parental aspirations: 'Parental aspirations are the single most important factor in better outcomes for children, more important than quality of group setting, school or teachers.'[49]

The task of parents, set forth by Sure Start, is to have proper 'parental aspirations'. Such aspirations may be difficult to measure, but they appear to be related to assimilation if we see parental tasks in relation to a theory of labour, they fall under the category of 'affective labour'. The form of service with a smile now required to be 'deserving of social services offered by Sure Start is embodied in the nod towards assimilation and eagerness for employment'. The focus on 'parental aspirations' sets Sure Start apart from Johnson's Great Society, Head Start and The Black Panther's Breakfast Program.

The Black Panther Party and Johnson viewed the family's role in poverty very differently. Individual moral failure and the concept of a culture of poverty are both linked to the views of many about family and community. While some focus on children, others focus on the family. Califano quotes a speech of Johnson's in 1965: 'Perhaps more importantly, radiating to every part of life, is the breakdown of the Negro family structure.'[50] He situated this breakdown into the context of historical oppression and persecution. It was implied that the dominant culture was responsible for this oppression and persecution. The approach to child poverty was to help the families of poor children.

The eradication of poverty was not the work of families in the analysis of the Black Panther Party. More than supply-side actions were thought to be required. Within the context of educational reform, more than additional classrooms were sought. In what Self refers to as the second stage of the Black Panther Party, between 1971 and 1973, the 'Base of Operation Campaign' provided, a detailed critique of the East Bay Metropolis of Oakland: the culprits identified 'included the destruction of traditional neighbourhoods by construction of freeways; segregated schools systems, urban renewal in the form of the removal of blacks', and 'a suburban noose of segregated peripheral cities with a solid tax base and white residents who worked in Oakland and spent their money elsewhere'.[51] Supply-side tactics such as redirecting resources that had been 'funneled away' were conceptualized by the Black Panther Party within the larger framework of the relationship of challenging the state through the patrolling of the police and their anti-colonial politics.

Conclusion: The Border Machine

Judia Weldes and Mark Laffey are persuasive, in their critique of Empire, about the complexity of the border: in some instances, we find borders becoming more open; however, there are many examples of the militarization borders, as in the US–Mexico border region. Since 9/11, the Immigration and Naturalization Service (INS) now operates under the umbrella of Homeland Security (Immigration and Customs Enforcement (ICE)). In my book *Border Writing*, I did not include the human rights monitor as part of the Border Machine.[52] Now, I would include human rights activists such as Robert Martinez, of the American Friends Service Committee, his successor Christian Ramirez, Victor Clark Alfaro and the many grass-roots organizers who seek to advocate for immigrant communities.

I want to address Johnson's advocacy of the poor, along with the Black Panther Party's monitoring of the police, and Sure Start in relation to the theoretical model of the Border Machine. Johnson's Great Society played a crucial role in bringing attention to Appalachia, and to poverty among whites as well as African Americans and Latinos. In the case of the Black Panther Party, 'by challenging the police and aligning themselves with the Vietnamese, Panthers exercised what Bourdieu calls "symbolic violence" against the state itself'.[53] The postnational theory of the state suggested by the Black Panther Party is linked to monitoring state actors, the police, armed with law books, and to solidarity with the Third World. Self writes:

> Unlike most black intellectuals in the 1930s, both radical and liberal, who saw the nation-state as the horizon of class struggle, the Panthers inherited the legacy of those black radical internationalists who, in the 1940s and 1950s, began to see beyond the limits of the nation-state to the capitalist foundations of a global colour line.[54]

The ability to see beyond the limits of the nation-state is suggested by black radical internationalists, including the Black Panther Party, the work of the Subaltern Studies Group and current discussions of border thinking.

These findings further suggest that in both the UK and the US it is necessary to do research on and to formulate complex social policies regarding immigration, education, assimilation and capital defined as economic, social and cultural in relation to neo-liberalism and social democracy. Policies will need to be built on a commitment to social justice and to a respect for ethnic diversity. The Black Panther Party operated within the context of the Civil Rights movement. Johnson developed his Great Society program within the context of this movement as well; however, he also passed the 1965 Immigration Bill. It is immigration, not civil rights, that forms the backdrop of the Sure Start programme. The socio-historical context in which the programme is developing is very different from that of the Black Panther in the late 1960s. The Black Panther Party, which operated during the Vietnam era, did not position itself primarily as a moral force, but rather as a political force.

The Black Panther Party had an inclusive social justice agenda. In contradiction to underlying assumptions of Sure Start, the eradication of poverty was not the work of families. In the analysis of the Black Panther Party, more than supply-side actions were thought to be required. Supply-side tactics such as redirecting resources that had been 'funneled away' were conceptualized by the Black Panther Party within the larger framework of the relationship of challenging the state and through anti-colonial politics.

The emphasis on social cohesion and inclusion in scholarship on Blair should not obscure Bergsonian 'zones of indetermination' within the contemporary cultural landscape of the contemporary, multicultural UK. The Black Panther Party's inner-city zones can be viewed in relation to Bergsonian zones. By focusing on the *lumpenproletariat*, defined as including the unemployed, the Black Panther Party moved leftist political discourse away from an emphasis on the factory and proletariat and towards the poorest urban neighbourhoods and inhabitants of the margins. Their discursive move opened up many spaces for discussing ethnicity, racism and post-colonialism in the 1980s, 1990s and the first decade of the twenty-first century. The insight of post-colonial critics that there is a 'border thinking' that is different from eurocentric thought can give insight into some of the challenges faced by the dominant culture and the cultures of ethnic minorities in the UK. There are multiple cultural borders within cities in the UK and the US; it is the border figure, often an urban black and minority ethnic (BME) person in the UK and an urban undocumented worker in the US, who negotiates complex social, economic and cultural boundaries.

Notes

[1] Furedi, Frank, 'Save us from the politics of behaviour'. *Spiked* (11 September 2006).

[2] See video clips from *MayDay*, dir. Roz Payne (Newsreel Collective, 1969). Available at http://lib.berkeley.edu/MRC/pacificapanthers.html, accessed on 18 May 2008. The term 'serve the children' is used. Newton is credited by one of the speakers with making the Breakfast Program possible. The ten-point platform, as well as its reach, which included poor whites in Appalachia, is referenced.

[3] The Breakfast Program, including menus in various cities, are discussed in 'Revolution for Breakfast' (KPFA UC Berkeley Library Social Activism Sound Recording Project: The Black Panther Party, 1995). Available at www.lib.berkeley.edu/MRC/pacificapanthers.html, accessed on 18 May 2008.

[4] An excerpt of Norman Glass's article 'Origins of the Sure Start Programme', in which Glass made this claim, is available on the Sure Start website. The article originally appeared in 1999 in *Children & Society*. See Glass, Norman, 'Origins of the Sure Start local programmes'. *Children & Society* 13 (1999). Available at www.surestart.gov.uk/_doc/P0001720.doc, accessed on 18 May 2008.

[5] Ibid.

[6] See Chomsky, Noam, 'Chomsky replies to multiple questions about anarchism'. Available at www.zmag.org/chomsky_repliesana.htm, accessed on 18 May 2008.

[7] Schwartz, Joel, 'Moral reform, learning from the past'. *Public Interest* (Spring 1998), para. 1.

[8] Ibid. para. 2.

[9] I am not denying that religion may sometimes play a progressive role. Religious progressives in the US are currently discussing alternatives to corporatism. A California-based group that includes Catholics and Protestants defines corporatism in its relation to both private companies and state control. They are seeking alternatives that will enhance democracy and economic participation; they are concerned with the 'unfettered mobility of capital' and 'unrestricted uses of least costly labour' (California Council of Churches, 'Building a moral economy in a global world'. *Justice Seekers*. 10/1 (2007), 2–3 at 2). Current topics within this community include 'what benefits to obtaining more direct participation in economic decisions might come to us as individuals, families, communities, nation' (ibid. at 3)? They share a desire to build 'a moral economy in a global world'

(ibid.). Baker's arguments in *The Conservative Nanny State* echo the progressive religious view that 'human well-being is as important as making money'. They argue that there is biblical support for the following view: 'poverty was not a sin; creating poverty in others was' (ibid. at 2).

10 Hicks, D. Emily, *Border Writing, the Multidimensional Text* (Minneapolis: University of Minnesota Press, 1991).

11 Brah, Avtar, *Cartographies of Diaspora* (London: Routledge, 1996), p. 204.

12 Mignolo, Walter D., *Local Histories/Global Designs: Essays on the Coloniality of Power, Subaltern Knowledge and Border Theory* (Princeton: Princeton University Press, 2000), pp. 2–3.

13 See Grosfoguel, R., 'Decolonizing Political-Economy and Post-Colonial Studies: Transmodernity, Border Thinking, and Global Coloniality' (2007). Available at www.afyl.org/descolonizingeconomy.pdf, accessed on 18 May 2008. He refers to the work of Gloria Anzaldua as well as to Walter D. Mignolo's term 'critical border thinking', put forward in *Local Histories/Global Designs*. I have written about the border subject in *Border Writing*. See also Dennis Conway, 'Globalizing from below, coordinating global resistance, alternative social forums, civil society, and grassroots networks', in Dennis Conway and Nik Heynen (eds), *Globalization's Contradictions, Geographies of Discipline, Destruction and Transformation* (London: Routledge, 2006), pp. 212–25.

14 Deleuze, Gilles and Guattari, Felix, *Kafka*, trans. Dana Polan (Minnesota: University of Minnesota Press, 1986); Hicks, *Border Writing*, pp. xiii–xxiv.

15 Hicks, *Border Writing*.

16 Ibid.

17 Grosz, Elizabeth, *The Nick of Time: Politics, Evolution and the Untimely* (Chapel Hill: Duke University Press, 2004), p. 169.

18 Sargent, Lydia (ed.), *Women and Revolution, A Discussion of the Unhappy Marriage of Marxism and Feminism* (Boston: South End Press, 1981).

19 Callinicos, Alex, *Against the Third Way: An Anti-Capitalist Critique.* (Cambridge: Polity, 2001), p. 542, quoted in Hopkinson, Shane, 'New Labour's cloak for neo-liberalism', *Links, International Journal of Socialist Renewal*, 21 (2002). Available at http://links.org.au/node/93, accessed 27 June 2007.

20 Hopkinson, 'New Labour's cloak', para. 8.

21 Ibid. para. 9.

22 Ibid. para. 10.

23 Ibid. para. 9.

24 Ward, Lucy, 'Sure Start failing ethnic minorities, says report'. *Guardian* (10 July 2007).

25 Califano, Joseph A., 'What was really great about the great society, the truth behind the conservative myths', *The Washington Monthly* (October 1998), p. 6.

26 Ibid. p. 4.

27 Self, Robert O., 'The Black Panther Party and the long civil rights era', in Jama Lazerow and Yohuru Williams (eds), *In Search of the Black Panther Party* (Durham: Duke, 2006), pp. 15–56 at p. 41.

28 Zetter, Roger et al., *Immigration, Social Cohesion and Social Capital: What are the Links?* (Oxford: Oxford Brookes University Press, 2006), p. 17.

29 Ibid. p. 22.

30 London School of Economics researchers Ian Gordon, Tony Travers and Chris-
    tine Whitehead, in 'The Impact of recent immigration on the London economy',
    report that unemployment has not increased, but the demands for public ser-
    vices has increased.

31 Johnson, Lyndon B., 'Remarks at the signing of the immigration bill' (October 3
    1965).

32 Baker, Dean, *The Conservative Nanny State: How the Wealthy Use the Government to
    Stay Rich and Get Richer* (Morrisville: Lulu, 2006).

33 Self, 'The Black Panther Party'.

34 Ogbar, Jeffrey O. G., 'Brown power to brown people: Radical ethnic national-
    ism, the Black Panthers, and Latino radicalism 1967–1973', in James Lazerow
    and Yohuru Williams (eds), *In Search of the Black Panther Party, New Perspectives on
    a Revolutionary Movement* (Durham: Duke University Press, 2006), pp. 252–86 at
    p. 258.

35 Singh, Nikil Pal, *Black is a Country, Race and the Unfinished Struggle for Democracy*
    (Cambridge: Harvard, 2005).

36 Hartman, Saidya V., *Scenes of Subjection: Terror, Slavery and Self-making in Nineteenth-
    Century America* (New York: Oxford University Press, 1997).

37 Weldes, Judah and Mark Laffey, 'Representing the international: Sovereignty
    and modernity', in Jodi Dean and Paul Passavant (eds), *The Empire's New Clothes*
    (London: Routledge, 2004), pp. 121–42.

38 Califano, 'What was really great'.

39 Suring, Kenneth, 'Reinventing a physiology of collective liberation: Going
    "beyond Marx" in the Marxism(s) of Negri, Guattari and Deleuze', in Gary
    Genosko (ed.), *Deleuze and Guattari: Critical Assessments of Leading Philosophers*
    (London: Routledge, 2001), pp. 605–25 at p. 619.

40 Bagley, Carl, Ackerley, Claire and Rattray, Julie, 'Documents and debates, social
    exclusion, Sure Start and organizational social capital: Evaluating inter-disciplinary
    multi-agency working in an education and health work programme', *Journal of
    Educational Policy*, 19/5 (2004), 595–607, para. 1.

41 Davies, Jonathan S., 'The social exclusion debate'. *Policy Studies*, 26/1 (2005),
    3–27 at 3.

42 Califano, 'What was really great', p. 2.

43 See Neil, Earl A., 'Black Panther Party and Father Neil' (22 September 2007).
    Available from www.itsabouttimebpp.com/Our_Stories/Chapter1/BPP_and_
    Father_Neil.html, accessed on 18 April 2008. The undated article was written
    before 2002. Neil writes that the Black Panther Party's Breakfast Program began
    in 1969, which it was the 'first nationally organized breakfast program' and that
    it spread across the country (para. 9).

44 Bagley et al., 'Documents and debates'.

45 Bagley, Carl and Ackerley, Claire, 'I am much more than just a mum: Social Cap-
    ital, Empowerment and Sure Start', *Journal of Education Policy*, 21/6 (2006),
    717–34.

46 Hardt, Michael and Negri, Antonio, *Multitude, War and Democracy in the Age of
    Empire* (New York: Penguin, 2004), p. 108; Hardt, Michael and Negri, Antonio,
    Labor of Dionysius, a Critique of the State Form (Minneapolis: University of Minnesota

Press, 1994); Hardt, Michael and Negri, Antonio, *Empire* (Cambridge: Harvard University Press, 2001).

47 Blair, Tony, 'Tony Blair: Social Exclusion Speech in Full' (2007). Available at www.epolitix.com/EN/News/200609/83f43492-4145-4f17-a2a0-90ea840bf108. htm, accessed on 19 May 2008, para. 80.

48 'Sure Start path to success', *Inside Out, Working Together with Families and Communities* (New South Wales Government Department of Community Services, 2006), para. 4.

49 Ibid.

50 Califano, 'What was really great'.

51 Self, 'The Black Panther Party', p. 41.

52 Hicks, *Border Writing*.

53 Singh, 'Black is a Country', p. 84.

54 Self, 'The Black Panther Party', p. 37.

Chapter 11

'Putting the responsible majority back in charge': New Labour's Punitive Politics of Respect

Phil Edwards

Introduction

The concept of anti-social behaviour is among New Labour's key legislative innovations. Unknown to English law prior to 1997, anti-social behaviour was addressed by provisions in the Crime and Disorder Act 1998, the Police Reform Act 2002 and the Criminal Justice Act 2003, as well as receiving an Act of its own (the Anti-Social Behaviour Act 2003). As these dates suggest, the concept became particularly prominent during Tony Blair's second and third terms as Prime Minister (2001–7). Anti-social behaviour – together with the associated remedy of the Anti-Social Behaviour Order (ASBO) – was a prominent feature of the 'Respect agenda', a framework for social policy associated with Blair personally and with David Blunkett (Home Secretary between 2001 and 2004).

In this chapter, I examine the ideological roots of the 'Respect Agenda' by reviewing statements made by Tony Blair, who set out his views on anti-social behaviour on many occasions between 1988 and 2006. I argue that Blair has developed a complex and coherent model of how individuals should relate to one another within a contemporary community, and of how they may legitimately be coerced into doing so. The roots of this authoritarian variant on communitarianism are then traced back to two authors whom Blair has explicitly cited as intellectual influences: Thomas Hobbes and John Macmurray. I argue that Blair's fusion of Hobbesian liberal absolutism with Macmurray's moral communitarianism results in a model of society permeated by an intrusive moralism, underpinned by state coercion.

Tony Blair: 'How do we live together?'

In 1993, the Shadow Home Secretary – Tony Blair – set out his thoughts on crime in the left-wing magazine *New Statesman and Society*:

> We should be tough on crime and tough on the underlying causes of crime. We should be prepared and eager to give people opportunities. But we

are then entitled to ask that they take advantage of it, to grant rights and demand responsibilities.

. . .

crime, ultimately, is a problem that arises from our disintegration as a community, with standards of conduct necessary to sustain a community. It can only be resolved by acting as a community, based on a new bargain between individual and society. Rights and responsibilities must be set out for each in a way relevant for a modern world.[1]

Still earlier, in 1988, Blair (then a back-bencher) had warned in the *Times* of 'the new lawlessness' represented by rising levels of gang violence. He related this development to 'the decline in the notion of "community", of the idea that we owe obligations to our neighbours and our society as well as ourselves':

When a sense of community is strong, that adds its own special pressure against anti-social behaviour. Instead, we have learnt to tolerate what should not be tolerated. . . . We are living in a society where increasingly the term is itself becoming meaningless, where social responsibility and the duties that come with it are seen simply as a drag anchor on our private pleasure.[2]

These brief excerpts foreground three ideas which would recur throughout Blair's career. First, the concept of 'community' is prized: 'community' is an ideal which present-day societies should strive to realize. The fundamental characteristic of a community is the combination of rights and obligations, or of opportunity and responsibility: the state may 'grant rights' but it should also 'demand responsibilities'. Crucially, these obligations and responsibilities are horizontal rather than vertical, connecting members of the community one to another: a community is a society uniting its members through ties of reciprocal obligation.

Thus in 1999, addressing the National Council of Voluntary Organisations, Blair argued: 'individuals realise their potential best through a strong community based on rights and responsibilities. I have always believed that the bonds that individuals make with each other and their communities are every bit as important as the things provided for them by the state.'[3] In 2000, addressing the Global Ethics Foundation in Tübingen, he developed the argument further: 'you can't build a community on opportunity or rights alone. They need to be matched by responsibility and duty. That is the bargain or covenant at the heart of modern civil society.'[4]

This line of thinking culminated in the 2006 Respect Action Plan, launched by Blair in these terms:

Respect is a way of describing the very possibility of life in a community. It is about the consideration that others are due. It is about the duty I have to respect the rights that you hold dear. And vice-versa.

. . .

the change has to come from within the community, from individuals exercising a sense of responsibility. Rights have to be paired with responsibilities.[5]

In turn, this horizontal network of mutual obligations, of paired rights and responsibilities, is based on an assertion of equality among the community's members – or rather 'equal worth'. In his Tübingen speech Blair described 'the equal worth of all' as 'the central belief that drives my politics', and clarified the concept thus: 'Note: it is equal worth, not equality of income or outcome; or, simply, equality of opportunity. Rather it affirms our equal right to dignity, liberty, freedom from discrimination as well as economic opportunity.'[6] The following year, addressing the Christian Socialist Movement, he argued:

> Our values are clear. The equal worth of all citizens, and their right to be treated with equal respect and consideration despite their differences, are fundamental. So too is individual responsibility, a value which in the past the Left sometimes underplayed. But a large part of individual responsibility concerns the obligations we owe one to another. The self is best realised in community with others. Society is the way we realise our mutual obligations – a society in which we all belong, no one left out.[7]

The community – founded on a network of reciprocal obligations, owed by every member to every other on the basis of their equality of worth – is a well-developed and consistent theme in Blair's speeches and writings on the theme of anti-social behaviour.

Secondly, this notion of community is counterposed to crime and disorder, which are conceptualized in terms of heedless, self-seeking individualism ('our private pleasure'). There is a significant ambivalence here. Blair argues that individuals are able to act anti-socially as a *result* of the decline of community ('crime . . . arises from our disintegration as a community'). At the same time, he suggested that anti-social behaviour is spreading and growing independently, and that this growth is a *cause* of further community decline ('we have learnt to tolerate what should not be tolerated').

The first of these oppositions – anti-social behaviour as a morbid symptom of community decline – recurred when Blair was interviewed by Jeremy Paxman in 2002: 'I think the anti-social behaviour, the vandalism, the graffiti, the lack of respect for people, I think that's all part of a society that has lost its way and I want to create a society where we have opportunity for people, while we demand responsibility from them.'[8] However, the more active formulation – anti-social behaviour as a malignant growth tending to destroy the community from within – was much more prominent in Blair's later statements. A typical formulation is the assertion that anti-social behaviour is 'as corrosive to community life as more serious crime'[9] Similarly, in a 2005 speech on parenting, Blair argued, 'It is not criminal acts that are bad in themselves . . . it is what they cumulatively indicate, which is a disrespect for other people, for their rights, for the community.'[10]

The third distinguishing feature of Blair's communitarian rhetoric is that 'community' is not articulated as a utopian concept – an ideal to which any existing society could aspire, but which none could hope to achieve – but as a historically real state of affairs, which has been lost over time but can be rebuilt. Blair's 2000 speech to the Women's Institute expresses this notion succinctly:

> The idea of community is as old as time. What makes it tick are the values of responsibility to, and respect for, others. These are traditional values, good old British values. But here's the challenge. The spirit of this age is democratic. We won't rebuild community on the basis of doffing your cap or hierarchy. The rich man in his castle, the poor man at his gate: it won't wash any more.[11]

Community is associated with a past condition of stable hierarchy and deference: by implication, progress towards equality had encouraged self-seeking individualism, which tended to dissolve community. At the beginning of his third term of office, Blair returned to the theme:

> I've been struck again and again in the course of this campaign by people worrying that in our country today, though they like the fact we have got over the deference of the past, there is a disrespect that people don't like. . . . I want to make this a particular priority for this government, how we bring back a proper sense of respect in our schools, in our communities, in our towns and our villages.[12]

Launching the 'Respect Agenda' in 2006, Blair explicitly linked modernity with lack of respect for authority, and proposed that its place should be taken by mutual respect among individual citizens.

> A modern market economy needs the attributes of innovation, creativity, entrepreneurial spirit. These qualities thrive best when we can be critical of authority. . . . But to help communities in the modern world restore respect, these changes in lifestyle need to be accompanied by a new settlement between people, a new *modus vivendi*.[13]

He concluded: 'We are not looking to go back to anything. We have left behind an era in which we refused to respect people because of who they *were*. The only reason to withhold respect is because of what people *do*.'[14]

The respect agenda: 'Rules, order and proper behaviour'

Community is based on mutual respect among equal individuals. Anti-social behaviour both benefits from the decay of community and damages it further. Community has been lost but can be rebuilt. Considered as a political philosophy, this combination of ideas has some curious features. It is essentially *moralistic*: both the problems it diagnoses and their solution are rooted in individual behaviour rather than broader social factors. Growing social equality and the decline of deference are blamed for the dissolution of community, but also celebrated for their contribution to 'a modern market economy'; large-scale changes in society are accepted as being benign, or at worst irreversible. 'The bonds of cohesion have been loosened. They cannot be tied again the same way.'[15]

The fault thus lies not with changes in society, but with the way a minority has exploited them.

> The 1960s saw a huge breakthrough in terms of freedom of expression, of lifestyle, of the individual's right to live their own personal life in the way they choose. . . . It was John Stuart Mill who articulated the modern concept that with freedom comes responsibility. But in the 1960s revolution, that didn't always happen . . . some took the freedom without the responsibility.[16]

Equally, the solution is for people, as individuals, to behave better – to play by the rules. 'People do not want a return to old prejudices and ugly discrimination. But they do want rules, order and proper behaviour.'[17]

It follows that the anti-social behaviour agenda is deeply *divisive*. If community is a realizable state, but one which is imperilled by the actions of a minority of selfish individuals, then those individuals need to be dealt with – both for the sake of their own reform and to prevent them from causing any more damage. In this context, Blair's 2006 formulation on respect and equality – 'We have left behind an era in which we refused to respect people because of who they *were*. The only reason to withhold respect is because of what people *do*' – is double-edged. It implies that mutual respect, among individuals of equal worth, may be withdrawn – and perhaps that some people's equal worth is more equal than others'. Continuing membership of the 'society in which we all belong, no one left out'[18] is implicitly conditional on each person contributing to the community by acting respectfully. Withdrawal of respect would set the individual outside the community – and, in the process, cancel the community's obligations to the person excluded: henceforth their well-being would be a secondary consideration to that of the community they had offended against.

Blair has consistently emphasized the damage done by anti-social behaviour to the community and its values. As early as 1997, he argued that the Community Safety Order (henceforth CSO) 'would give the power to local authorities and the police to put people under an obligation to behave them-selves', adding: 'Some people say that it is a very draconian thing to do but I think you are entitled to certain minimum standards of behaviour from people if you are living next door to them.'[19] In 2002 Blair explicitly associated crime and punishment with a wide range of non-criminal rule-breaking and deviance, under the general heading of disrespect: 'Tough on crime – and on those who break the rules: those who don't turn up for school, who won't take a job when it is offered, those who commit crimes and threaten our basic values of decency and mutual respect.'[20] Failing to participate in employment and education in approved ways is now a threat – on a par with crime – to 'decency and mutual respect'.

For the sake of the responsible majority, action must be taken against the minority posing this threat. 'It is about respect for other people. . . . It's about hard-working families who play by the rules not suffering from those that don't. . . . For too long, the selfish minority have had it all their own way. That's changing.'[21] Speaking to Paxman, Blair went so far as to advocate withdrawing state benefits from claimants who refused to 'give anything back' by behaving responsibly: 'if your child is engaged in persistent truanting, refusing to cooper-ate, and the police and the education welfare officers and the school and every-one is at their wits' end, well, I'm sorry, but we shouldn't carry on paying out benefit to you in circumstances where you are not prepared to give anything back to society.' The question of how the – presumably impoverished – claim-ant would cope without benefits was brushed aside ('you might as well say that a family that is of low income should never be fined'). Later in the same interview, Blair explicitly dismissed any concern for the welfare of anti-social offenders: 'As you know some families have been evicted with the anti-social behaviour orders. But in the end what happens is in those areas the other families can live in a bit of peace and quiet.'[22]

Finally, this project of moral renewal for the many and punishment for the disrespectful few is also a populist appeal for *authoritarian mobilization*. Many of Blair's statements on anti-social behaviour are characterized by an almost revolutionary urgency:

> I am pleased that 50 per cent of Crime and Disorder Reduction Partnerships have dedicated anti-social behaviour teams – but I am worried about those communities who don't. . . . Until action is taken in every community where it is needed, we can't rest.[23]

Sometimes the government is seen as driving through urgently needed change, in the teeth of an entrenched establishment:

> For eight years I have battered the criminal justice system to get it to change. And it was only when we started to introduce special anti-social behaviour laws, we really made a difference. And I now understand why. The system itself is the problem.[24]

Sometimes the government is portrayed not as initiating change from above but as responding to the moral awakening of the decent majority. '[People] want a society of respect. They want a society of responsibility. They want a community where the decent law-abiding majority are in charge; where those that play by the rules do well; and those that don't, get punished.'[25] 'Anti-social behaviour is not evidence of a flawed moral sensibility in the British people. On the contrary, the need to act comes from the pressing moral urgency of the people.'[26] In all cases the need is for more action by government agencies: more intervention, more control, more punishment.

In short, the anti-social behaviour agenda – as described by Tony Blair – is a coherent project for the progressive regulation, stigmatization and punishment of groups within society which are seen to be responsible for disorderly, chaotic and disrespectful behaviour. This is justified on the grounds that disorderly behaviour is intrinsically damaging to the social order, irrespective of its actual effects. It is underpinned by the moral mobilization of those groups in society who regard themselves as responsible and law abiding, in support of the government and the police and against disfavoured minorities. Having reached this point, it comes as something of a surprise to remind ourselves that Blair has always described himself as a Christian, and claimed that his religious faith underpins his political philosophy. It's not immediately obvious, not to put too fine a point on it, how you get here from there.

In order to identify the sources of Blair's thought, it's worth focusing on two key concepts: the community of equal worth and the society bound by covenant. Blair returned repeatedly to these concepts. Addressing the Global Ethics Foundation in Tübingen in 2000, Blair said:

> The traditionalist mourns the passing of the old familiarities, points to the greater stability of family life in the past; points to the ugliness and disorder of much of the new world. The moderniser sees its opportunities; rejects the prejudices of the past, the old hierarchies, is impatient to grasp the material benefits modernity brings.
>
> . . .
>
> The resolution of this conflict lies in applying traditional values to the modern world; to leave outdated attitudes behind; but re-discover the essence of traditional values and then let them guide us in managing change. The theologians among you will say it is reuniting faith and reason.
>
> What are the values? For me, they are best expressed in a modern idea of community. At the heart of it is the belief in the equal worth of all – the central belief that drives my politics – and in our mutual responsibility in creating a society that advances such equal worth. Note: it is equal worth, not equality of income or outcome; or, simply, equality of opportunity.
>
> . . .

you can't build a community on opportunity or rights alone. They need to be matched by responsibility and duty. That is the bargain or covenant at the heart of modern civil society. Frankly, I don't think you can make the case for government, for spending taxpayers' money on public services or social exclusion, in other words for acting as a community – without this covenant of opportunities and responsibilities together. If we invest so as to give the unemployed person the chance of a job, they have a responsibility to take it or lose benefit. And on crime, I have no hesitation about being very hard on it. It's not just that the vulnerable suffer most from crime. It is that it breaks the covenant between citizens.[27]

In 2006, launching the 'Respect Action Plan', he argued:

Respect is a way of describing the very possibility of life in a community. It is about the consideration that others are due. It is about the duty I have to respect the rights that you hold dear. And vice-versa. It is about our recipro-cal belonging to a society, the covenant that we have with one another. More grandly, it is the answer to the most fundamental question of all in politics which is: how do we live together? From the theorists of the Roman state to its fullest expression in Hobbes's *Leviathan*, the central question of political theory was just this: how do we ensure order? And what are the respective roles of individuals, communities and the state?

Legal stricture will never be enough. Respect cannot, in the end, be con-jured through legislation. Government can provide resources and powers. It can do its best to ensure that wrong-doing is detected, that its powers against offenders are suitable, that its systems are expeditious and its enforcement strong. And the British system, like others, in the modern world, has not been good enough against these standards. But, ultimately, the change has to come from within the community, from individuals exercising a sense of responsibility. Rights have to be paired with responsibilities.

. . .

a modern market economy needs the attributes of innovation, creativity, entrepreneurial spirit. These qualities thrive best when we can be critical of authority, when people can make the most of themselves without feeling constrained by their background. This is precisely the ideal of the open soci-ety that we value. All of this is true. But to help communities in the modern world restore respect, these changes in lifestyle need to be accompanied by a new settlement between people, a new *modus vivendi*.[28]

Two phrases stand out here: 'the equal worth of all' and 'the covenant that we have with one another'. Tracing these concepts to their intellectual roots will help to clarify how a sincerely held Christian faith can be said to inform Blair's political views, and in particular how it underpins the divisive authoritarian moralism of the anti-social behaviour agenda.

Hobbes: 'A common power to keep them all in awe'

'Covenant' is an unusual word for a twentieth-century British politician to use. In Jewish-Christian Scripture, the term is generally used in the context of a covenant between God and humanity. The concept of a community held together by a covenant among its members has very different roots.

According to Blair, Hobbes' *Leviathan* is the 'fullest expression' of 'the central question of political theory . . . how do we ensure order? And what are the respective roles of individuals, communities and the state?' If we follow this lead, we find that Hobbes is also concerned with articulating a relationship between horizontal covenants and the creation and maintenance of a law-abiding community:

> A Common-wealth is said to be Instituted, when a Multitude of men do Agree, and Covenant, Every One With Every One, that to whatsoever Man, or Assembly Of Men, shall be given by the major part, the Right to Present the Person of them all, (that is to say, to be their Representative;) every one, as well he that Voted For It, as he that Voted Against It, shall Authorise all the Actions and Judgements, of that Man, or Assembly of men, in the same manner, as if they were his own, to the end, to live peaceably amongst themselves, and be protected against other men.
>
> . . .
>
> Because the Right of bearing the Person of them all, is given to him they make Soveraigne, by Covenant onely of one to another, and not of him to any of them; there can happen no breach of Covenant on the part of the Soveraigne; and consequently none of his Subjects, by any pretence of forfeiture, can be freed from his Subjection. . . .
>
> because the major part hath by consenting voices declared a Soveraigne; he that dissented must now consent with the rest; that is, be contented to avow all the actions he shall do, or else justly be destroyed by the rest . . . whether his consent be asked, or not, he must either submit to their decrees, or be left in the condition of warre he was in before; wherein he might without injustice be destroyed by any man whatsoever.[29]

The reference to a 'condition of warre' in the third point can be clarified by referring to an earlier passage:

> during the time men live without a common Power to keep them all in awe, they are in that condition which is called Warre; and such a warre, as is of every man, against every man.

. . . To this warre of every man against every man, this also is consequent; that nothing can be Unjust. The notions of Right and Wrong, Justice and Injustice have there no place. Where there is no common Power, there is no Law: where no Law, no Injustice.[30]

The necessary corollary of a society united 'by Covenant . . . of one to another' is that anyone who breaks the covenant risks exclusion from the society. On this point, Hobbes is terse but explicit:

he that dissented must now consent with the rest . . . whether his consent be asked, or not, he must either submit to their decrees, or be left in the condition of warre he was in before; wherein he might without injustice be destroyed by any man whatsoever.

Peace, the rule of law and the possibility of justice can obtain only within a commonwealth, established on the basis of common submission to a sovereign power. Once such a commonwealth has been established, its decrees are binding on all its members: anyone who dissents from them must submit. Crucially, this submission is motivated not by the punitive power of the sovereign, but by the second-order imperative that the power of the sovereign should remain unchallenged. The rapacity of other individuals is the greatest threat to an individual's ability to live in peace, Hobbes argues; this is kept in check only by the power of the sovereign, which in turn is only binding within the commonwealth whose members are united in submission to it.

If dissenters from the decrees of the commonwealth will not submit to them, they must be excluded from the commonwealth – which will return them, as individuals, to a state of war. The argument is brutally symmetrical. In the state of nature, people will tend to compete for what they desire, by foul means as well as fair. The possibility of peace and the rule of law can only exist within a commonwealth, guaranteed by the unchallenged power of the sovereign ('Covenants, without the Sword, are but Words, and of no strength to secure a man at all').[31] However, a commonwealth is sustained by its members' consent or submission to its decrees; anyone who refuses to submit thereby ceases to be a member of the commonwealth. By so doing, they will forfeit the protection of the sovereign, and by the same token remove themselves from the scope of the rule of law. While members of the commonwealth behave lawfully among themselves, this is only guaranteed by their fear of the sovereign set over them all; the outlawed ex-member of the commonwealth may be treated as brutally as they please. Nor could their actions be criticized as unjust: since justice is only conceivable within the commonwealth, anyone excluded from the commonwealth 'might without injustice be destroyed by any man whatsoever'.

Blair's debt to Hobbes seems to include the idea of society being sustained 'by Covenant . . . of one to another, and not by [the government] to any of them', as well as the idea that it is only such a horizontal covenant which keeps lawlessness and chaos at bay. Blair's insistence on the reality of crime, and his association of crime with self-seeking individual desire, also seems authentically Hobbesian. Hobbes' admonition to readers who might accuse him of a pessimistic view of human nature is a clear precursor of the rhetoric used by politicians who see themselves as 'tough on crime':

> It may seem strange to some man, that has not well weighed these things; that Nature should thus dissociate, and render men apt to invade, and destroy one another: and he may therefore, not trusting to this Inference, made from the Passions, desire perhaps to have the same confirmed by Experience. Let him therefore consider with himselfe, when taking a journey, he armes himselfe, and seeks to go well accompanied; when going to sleep, he locks his dores; when even in his house he locks his chests; and this when he knows there bee Lawes, and publike Officers, armed, to revenge all injuries shall bee done him. . . . Does he not there as much accuse mankind by his actions, as I do by my words? But neither of us accuse mans nature in it. The Desires, and other Passions of man, are in themselves no Sin. No more are the Actions, that proceed from those Passions, till they know a Law that forbids them.[32]

For Hobbes – as for Blair – crime is to be expected when individuals are not restrained by the law. The exclusionary logic of Hobbes' definition of the commonwealth is also echoed in several of Blair's comments on anti-social behaviour: his suggestion that respect should be withheld 'because of what people *do*'; his invocation of 'a community where the decent law-abiding majority are in charge; where those that play by the rules do well; and those that don't, get punished'; and, less overt but perhaps most telling, his breezy indifference to poverty and homelessness when inflicted on the 'anti-social' ('in the end what happens is in those areas the other families can live in a bit of peace and quiet'). The divisiveness as well as the authoritarianism of Blair's thinking has a clear Hobbesian pedigree.

However, any account of Blair's thinking as Hobbesian runs up against the problem of the content of the imagined 'covenant'. Hobbes's covenant was not a moral undertaking: as we have seen, the members of the commonwealth are bound to a higher standard of behaviour only by the power of the sovereign which is set over them. The commonwealth is not a community defined in positive terms, constituted by the mutual respect of its members for one another's rights; there is no sense that such a community is possible or that it would be desirable. As the lines quoted above on security from crime suggests, Hobbes began from the assumption that people will get away with as much as they can; the function of a commonwealth is to ratify an agreement to limit how much this is. The reason why the rule of the sovereign restricts individual freedom is that an individual whose freedom is unrestricted will tend to use it against other individuals. For Hobbes, all behaviour is anti-social.

It follows from this that only a minimal 'covenant' can or should be administered. If members of the commonwealth infringe on one another's rights to life, liberty and property, they can justly be punished by the sovereign; if they dissent from the commonwealth's decrees, for instance by elevating their own conscience above its laws, they can justly be excluded from it. Beyond this (admittedly fairly advanced) point, the members of the commonwealth are not under any positive obligations.

> For seeing there is no Common-wealth in the world, for the regulating of all the actions, and words of men, (as being a thing impossible:) it followeth necessarily, that in all kinds of actions, by the laws praetermitted [i.e. omitted], men have the Liberty, of doing what their own reasons shall suggest, for the most profitable to themselves. . . . In cases where the Soveraign has prescribed no rule, there the Subject hath the liberty to do, or forbeare, according to his own discretion.[33]

This is the sense in which Hobbes can reasonably be seen as a liberal: the absolutism of *Leviathan* might preclude political dissent or appeals against sentencing decisions, but it stops short of proposing that citizens must act in certain ways if they are to form part of the commonwealth. Nor are any duties imposed on citizens in their relations with one another. The notion that there might be 'standards of conduct necessary to sustain a community', or that individuals might be bounden to respect one another's equal worth, would be foreign to Hobbes.

Macmurray: 'The sharing of our lives in fellowship'

As we have seen, Blair's social thinking combines echoes of Hobbesian absolutism with a very different vision of society: one in which mutual respect and equality of individual worth play a large part. Interviewed in 1994, Blair was quoted as saying: 'If you really want to understand what I'm all about, you have to take a look at a guy called John Macmurray.'[34] Macmurray (1891–1976) was a philosopher whose work, both as a popularizer and promoting his 'personalist' model of society, enjoyed a certain popularity in the mid-twentieth century. Brought up as an evangelical Christian, Macmurray left the church during the First World War; he joined the Society of Friends late in life, but had no institutional religious affiliation during his working life.[35] Despite this lack of practical religious engagement, Macmurray saw himself (and was seen) as a Christian writer.

Among Macmurray's central ideas was the distinction between 'community' or 'fellowship' on one hand and 'society' on the other, and the related distinction between 'personal' and 'impersonal' or 'functional' relationships. He argued that 'we should use the term "society" to refer to those forms of human association in which the bond of unity is negative or impersonal; and reserve for the contrasted forms of association which have a positive personal relation as their bond, the term "community" '.[36] The 'personal' life is

> the life that we live as persons, and we can live it only by entering into relationships with other people on a fully personal basis, in which we give ourselves to one another; or, to put the same thing the other way round, in which we accept one another freely for what we are, and in which therefore there is and can be no purpose other than the sharing of our lives in fellowship.[37]

A community, in these terms, should not be confused with a society:

> Like a society, a community is a group which acts together; but unlike a mere society its members are in communion with one another; they constitute a fellowship. A society whose members act together without forming a fellowship can only be constituted by a common purpose. They co-operate to achieve a purpose which each of them, in his own interest, desires to achieve, and which can only be achieved by co-operation. The relations of its members are functional; each plays his [*sic*] allotted part in the achievement of the common end. A community, however, is a unity of persons as persons.[38]

Viewed pragmatically, the distinction between personal and impersonal relationships simply corresponds to two modes of interacting, both of which are necessary for anyone living in a differentiated society. Within society, we 'associate with each other in order to achieve some purpose that we all share. Out of this there springs a life of social co-operation through which we can provide for our common needs and achieve common ends'.[39] However, this form of interaction is not without a cost: 'The satisfactory working of social life depends upon entering into relationships, not with the whole of ourselves, but only with part of ourselves'.[40] '[T]here is a central core of our life which is personal';[41] there is a fundamental need for people to be able to relate on a personal basis, in 'a relationship . . . which has no purpose beyond itself; in which we associate because it is natural to human beings to share their experience, to understand one another, to find joy and satisfaction in living together'.[42] Social co-operation is necessary for practical reasons, but personal relationships are an end in themselves: a free expression of the desire to share the experience of living.

It follows that personal relationships are built on a basis of equality. In the personal relationships which go to make up a community,

> [individuals are] related as equals. This does not mean that they have, as a matter of fact, equal abilities, equal rights, equal functions or any other

kind of *de facto* equality. The equality is intentional; it is an aspect of the mutuality of the relation. If it were not an equal relation, the motivation would be negative; a relation in which one was using the other as a means to his own end.[43]

A community is neither a biological family nor an artificially imposed society, and avoids the inequalities built into both; it is 'based neither on the blood-relationships of natural affinity, nor on the organized relationships of political or ecclesiastical groupings, but simply the practical sharing of life on a basis of their common humanity'.[44]

Macmurray's argument is cogent and coherent. We can readily appreciate the difference between a 'functional' relationship, in which 'one was using the other as a means to his own end', and a 'personal' relationship in which 'there is and can be no purpose other than the sharing of our lives'. The idea of extending this model of relationship to form a community – a network of voluntary obligations sustained by mutual respect and intentional equality – is a powerful ideal. What it cannot be, and does not claim to be, is a model of society. A church may be a community; a school may be a community – Macmurray in fact argued that education depended on personal relationships, and hence that a properly functioning school *must* be a community.[45] An entire society can never be a community, as it is necessarily organized along 'functional' and impersonal lines. It follows that to treat obligations to society as if they were obligations to community is both mystifying and exploitative, as it leads to individuals being exhorted to invest in a functional social bond as if it were a fulfilling personal relationship. Macmurray sharpened this point in a 1932 talk which contrasted 'social morality' with the 'human morality' of personal relationships. According to 'social morality', Macmurray argued, 'the purpose which ought to control our lives is not our own selfish purpose, but the social purpose . . . the goodness of our own individual lives depends upon our devoting them to the common good'. Macmurray dismissed this as 'a false morality': 'a denial of human reality' which 'treats everybody as a means to an end'.[46] Blair's belief in the ideal of Macmurray's 'community' appears to be sincerely held: his statements on respect, mutual responsibility and equality of worth bear the authentic Macmurrayan stamp. However, as Hale points out, what Blair has made of it is closer to Macmurray's 'social morality'.

Conclusion

Macmurray's influence alone might have given Blair a project for moral mobilization; as we have seen, Blair's actual thinking is equally marked by a divisive authoritarianism which can be traced back to Hobbes. The resultant hybrid is a particular kind of vision of 'community'. In the context of the 'Respect Agenda', responsibility and respect are invoked in authentically Macmurrayan terms, but the invocation is always accompanied by a drive to identify and punish those who do not belong in the community. In the Respect Action Plan (which has no authorial credit but carries Tony Blair's image and signature), we read:

> we have changed the culture of our public services and our communities so that the most visible signal of disrespect – serious anti-social behaviour and disorder – is tackled not tolerated, putting the responsible majority back in charge of their communities.
>
> . . .
>
> If we are to achieve the vision of the Britain that we all want, then there is no room for cynicism. We need to take responsibility for ourselves, our children and our families, support those who want to do the same – and challenge those who will not.
>
> . . .
>
> *every citizen has a responsibility* to behave in a respectful way and to support the community around them in doing the same.
>
> . . .
>
> Too many people still suffer from the anti-social behaviour of a minority and feel powerless to stop it.
>
> . . .
>
> When people feel confident, safe and supported, they will be able to come together with others in their neighbourhood to build trust, share values *and agree what is acceptable behaviour.*[47]

For Hobbes, it was every citizen's duty to refrain from lawbreaking and to consent to the decrees of the commonwealth. For Blair, this duty extends to meeting a positive standard of behaviour and assisting local institutions in enforcing it. For Macmurray, the community was an end in itself, and the fullest expression of human life treated as an end in itself. For Blair, building a trusting community makes it possible to agree the standards of behaviour which community members must meet or be excluded. This grotesque hybrid is as authoritarian and divisive as Hobbes, but without the framing liberalism that kept Hobbes' sovereign from governing every area of behaviour; it is as moralistic as Macmurray, but without Macmurray's belief in a universal human dignity which should not be coerced.

New Labour's anti-social behaviour legislation is not unique; in the US, particularly, 'zero tolerance policing' has been enthusiastically promoted as a means of driving down both crime and disorder. What is unusual about the

'Respect agenda' is its combination of a rhetoric of idealistic inclusiveness with practices that openly promote division. This combination of Macmurray and Hobbes – moral exhortation for the respectable majority, punitive exclusion for the disorderly – was Blair's distinctive contribution to Labour's law and order agenda. Hopefully it can now be spoken of in the past tense.

Notes

1. Blair, A. (1993), 'Why crime is a socialist issue', *New Statesman and Society*, 29 January, 27–28.
2. Blair, A. (1988), 'Anti-social behaviour article in the *Times*', 12 April, online at <www.number10.gov.uk/Page9738> [accessed 27 Oct. 2008].
3. Blair, A. (1999), 'Keynote speech, NCVO Annual Conference', 14 February, online at <www.number10.gov.uk/Page8072> [accessed 27 Oct. 2008].
4. Blair, A. (2000b), 'Speech to the Global Ethics Foundation Tübingen University', 30 June, online at <www.number10.gov.uk/Page1529> [accessed 27 Oct. 2008].
5. Blair, A. (2006), 'Prime Minister's speech launching the Respect Action Plan', 10 January, online at <www.number10.gov.uk/Page8898> [accessed 27 Oct. 2008].
6. Blair, 'Speech to the Global Ethics Foundation Tübingen University'.
7. Blair, A. (2001), 'Prime Minister's speech to the Christian Socialist Movement', 29 March, online at <www.number10.gov.uk/Page3243> [accessed 27 Oct. 2008].
8. Blair, A. (2002a), 'Interview with Jeremy Paxman', 16 May, online at <http://news.bbc.co.uk/1/low/programmes/newsnight/archive/1988874.stm> [accessed 27 Oct. 2008].
9. Blair, A. (2003), 'Prime Minister's speech to Criminal Justice Conference', online at <www.number10.gov.uk/Page4091> [accessed 27 Oct. 2008].
10. Blair, A. (2005b), 'Speech on improving parenting', 2 September, online at <www.number10.gov.uk/Page8123> [accessed 27 Oct. 2008].
11. Blair, A. (2000a), 'Prime Minister's speech to the Women's Institutes' Triennial General Meeting', 7 June, online at <www.number10.gov.uk/Page1526> [accessed 27 Oct. 2008].
12. Blair, A. (2005a), 'Prime Minister's speech on returning to 10 Downing Street', 6 May, online at <www.number10.gov.uk/Page7459> [accessed 27 Oct. 2008].
13. Blair, 'Prime Minister's speech launching the Respect Action Plan'.
14. Ibid.; emphasis in original.
15. Blair, A. (2005c), 'Keynote speech to the Labour Party's conference in Brighton', 27 September, online at <newsvote.bbc.co.uk/mpapps/pagetools/print/news.bbc.co.uk/1/hi/uk_politics/4287370.stm> [accessed 27 Oct. 2008].
16. Blair, A. (2004a), 'Speech on the launch of the five-year strategy for crime', online at <www.number10.gov.uk/Page6129> [accessed 27 Oct. 2008].
17. Ibid.
18. Blair, 'Prime Minister's speech to the Christian Socialist Movement'.

19. Blair, A. (1997), 'Speech on Law and Order', 13 June, online at <www.number10. gov.uk/Page1028> [accessed 27 Oct. 2008].

20. Blair, A. (2002b), 'Prime Minister's speech on tackling poverty and social exclusion', 18 September, online at <www.number10.gov.uk/Page1726> [accessed 27 Oct. 2008].

21. Blair, A. (2004b), 'Prime Minister's speech on Anti Social Behaviour', 28 October, online at <www.number10.gov.uk/Page6492> [accessed 27 Oct. 2008].

22. Blair, 'Interview with Jeremy Paxman'.

23. Blair, 'Prime Minister's speech on Anti Social Behaviour'.

24. Blair, 'Keynote speech to the Labour Party's conference in Brighton'.

25. Blair, 'Speech on the launch of the five-year strategy for crime'.

26. Blair, 'Prime Minister's speech launching the Respect Action Plan'.

27. Blair, 'Speech to the Global Ethics Foundation Tübingen University'.

28. Blair, 'Prime Minister's speech launching the Respect Action Plan'.

29. Hobbes, T. (1651), *Leviathan*, London: Andrew Crooke, chapter 18.

30. Ibid., chapter 13.

31. Ibid., chapter 17.

32. Ibid., chapter 13.

33. Ibid., chapter 21.

34. Quoted in Hale, S. (2002), 'Professor Macmurray and Mr Blair: The strange case of the communitarian guru that never was', *The Political Quarterly* 73/2, 192.

35. Stern, J. (2001), 'John Macmurray, spirituality, community and real schools', *International Journal of Children's Spirituality* 6, 25.

36. Stern, 'John Macmurray, spirituality, community and real schools', 31.

37. Macmurray 1961; quoted in Doddington, C. (2007), 'Individuals or persons – what ethics should help constitute the school as community?' *Ethics and Education* 2/2, 135.

38. Macmurray 1996; quoted in Stern, 'John Macmurray, spirituality, community and real schools', 31.

39. Macmurray 1935; quoted in Hale, 'Professor Macmurray and Mr Blair', 193.

40. Ibid.

41. Macmurray 1935: quoted in Doddington, 'Individuals or persons – what ethics should help constitute the school as community?', 135.

42. Macmurray 1935; quoted in Hale, 'Professor Macmurray and Mr Blair', 193–4.

43. Macmurray 1961; quoted in Stern, 'John Macmurray, spirituality, community and real schools', 33.

44. Macmurray 1936; quoted in Prideaux, S. (2005), 'John Macmurray and the "forgotten" lessons on capitalism and community', *The Political Quarterly* 76/4, 544.

45. Stern, 'John Macmurray, spirituality, community and real schools', 32.

46. Macmurray 1932; quoted in Hale, 'Professor Macmurray and Mr Blair', 196.

47. Home Office (2006), *The Respect Action Plan*, online at <www.homeoffice.gov.uk/ documents/respect-action-plan?view=Binary> [accessed 27 Oct. 2008], 1–2; emphasis added.

Bibliography

Blair, A. (1988), 'Anti-social behaviour article in the *Times*', 12 April, online at <www.number10.gov.uk/Page9738> [accessed 27 Oct. 2008].

— (1993), 'Why crime is a socialist issue', *New Statesman and Society*, 29 January

— (1997), 'Speech on Law and Order', 13 June, online at <www.number10.gov.uk/Page1028> [accessed 27 Oct. 2008].

— (1999), 'Keynote speech, NCVO Annual Conference', 14 February, online at <www.number10.gov.uk/Page8072> [accessed 27 Oct. 2008].

— (2000a), 'Prime Minister's speech to the Women's Institutes' Triennial General Meeting', 7 June, online at <www.number10.gov.uk/Page1526> [accessed 27 Oct. 2008].

— (2000b), 'Speech to the Global Ethics Foundation Tübingen University', 30 June, online at <www.number10.gov.uk/Page1529> [accessed 27 Oct. 2008].

— (2001), 'Prime Minister's speech to the Christian Socialist Movement', 29 March, online at <www.number10.gov.uk/Page3243> [accessed 27 Oct. 2008].

— (2002a), 'Interview with Jeremy Paxman', 16 May, online at <http://news.bbc.co.uk/1/low/programmes/newsnight/archive/1988874.stm> [accessed 27 Oct. 2008].

— (2002b), 'Prime Minister's speech on tackling poverty and social exclusion', 18 September, online at <www.number10.gov.uk/Page1726> [accessed 27 Oct. 2008].

— (2003), 'Prime Minister's speech to Criminal Justice Conference', online at <www.number10.gov.uk/Page4091> [accessed 27 Oct. 2008].

— (2004a), 'Speech on the launch of the five-year strategy for crime', online at <www.number10.gov.uk/Page6129> [accessed 27 Oct. 2008].

— (2004b), 'Prime Minister's speech on Anti Social Behaviour', 28 October, online at <www.number10.gov.uk/Page6492> [accessed 27 Oct. 2008].

— (2005a), 'Prime Minister's speech on returning to 10 Downing Street', 6 May, online at <www.number10.gov.uk/Page7459> [accessed 27 Oct. 2008].

— (2005b), 'Speech on improving parenting', 2 September, online at <www.number10.gov.uk/Page8123> [accessed 27 Oct. 2008].

— (2005c), 'Keynote speech to the Labour Party's conference in Brighton', 27 September, online at <newsvote.bbc.co.uk/mpapps/pagetools/print/news.bbc.co.uk/1/hi/uk_politics/4287370.stm> [accessed 27 Oct. 2008].

— (2006), 'Prime Minister's speech launching the Respect Action Plan', 10 January, online at <www.number10.gov.uk/Page8898> [accessed 27 Oct. 2008].

Doddington, C. (2007), 'Individuals or persons – what ethics should help constitute the school as community?' *Ethics and Education* 2:2.

Hale, S. (2002), 'Professor Macmurray and Mr Blair: The strange case of the communitarian guru that never was', *The Political Quarterly* 73:2.

Hobbes, T. (1651), *Leviathan*, London: Andrew Crooke.

Home Office (2006), *The Respect Action Plan*, online at <www.homeoffice.gov.uk/documents/respect-action-plan?view=Binary> [accessed 27 Oct. 2008].

Macmurray, J. (1932), *Freedom in the Modern World; Broadcast Talks on Modern Problems*, London: Faber & Faber.

Macmurray, J. (1935), *Reason and Emotion*, London: Faber & Faber.

— (1936), *Creative Society*, New York: Association Press.

— (1961), *Persons in Relation*, London: Faber & Faber.

— (1996), *The Personal World: John Macmurray on Self and Society*, Edinburgh: Floris Books.

Prideaux, S. (2005), 'John Macmurray and the "forgotten" lessons on capitalism and community', *The Political Quarterly* 76:4.

Stern, J. (2001), 'John Macmurray, spirituality, community and real schools', *International Journal of Children's Spirituality* 6.

Part III

Justice and International Order

Chapter 12

Tony Blair and the Commission for Africa: A Fig Leaf for Iraq or a Moral Imperative?

Paul Vallely*

Tony Blair's decision to set up the Commission for Africa received a mixed response when it was announced in 2004. Development activists took him at his word. This was, after all, the man who at the Labour Party conference in 2001 had described Africa as 'a scar on the conscience of the world'. They applauded the idea. But others dismissed it as a piece of political spin designed to offer some degree of appeasement to those on the Left who had been critical of his policy on Iraq.

The scepticism was understandable. Labour had achieved, after all, a mixed record on the implementation of what its first Foreign Secretary, Robin Cook, had in 1997, 12 days after coming into office, described as a foreign policy with 'an ethical dimension' which would 'put human rights at the heart of our foreign policy'.

On the plus side, in the early years, there had been Britain's intervention in Kosovo to end the massacre of Albanian Muslims by Serbia's Slobodan Milosevic. And Blair had also sent troops into Sierra Leone in 2000 to prevent rebels from overturning the democratically elected government. There had been a ban on the use and manufacture of anti-personnel landmines, as there was later to be on the use of cluster bombs. Labour had increased support for human rights lobby groups. And training for foreign troops by the British Army had been reshaped to include concern for human rights and the need for civilian accountability of the military. It had taken the overseas aid ministry out of the Foreign Office to separate aid from foreign policy and focus it on reducing poverty.

On the debit side, New Labour had refused to allow the extradition of Chile's former dictator, General Pinochet, when he turned up in the UK. It had approved a controversial £28 million military air traffic control system to the poverty-stricken, debt-ridden government of Tanzania. And Cook had controversially approved the delivery of nine British Aerospace Hawk jets to

* Paul Vallely, associate editor of *The Independent*, was seconded to the Commission for Africa and was co-author of its final report. He worked with Bob Geldof and Bono in lobbying the G8 ahead of the Gleneagles summit.

Indonesia, despite fears by human rights campaigners that they would be used for internal repression in East Timor. That, more than anything, underscored the central ambiguity at the heart of Labour policy. While Cook had talked about the 'ethical dimension', the Labour manifesto had stated: 'We support a strong UK defence industry, which is a strategic part of our industrial base as well as our defence effort'. In those days Britain was the world's second biggest arms exporter (Russia and France have since overtaken the UK) with arms exports worth £5 billion a year providing jobs for 150,000 people. Arms went to other unsavoury regimes too – China, Colombia, Pakistan, Saudi Arabia, Sri Lanka and Zimbabwe – and some 50% of the turnover of the Export Credit Guarantee Department[1] went to support arms sales.

This dichotomy reflected something that ran deep through Tony Blair's political personality. He was driven by two impulses, which were in tension and sometimes, perhaps, in contradiction. He had a strong sense of moral commitment. Yet he was the quintessential political pragmatist. His establishment of the Commission for Africa reflected both those motivating characteristics.

It was set up at the behest of a celebrity figure. Bob Geldof late in 2003 visited Ethiopia, where famine was threatened on the scale of the great drought of 1984 and 1985 which prompted the Live Aid concerts which had raised more than $100 million for Africa. Geldof despaired that all his work of two decades before had come to naught. From Addis Ababa he rang Downing Street. Tony Blair took the call, patched through to Evian in France, where the Prime Minister was attending a summit of the world's eight most powerful nations, the G8.

'It's happening again', Geldof exploded.

'Calm down', said the prime minister, 'and tell me what the problem is'.

'I can't calm down', said Geldof. 'Twenty years after Live Aid and things are no better. In some ways they're getting worse. What happened to all the early warning systems we put in? What happened to the improvements in EU aid – they're double-counting again. None of it is working. And there are all these new forces of the globalized economy at play which nobody properly understands. Africa is fucked.'

'Come and see me when you get back', said Blair.[2]

Geldof did.

Charity and justice

The charitable impulse which had driven Live Aid, Geldof had concluded, had not been enough; what was needed was structural change. Not charity but justice became his slogan. A Marshall Plan for Africa was required if the continent were ever to stand on its own feet. It was time to take another look at Africa in the same way that the Brandt Commission had looked at the relationship between the North and the South 25 years earlier. Blair – and Brown to whom Geldof also talked – agreed. They set up the Commission. I was party to much of the detail after Geldof insisted that I was brought into the process. I had been *The Times* correspondent in Ethiopia, and later across Africa, during the great famine of 1985 which had inspired Geldof to launch first Band Aid and then Live Aid. After the concert I had accompanied Geldof on a journey across Africa – through Mali, Burkina Faso, Niger, Chad, Sudan and Ethiopia – to decide how the money raised by Live Aid should be spent. Geldof and I worked together on various development issues over the two decades that followed. When the Commission was agreed upon Geldof insisted that I joined the team to bring the skills of a professional writer to bear on the Commission's final report to ensure that it was accessible to the widest possible readership.

From the outset it was clear that both sides of Blair's political character were in evidence here. He saw a moral imperative that something had to be done about the plight of the world's poorest people in the world's most neglected continent. The depth of Blair's sense of that was incontestable. In 1997, before he became Prime Minister, being aid minister had about as much kudos in British politics as being put in charge of Northern Ireland. It was the job no-one really wanted. Britain's aid budget had been cut and cut, year after year under the Conservatives. Blair changed all that. He brought the aid minister into the Cabinet. He commissioned the first White Paper on development for quarter of a century with the title 'Eliminating World Poverty: Making Globalisation Work for the Poor'. Blair steadily increased the budget for overseas development. Today British aid is nearly three times what it was ten years ago. In Blair's final year as Prime Minister it increased by 13% to £5.4 billion for 2007/08. Raising the priority of the world's poor was one of the consistent commitments of Blair's time in office.

But there was in all that a political pragmatist at work. In his introduction to that White Paper he spelled out the twin drivers of his vision: world poverty was 'the greatest moral challenge facing our generation', he wrote, but addressing it was 'also in the UK's national interest' since 'many of the problems which affect us – war and conflict, international crime and the trade in illicit drugs, and the spread of health pandemics like HIV/AIDS – are caused or exacerbated by poverty'. Tony Blair knew that Live Aid had in its day attracted the biggest audience the world had ever seen and it had raised more for charity than any other single event in world history. Geldof had a power which could not be ignored, and which could perhaps be harnessed. Blair knew that intuitively because he, like Gordon Brown, was a child of the Live Aid generation. He had been among the 1.5 billion people watching Live Aid that day – an event which Gordon Brown has described as the single most important public event in the lives of two generations. Blair shared his generation's attitude to celebrity; in private with Geldof he, not the fading pop musician, was the one who was star-struck. The same was true of George Bush; put him alongside Bono and it was the world's most powerful politician who was the one wanting a photo to be taken of them together.

Broad-brush morality

In February 2004 Blair announced a Commission for Africa made up of 17 Commissioners, a majority of them African, from the worlds of government, business and the development sector. They included two prime ministers, a president, two finance ministers, representatives of key G8 countries and China, and key movers in Africa's private sector.[3] Blair saw it as a vehicle with which to put Africa (along with climate change) at the top of the agenda for Britain's simultaneous presidencies of the G8 and the EU in 2005. But it was a moral agenda, without any clear idea initially of how this might best be done, what specific outcomes should be sought or whether recommendations should be addressed primarily to African leaders or the rest of the international community. There were no Terms of Reference. Its modus operandi remained undecided. Indeed, so much so that some Western governments were wary that it was a Trojan Horse designed to push them into commitments they might not welcome – and, by contrast, governments within Africa feared it might be another attempt to impose an external agenda on the continent, undermining the mechanisms and strategies Africans had set up for themselves – the African Union, New Partnership for Africa's Development (NEPAD) and Africa Peer Review Mechanism.

Fears that this was to be a Western-imposed agenda rather than one springing from the analysis of Africans were compounded when senior officials in Commission's London-based secretariat early on drew up a set of 'Emerging Conclusions' which were circulated to Commissioners. The Commissioners promptly batted them back with the rejoinder that they would come to their own conclusions, and not before they had done a lot more listening to Africans.

Blair was surprisingly relaxed about this demonstration of independence on the part of the Commission's members. Nor was he fazed by a number of counter-intuitive suggestions made by its members. He was content to accommodate the fairly radical demand of the Ethiopian Prime Minister, Meles Zenawi, that the Commission should reject the received orthodoxy in international trade negotiations that every concession made by rich countries had to be matched in some way by a quid pro quo from developing nations. Geldof backed that insisting 'the idea that we have to get something out of any negotiations in which we give something to Africa is morally repugnant. Moreover it doesn't grow out of any serious economic need so much as out of political ideology.'[4] But neither did Blair demur at the insistence of the South African finance minister, Trevor Manuel, that Africa could not efficiently cope with the amounts of cash that would flow from Bob Geldof's initial idea that global aid to Africa should be quadrupled; Africa did not have the 'absorptive capacity' – the planners, technicians, engineers or civil servants – to spend such amounts efficiently.

Geldof, reluctantly, also came to accept that truly massive transfers of aid were not realistic, though he argued for a medium-term building of the capacity which would permit far greater increases in aid in the future. His main concern, he told Blair privately after the second meeting of the Commission in Addis Ababa, was that the paradox that

> if we come up with something very radical you won't be able to sell it in the G8, but if we don't produce something radical I won't be able to sell it to the public in the G8 countries where people intuitively feel that we have to do something big and different if we are to get Africa out of its nightmare.[5]

There were, Geldof suggested 'a few touchstones of radicalism which for me are a minimum baseline'. The first was Meles Zenawi's idea about non-reciprocal liberalization on market access, discussed above. A second touchstone was the need for the Commission to include capacity-building as a major component in its recommendations: arguments about absorptive capacity were 'all too often an easy excuse for doing nothing. The truth is that people only start creating capacity once there is money on the table . . . an aggressive "[anti-] corruption and capacity" fund should be a key "big idea" component.' And a third touchstone was reform of the International Monetary Fund and other international financial institutions which often had become impediments rather than instruments as far as Africa is concerned.

Blair's handwritten reply was revealing for the way in which it intermingled a sense of moral purpose with an eye for the necessary political manoeuvrings. He agreed with Geldof's analysis that the dilemma was 'how to get measures realistic enough to pass G8 leaders; but visionary enough to inspire the outside world'[6] and then set out a tactical plan for achieving that. It was essential to accept, he argued, that G8 governments should be given the room to manoeuvre on how the increases in aid and debt cancellations should be achieved: individual rich nations had to be allowed to 'find their own way' on this. He wanted the Commission to push hardest on trade where it would be tough for G8 leaders publicly to resist basic moral arguments about the need for equity and fair dealing in granting poor nations access to G8 markets. The third essential, he insisted, was to get 'real buy-in from African leaders'. Overall what was needed was 'to put together a sufficient package that even where there is resistance on individual items, or a feeling that it doesn't go far enough, the sum of the parts is significant enough'.[7] Blair's end in all this was visionary, but his tactics were those of *realpolitik*. It was a characteristic combination.

Public and private religion

Many political commentators have mocked Blair, suggesting that his 'religion' is either detached and deeply privatized or else that he is hypocritical or self-deluded. In part that grows out of a misconception popular among secularists, and perhaps best summed up in the parody of Blair as an evangelical charismatic who hears the voice of God in his ear, presumably whispering: 'Invade Iraq'. This is to misunderstand what it means to be religious in the Catholic tradition, to which Tony Blair eventually converted, but which had shaped his religious world-view for several decades. That tradition is altogether more intellectual and psychologically grounded. It is a way of 'doing God'[8] which is more assimilated and internalized. Blair's Christianity was about being part of a community and a shared moral tradition which, through regular exposure to the gospel, shaped the kind of person he was, informing and moulding his conscience and informing his moral world-view – against which background he made decisions based on the evidence as he saw it, the advice of others and his own political judgements. Everything Blair has said about his faith presupposed this, though he was too hesitant to launch into such explanations for fear that 'doing religion' would inevitably be misconstrued by his political critics and opponents.

Privately he was less coy. Just before his first 1997 landslide election victory Blair wrote to Cardinal Hume. The letter, which has never been published,[9] was warm in tone and acknowledged the common agenda between his vision for New Labour and the social teaching of the Catholic church which lay at the heart of the bishops' document titled *The Common Good*.

The pillars of Catholic Social Teaching are the concepts of the common good – 'the sum total of those conditions of social living, whereby human beings are enabled more fully and more readily to achieve their own perfection';[10] of solidarity – 'a firm and persevering determination to commit oneself to the common good; that is to say, to the good of all and of each individual because we are all really responsible for all';[11] and of subsidiarity – the idea that the state should not take over what individuals or groups can do or that decisions should be taken at the lowest level possible which is compatible with good government. Together they constitute the combination of rights and responsibilities so characteristic of Blairism.

These principles could be seen at work in a variety of Blair's domestic policies and philosophies: from stakeholding and devolution, to the minimum wage and statutory holidays, from the human rights act and civil partnerships to family tax credits, lifelong learning and Sure Start nurseries, from paternity leave and the increase in maternity pay to getting lone mothers back to work and welfare reform.[12] His sense of social justice went wider than a mere sense of entitlement. A similar moral balance informed his views on foreign policy.

It was pretty clear from anyone up close to Blair in dealing with the Commission for Africa that he was motivated by something beyond the usual considerations of daily politics. 'I fear my own conscience on Africa', he said at the launch of the Commission's Africa report in March 2005. 'I fear the judgement of future generations, where history properly calculates the gravity of the suffering. I fear them asking: but how could wealthy people, so aware of such suffering, so capable of acting, simply turn away to busy themselves with other things?'

He was emotionally engaged; that much was clear when, in Addis Ababa, in a room with barely half a dozen people present Geldof introduced him to Birhan Woldu, the young woman whose image as a child, at the brink of death, had been the single most memorable image in the original Live Aid concert – and who was 20 years on a successful agricultural studies graduate.

And there was about him in private a fire and a vision that burst out of narrow political self-interest. Indeed sometimes it ran counter to usual political considerations. Blair knew that his continued lobbying of his fellow G8 leaders on Africa was irritating them. At one point the German Chancellor, Gerhard Schroeder – in a desperate attempt to find some common ground with George Bush, with whom relations were still icy after Germany's opposition to the invasion of Iraq – said privately to Bush: 'Blair is being a real pain in the arse about this Africa stuff, isn't he?' To which Bush replied: 'Yeah, I wish he'd give it a rest.'[13]

It is to Tony Blair's credit that he never did give it a rest, not even when he was preoccupied by winning the Olympics for Britain (the announcement of which was made by the International Olympic Committee on the very morning of the first day of the Gleneagles summit) or responding to terrorist bombers on the streets of London – forcing Blair to quit the summit to fly to London and address the crisis. He kept going back to the business of getting a better deal for Africa.

Bombs and a blueprint

The London bombings had a mixed impact on the outcome of the Gleneagles summit. British negotiators at Gleneagles felt the suicide bombings in London in which 52 people died and 700 were injured, disposed other G8 leaders to give Blair the package he wanted on aid as an act of solidarity against the terrorist bombers. But the crisis took Blair away from Gleneagles on the day when trade was to be discussed, wiping away the prospect of a significant reduction in rich country farm subsidies, to which George Bush and Jacques Chirac were edging, but which, in Blair's absence, was scuppered by the EU President, Jose Manuel Barroso. It is hard to say whether a deal on export subsidies was lost; some insiders at Gleneagles suspected Chirac of gamesmanship, but others felt that Blair might truly have secured some real progress had he not been called away.

But the Commission report had established an effective blueprint on which Gleneagles significantly delivered, prompting the UN Secretary General Kofi Annan to describe it as 'the greatest summit for Africa ever' though critics in some aid agencies suggested that it had fallen far short of what was required. Certainly Blair did not succeed in everything he tried for. On debt he had a great success; $ 41.9 billion has been written off in 19 of the poorest countries.[14] And the release of money which had been set aside to service debts has meant that health care is now free in Zambia, roads are being built for farmers in Ghana, Nigeria will get 3 million more children into school by 2009, and much more. On aid, the picture was more mixed. Gleneagles promised to double aid to Africa by 2010. By the time Blair left office his G8 colleagues had delivered only 10% of that. And though that has brought some successes: the number of people receiving Aids treatment in Africa, for example, has increased tenfold, it is still well-short of what was promised because other rich nations – most particularly Germany, Canada and Italy – have not paid up as Britain has. On trade, the area he privately felt the rich world was most morally remiss, a deal eluded him almost entirely.

'It is in the nature of politics that you do not achieve absolutely everything you want to achieve', he said at the press conference at the end of the Gleneagles Summit in July 2005, 'but nonetheless I believe we have made very substantial progress indeed. . . . All of this does not change the world tomorrow, it is a beginning, not an end.'

Interestingly Geldof underwent a parallel experience in terms of compromise. He had to learn how limited was the room for political manoeuvre – with the French on the question of farm subsidies, with the Germans who said they would keep their promises on aid but then tried to knock down all the mechanisms proposed to raise it – from the International Finance Facility which Gordon Brown had devised to finance the Commission package to the French proposal to add a levy to tickets for air travel.

Blair's role in all this was revealing. It was Gordon Brown who led on the substantial deal on debt cancellation; Brown, for whom Africa is a visceral moral issue, had spent over a year manoeuvring his fellow finance ministers into a deal to cancel multilateral debt to the continent's poorest nations. And it was Hilary Benn, a Development Secretary utterly in command of his brief, who kept across the detail of the development issues.[15] But it was Blair who set the parameters of the Commission's considerable achievement by his choice of commissioners – and the balance of interests between the radical and the politically achievable, the African and the Western assumptions brought to the process. He was prescient in his appointment of a Chinese member of the commission, at a time when the massive impact of Chinese investment on Africa – and their determination to pursue a very different path from the good governance conditionality that had characterized Western approach in Africa – had not become generally understood. But Blair, who was a consummate chairman in the Commission sessions, stayed out of the final processes of internal negotiation within the Commission, between the activist viewpoint pressed by Geldof, the Washington-consensus embodied by President Chirac's representative, Michel Camdessus,[16] and the unexpected (to many) perspectives of the African members on issues including culture, absorptive capacity and the primary importance of peace and security as a prerequisite for development.[17] In all that Blair allowed the Commission the autonomy to find as it saw fit. He and his staff did not interfere in the drafting process of the Commission's report.

Perhaps most significantly Blair happily endorsed the Commission's decision to replace the old paradigm of aid conditionality with a model based on partnership – by which it meant not a narrow set of specific contracts between African governments and rich nations, which risks becoming adversarial and unpredictable, but one based on solidarity and mutual respect. The basic pact at its heart was that Africa had to do the right thing, not because donor nations told it to but because there was a growing realization on the continent that Africa could not keep avoiding the tough decisions. Similarly the West had to do the right thing – stopping hindering Africa's development, and starting to help that development far more effectively – not as its half of the bargain for Africa's compliance but because it was self-evidently right to do so. Doing the right thing for its own sake was good theology as well as better politics.

But what perhaps most surprised those involved in the Commission was that, at the launch of the report, Tony Blair declared that he supported the report in its entirety, and would make it British government policy, with the objective of making it G8 policy too. He took a risk in doing that. Other G8 leaders, it became clear, were not so enthusiastic. The Canadians and Americans insisted that their constitutions forbade them from front-loading aid in the way the Commissioners wanted. Interestingly when Bono privately tried to twist the arm of the US Secretary of State, Condoleeza Rice on this by telling her that during U2's US tour he would get 10,000 fans a night to call the White House, she simply replied: 'We can take the calls.' That was when Geldof finally decided to launch Live 8 – 'something so fucking *big*', he said, 'that even *they* can't ignore it'.

In the event the threat was enough. As soon as the Live 8 concerts were announced things began to change. In the pre-summit 'sherpa' meetings there was a sudden shift in attitudes. The German and American sherpas – in whose

countries there had been a huge amount of media coverage and pressure –
suddenly began to talk about things that weren't on their agenda before. Within
weeks the EU agreed a virtual doubling of its combined aid by 2010. And the
month after the G7 finance ministers agreed a deal to cancel $40 billion of
poor countries' debts. In Richard Curtis's film production offices in Notting
Hill, from which Live 8 was organized, Geldof got calls from Paul Wolfowitz –
the one-time architect of the war in Iraq, and then newly arrived at the World
Bank – telling him what to push George Bush on. (On Aids and education, an
area in which the US president was already being prodded by his wife Laura,
who had undertaken a tour of Africa and developed a special concern for girls'
education; one of President Bush's daughters had been working privately as a
volunteering with young AIDS sufferers at a Cape Town children's hospital.)
Bush made the concessions at the last minute in Scotland.

Some critics suggested that this was all gamesmanship and that the G8 leaders made no more concessions at Gleneagles than they would have intended
all along. But the size of the Make Poverty History and Live 8 campaigns mat-
tered. Those who saw the politicians up close, realized they were scared by the
size of the global anti-poverty lobby. More than 3 billion people watched Live
8 – half the population of the world. Geldof and Bono took to Blair and Bush a
briefcase containing 38 million names in the biggest petition ever assembled.
The intense political pressure on the world's leaders bore real fruit – and Blair
colluded in that. He allowed the report of the Africa Commission to be far
more radical than many people had expected. And he secured at Gleneagles
far more than any political realist could have hoped for. The world's politicians
have still not yet delivered all that they promised. By the time Blair left office
his G8 colleagues had paid out on just 10% of their Gleneagles pledges. Even so,
add that to the $41.9 billion delivered in debt cancellation and it was a signifi-
cant step forward. Between them the Commission for Africa, MPH and Live 8
has already produced 400 times more for poor Africans than Live Aid did two
decades earlier. If the promises to raise annual global aid flows by $25 billion a
year are kept that would be the equivalent of five Live Aid concerts every week.

Purpose and pragmatism – an activist agenda

That achievement says a lot about the balance between idealism and political
pragmatism in Tony Blair. As a Prime Minister he was, above all else, an activist. He was a man with a sense that he had a duty to intervene to try to rectify
wrong where he found it. After years of the Douglas Hurd do-nothing school of
foreign policy, which led Britain to walk away from ethnic cleansing in Bosnia
and turn its back on genocide in Rwanda, this was a significant shift.

Posterity may well determine that he was right about Kosovo but wrong
about Iraq. But what is clear is that he drew on the same combination of moral

purpose and political pragmatism in making decisions on both, and on so much else. He made an unashamedly moral case for Africa at Gleneagles – but he also deployed arguments about poverty creating a breeding ground for terrorism designed to win George Bush over to the Gleneagles deal. As on climate change, where Britain was early on the international leader in pressing for collective world action, he mixed arguments about self-interest (and new business opportunity with carbon capture technologies) with high-minded admonitions about our stewardship of the planet for future generations. Blair saw no conflict in this. Rather he believed that the interplay of moral imperatives and national self-interest was a creative one, creating an unanswerable case for action.

A common criticism of Blair was that he developed an 'autopilot foreign policy' which tied Britain to the coat-tails of the US. But those close to Blair know that what drove him is not merely a sense of strategic alliance (though that was important) but one of right and wrong. Where the two clashed – as with Iraq where Blair knew that war would be domestically damaging – he allowed his moral vision to dominate. And where things are wrong, Blair instinctively felt, Britain had the responsibility to ride in on a white charger and save the day. The world will be a lot quieter without him. But it may not necessarily be a better place.

Notes

1 These guarantee that if a foreign country defaults on paying for British goods the government will recompense the exporter.
2 Private conversation with Geldof.
3 The members were:

- Tony Blair (Chair) – Prime Minister (UK)
- Fola Adeola – Chairman of the FATE Foundation (Nigeria)
- K. Y. Amoako – Executive Secretary of the Economic Commission for Africa and Under-Secretary-General of the United Nations (Ghana)
- Nancy Kassebaum Baker – former Senator (US)
- Hilary Benn – Secretary of State for International Development (UK)
- Gordon Brown – Chancellor of the Exchequer (UK)
- Michel Camdessus – former managing director of the IMF (France)
- Bob Geldof – musician and founder of Live Aid (Ireland)
- Ralph Goodale – Finance Minister (Canada)
- Ji Peiding – Member of the Standing Committee of the National People's Congress and its Foreign Affairs Committee (China)
- William S. Kalema – Chairman of the Board of the Uganda Investment Authority (Uganda)
- Trevor Manuel – Minister of Finance (South Africa)
- Benjamin Mkapa – President of Tanzania
- Linah Mohohlo – Governor of the Bank of Botswana

- Tidjane Thiam – Group Strategy and Development Director Aviva PLC, (Côte d'Ivoire)
- Anna Tibaijuka – Director of UN HABITAT and Under-Secretary-General of the United Nations (Tanzania)
- Meles Zenawi – Prime Minister of Ethiopia

[4] Private letter to Blair, 14 October 2005.

[5] Ibid.

[6] Unpublished letter from Blair to Geldof, 25 October 2005.

[7] Ibid.

[8] Blair's director of strategy Alastair Campbell in 2003 famously interrupted an interview with David Margolick of Vanity Fair to prevent the Prime Minister from answering a question about his religious faith. 'We don't do God', Campbell interjected.

[9] Private conversation with a senior bishop.

[10] *Mater et Magistra* (1961) Pope John XXIII.

[11] *Sollicitudo Rei Socialis* (1987), Pope John Paul II.

[12] For a fuller discussion of the philosophical basis of this approach see my 'Towards a New Politics: Catholic Social teaching in a Pluralist Society' in *The New Politics: Catholic Social Teaching for the 21st century*, ed. Paul Vallely, SCM, 1998.

[13] Private conversation with a senior colleague of Gerhard Schroeder.

[14] When fully implemented the Multilateral Debt Relief Initiative will provide over $50 billion worth of debt relief.

[15] Though when it came to the detail on aid in the Gleneagles deals it was Blair and Brown's special advisers, Justin Forsyth and Shriti Vadera, along with the British sherpa, Sir Douglas Jay, the head of the British Diplomatic Service, who made the running. Even so the triumvirate of Blair, Brown and Benn may turn out to have been something of a golden age for development issues in recent British politics.

[16] Camdessus was formerly the managing director of the Washington-based IMF.

[17] There was much wrangling about the detail with Commissioners, particularly the African ones, demanding detailed changes right until the 11th hour and beyond. Indeed 24 hours after the document was supposed to be at the printers, to meet the deadline for the launch, there was a stand-off between Geldof and Camdessus on three key issues. Geldof demanded that the Commission must insist that poor countries should no longer be forced to liberalize their markets in return for aid or debt relief; eventually Camdessus conceded the point. Geldof also insisted that it was not enough for the Commission to say that ways must be found to allow poor people to participate in economic growth; it was important, too, to assert that the impact of policies designed to increased growth should not negatively affect the poorest. He won in that too. Where Camdessus prevailed was in insisting on debt relief rather than full debt cancellation (the latter means writing of the entire debt, interest and capital, whereas relief merely means writing off interest payments, in this case for a ten-year period). In the event this was overturned by the Bush administration at Gleneagles in favour of the more radical cancellation option.

Chapter 13

Soul Brothers? Blair, Bush and the Compact between Liberal Interventionism and Conservative Nationalism

Inderjeet Parmar

This chapter explores the reasons why former Prime Minister Tony Blair unfailingly supported the foreign policies of President George W. Bush. This issue is a vexed one, eliciting simplistic interventions: Blair was Bush's 'poodle'; Blair was Bush's 'foreign secretary'; or that Blair was a 'neo-conservative'. This chapter rejects these characterizations. Instead, I argue that the two leaders shared certain moral outlooks on and diagnoses of the international scene and, after 9/11 in particular, their prescriptions for 'solving' global problems by 'remaking the world' became virtually identical, at least at a rhetorical level. Ultimately, the Bush–Blair compact reflected a new unity between previously divergent political and ideological tendencies, American conservative nationalism and liberal humanitarian interventionism.

In the aftermath of 9/11, Bush and Blair forged a very strong relationship personally and between their governments. Prior to the attacks, there had been numerous issues that divided the two men and their administrations: America's refusal to back an International Criminal Court, to ratify the Kyoto environmental treaty on reducing green house gas emissions to prevent global warming, and America's National Missile Defence strategy. In each of these cases, the US was bucking the global trend, acting unilaterally, much to the dismay of Tony Blair.

In addition to specific policy differences, Bush and Blair were divided by their political philosophies. As a right-wing Republican, Bush supported cutting taxes, deregulating industry and scaling back the role of government. Blair, conversely, was a leading champion of the 'Third Way'. While Blair saw Bill Clinton as a model leader whose winning electoral strategies were worthy of emulation, Bush and the Republicans detested Clinton's liberalism, sexual promiscuity and his avoidance of the draft during the Vietnam War. The differences between Bush and Blair were large.

How did they manage to overcome such strong differences of outlook? This chapter aims to address this question by, first, examining the social backgrounds of the two leaders, and the development and nature of their ideas about their countries and the world. The chapter aims to show who these men really are, where they come from, what they think, and what they aspire to for their countries.

The conceptual approach is to examine the development of each leader's world-view over time, from school through university and into world politics. It is not a 'great man' approach to history which ignores long-term historical or strategic factors. Rather, it suggests that individual leaders can be highly influential. They can restructure relations and institutions especially if they use crises effectively and their 'definition of reality' becomes widely accepted and marginalizes alternative definitions.

Individual leaders, of course, embody and are constrained by structural factors, which intertwine with their innovative roles and capacities. The balance between the individual's power to restructure versus the individual as 'structure-embodiment' depends on the leader's own history, character and capacities, as well as the structure of political opportunities. This chapter concerns two leaders in what they defined as existential war crises brought about by the Al-Qaeda terror attacks on the World Trade Center, New York, and the Pentagon, Washington, DC, on 11 September 2001. War crises are critical junctures that tend to focus the power of decision even more than usual on the roles, character and styles of leaders, maximizing their potential for innovative action.

In this chapter, I see Blair as an innovative leader with agency but also as the bearer of historically and institutionally embedded culture, values and ideas. In the specific context of the 1990s and after, Blair was able to exercise significant political influence. He has, in part at least, come to his foreign policy positions through a quite profound development in Anglo-American liberal internationalism which has at its heart 'democratic peace' theory.[1] At its crudest, the democratic peace thesis suggests that since democracies do not fight wars against one another, democratizing the world would be the best way of ensuring global security against military and terrorist aggression. As Blair told an American audience in 1999, 'If we can establish and spread the values of liberty, the rule of law, human rights, and an open society then that is in our national interests too. The spread of our values makes us safer'.[2] Blair was also familiar with the work of Immanuel Kant, whose work he had read as an undergraduate at Oxford. Kant was the originator of democratic peace theory, publishing *Perpetual Peace* in 1795.[3] Additionally, Blair placed his doctrine of international community 'in a line stemming from Dante's "world law" to Erasmus's Council of Just Men'.[4] Finally, Blair was comfortable with being compared with President Woodrow Wilson – who famously waged a war to 'make the world safe for democracy'.[5] There is nothing inherent in democratic peace theory that argues for democracy promotion by force, however, but that is the way this theory was promoted by some leaders after 9/11. Consequently, Blair argued for military intervention for halting humanitarian crises and promoting democracy despite the inevitable violation of national sovereignty this necessitated.

The 'Responsibility to Protect' principle of the liberals of the 1990s now includes a 'duty to prevent'.[6] Liberal interventionists insist on this principle to prevent ethnic cleansing, intervening in 'failed states' and brutal dictatorships. To be sure, though not all liberal humanitarian interventionists supported the 2003 war on Iraq, their logic suggests that such a stance was entirely fitting.[7]

George W. Bush, conversely, arrived at his foreign policy positions through traditional American conservative nationalist-internationalism. This tendency was unenthusiastic about US interventions in Bosnia and Kosovo because of the belief that America was ill-fitted to be the world's 'nation-builder'. Conservative nationalists focused on US interventions on behalf of her 'vital interests', actions to promote American power in a unipolar world.

9/11 changed the structure of political opportunities by bringing together liberal interventionists and conservative nationalists. Curiously, their union might well have played a critical role in heralding the so-called neo-conservative moment and the related belief that the Bush administration's foreign policies had been 'hijacked' by 'neo-cons' such as Paul Wolfowitz and Richard Cheney, who were, in turn, close to the most visible organization of that ideological grouping, the Project for a New American Century (PNAC). By association, Prime Minister Blair was declared guilty of being a 'neo-con' by Clare Short, the-then secretary of state for international development.[8] In practice, what appears to have occurred is the union of liberal interventionism and conservative nationalism, as personified by the alliance between Bush and Blair. It was only after 9/11 that 'democracy promotion' – a balance of power favouring freedom – became the central rhetorical principle of the Bush administration.[9] Bush and Blair personify the combination of 'muscle and morality' that is emblematic of US foreign policy since 9/11 and which led directly to the Afghanistan and Iraq wars and, indeed, threatens to spill over into military interventions in Iran and Syria.

Summed up, an imperial tendency has emerged as a powerful force in Anglo-American foreign affairs, reminiscent of an earlier age. Democratic peace theory is its ideological higher truth, Britain and America the powers chosen by destiny to impose it on selected parts of the world. This is a twenty-first-century version of the imperial civilizing mission and of manifest destiny, welcomed by some and rejected by others as hubris. American-style political and economic capitalist democracy is declared suitable for export in a globalizing world, another self-evident truth. The mission relies on the former colonial world forgetting Britain's record of imperial domination, and amnesia about America's post-1945 record of military interventions against leftist-nationalist governments and installation of right-wing military juntas.

Three specific reasons why Blair backed Bush

First, Blair was on a neo-imperial mission to 'remake the world' – at least in part; this has deep roots in his philosophical, religious and political evolution. Relatedly, George W. Bush, as a Texan, imbibed a version of the empire thesis. Secondly, Blair and Bush shared independently arrived at diagnoses of the errors of Anglo-American foreign policies after the end of the cold war, rejecting the 1990s as years of drift and lost opportunities to reorder the world and cement American power. Thirdly, both leaders saw 9/11 as an ideal opportunity to reform the world, to promote/construct an imperial world order through a robust Anglo-American alliance.

This chapter explores the evolution of Blair's outlook showing similarities and convergences with that of President Bush. The evidence refutes claims that Blair was Bush's 'foreign minister'. The article shows that Blair is a liberal imperialist who believes that the world needs to be remade by an active Anglo-American alliance.

Bush, Blair and 9/11

9/11 ought not to be underestimated in its impact on Anglo-American relations and international affairs. While significant shifts in US strategy were evident prior to 9/11, the spectacular effects of the murderous attacks on the World Trade Center made politically possible the implementation of a more robust, unilateral, pre-emptive *and* preventive, more lethal military strategy. Bush is heir to the bureaucratic-political-military shift in American thinking after the collapse of the Soviet bloc, as were the Bush senior and Clinton administrations. But 9/11, America's new Pearl Harbor, *catalysed* everything – it made *politically possible* a reordering of the world and America's place in it.[10]

9/11 also represented an excellent opportunity to Tony Blair, who saw 9/11 as a chance to promote Britain's global role as defender of its own interests, as leader of Europe, and as a loyal US ally.[11] According to Peter Riddell, the Bush–Blair relationship was comparable to that of the original founders of the special relationship: President Franklin Delano Roosevelt and Winston Churchill.[12] That special character was evidenced on 20 September 2001, when Bush outlined to his National Security Council 'America's determination to win the war [on terror]'. America would respond so robustly to Al-Qaeda and 'our enemies', Bush promised, that 'Two years from now *only the Brits may be with us.*'[13] The loyalty of Blair's government was taken as read.

How did the two leaders overcome their various ideological and political differences? What role did their world-views play in bringing them together on policies to be pursued post-9/11, that is, wars on Afghanistan and Iraq?

It is argued below that significant shared features of Bush's and Blair's backgrounds and development account for the strength of their alliance.

Blair's schooling

Tony Blair: born in Scotland, brought up in England, with a brief interlude in Australia. His father was a law lecturer at Durham University, a successful barrister and chairman of his local Conservative Party. Blair was educated at 'the Eton of Scotland' – Fettes College. Founded in 1870, Fettes was an English-style public school which, Blair noted, was driven by 'a powerful sense of duty and . . . inspirational teaching', fitting students 'to carry into the future the torch of liberal values, duty and open-mindedness first lit back in 1870'.[14]

Fettes College, founded in Queen Victoria's long reign, a few years before she was unveiled by Prime Minister Disraeli as the Empress of India, bore all the hallmarks of the self-confidence of its era. It reflected the 'muscular Christianity of the new age', the desire to create through a Spartan spirit, men who would build and run the Empire.[15] Fettes College may have contributed significantly to planting the seeds of Blair's later 'conversion' to Christian Socialism. As the College's biographer emphasizes, Fettes was home to a 'pioneering spirit and interest in social reform . . . [a] brand of mild Christian socialism'. In fact, the College drew praise from William E. Gladstone, the then Prime Minister in whose footsteps, as a social moralist, Tony Blair has followed.[16]

Blair was a natural sportsman, captaining the school cricket and basketball teams. Again, in this the College, and Blair, followed the nineteenth-century tradition of promoting sports for building muscles and character, for channelling aggression. Even by Blair's time there, life at Fettes was Calvinistic, 'rigorous' and based on a 'strenuous ethic'.[17]

In many ways, Bush's schooling mirrored Blair's. Phillips Academy, Andover, was elitist, formal and physically demanding. It was founded by Calvinists, a tough academy, 'a rigorous institution with a survival-of-the-fittest ethos.' Its then headmaster, John Kemper, had been to West Point and was descended from 11 generations of soldiers. Andover was a 'steely' place where there were physical fitness tests and compulsory building-climbing exercises.[18] Muscular Christianity was not on the curriculum at Andover; it was in the very (cold) New England air. An academically rigorous institution, Bush suffered at Andover but worked reasonably hard and, in addition to cheerleading, joined the Phillips Society, helping with local community projects. He was carrying on an old east coast tradition of public service, values which his parents had encouraged by their own example in Midland, Texas.[19]

If Bush did not take advantage of the academic privileges of Andover, it was the setting for the early development of a reasonably coherent conservative world-view. The only book, in addition to the Bible, that Bush ever read, was Senator Barry Goldwater's, *The Conscience of a Conservative*. Goldwater's book opposed black civil rights legislation (specifically desegregating schools), supported states' rights (the traditional defence of racial segregation), cutting taxes, reducing welfare and aggressively curbing Soviet power. According to his Andover room-mate, Bush had read enough to explain Goldwater's conservatism and say why his family thought it was so interesting.

The chapter on 'The Soviet Menace' in Goldwater's tract repays reading; it is an aggressive call for rolling back international communism, rather than 'appeasing' or 'negotiating' with it. After 1945, Goldwater explains, the US 'were not only master of our own destiny; we were master of the world. . . . The most powerful nation the world had ever known.' (The parallel positions of the US in 1945 and 1989, when the Soviet Union collapsed, are clear.) By 1960, however, 'we are in clear and imminent danger of being overwhelmed by alien forces'. There is a revolutionary movement bent on global domination, 'that operates conspiratorially in the heart of our defenses . . . [with] an ideology that imbues its adherents with a sense of historical mission . . .' (If for communism we substitute Islamic terrorism or fundamentalism, the parallels between 1960 and post-9/11 era are obvious.) Our goal, Goldwater argues, must be 'victory' over communism, not negotiation or surrender, and we must be willing to wage war (using limited tactical and strategic nuclear weapons as necessary), within a modernized military, in order to achieve it. The United Nations, Goldwater claimed, is in part a 'Communist organization' and of limited value. In the struggle for victory over communism, we must view 'the UN as a possible means to that end', and not an end in itself.[20]

The young George W. Bush read this book in enough detail to be able to outline its message to a school friend. The book's influence should not be overstated but neither should it be dismissed. It suggests Bush was beginning to form the basis of a coherent conservative world-view, and that that outlook was introduced by his parents. Father was, indeed, a Goldwater conservative, running such a congressional campaign in 1964.[21]

Blair, Oxford and the development of his religious politics

Blair's university education was at St John's College, Oxford, reading law. Although he graduated and went on to become a London barrister, Oxford actually better prepared him for a career in politics by providing the context of the future prime minister's religious politics.

Blair claims to be a Christian socialist in the traditions of R. H. Tawney, A. H. Halsey and many other labour philosophers.[22] Unlike most, or in fact all other Labour prime ministers, however, Blair wears his beliefs on his sleeve. Indeed, he declared in 1996 that 'Jesus was a modernizer', alluding to some perceived divine legitimacy of the New Labour 'Project' to transform British politics and the Labour Party. For Blair, religious beliefs are for everyday life, including political life. In his view, Jesus stood for equality, social justice and fairness, and is the model for Blair's own vision of how a just society ought to be ordered and led. He rejects the rampant individualism of Thatcher's Conservatives in favour of strengthening the social, community basis of individualism.[23]

In that regard, he is the disciple of a now-forgotten Scottish philosopher, John Macmurray, whose ideas were introduced to Blair at Oxford by Peter Thompson, an Australian fellow student and former priest. Macmurray argued that traditional liberalism often began with the isolated individual who, for self-interest, developed a sense of community for utilitarian ends. The society was just the sum of its individuals. Macmurray argued that, in fact, the individual is, in part, a product of social relationships, of a community. In the relationship between the community and the individual, both owe each other social obligations. The community looks after the individual, but the individual must also serve the community; there are rights and duties. There is a human impulse, according to this view, to serve, to do our duty to the community.[24]

To Blair, Macmurray may well have been his first glimpse of the 'Third Way' that he later championed. Macmurray, according to Blair, confronted the 'critical political question of the twenty-first century: the relationship between the individual and society'. While the twentieth century saw the rise of state intervention and welfare states, to fight poverty and deprivation, followed by a reaction to them in New Right individualism (Thatcherism and Reaganomics), the new millennium's problem is how to 'construct a new settlement for individual and society today. We have reached the limits of narrow selfish individualism; but have learnt the mistakes that collective power can make.' A middle ground, between an all-powerful nanny state and selfish individualism must be found and implemented in the real world. Macmurray's Christian socialism was a philosophy connected with the world, 'not an abstraction from it', a great strength, Blair argues, in finding 'spiritual meaning' without a 'retreat from reason'. Philosophy, 'to be at all relevant . . . must either increase an understanding of the world or our ability to change it', Blair contends, and Macmurray's thought passes both tests with 'flying colours'.[25]

Macmurray was himself heavily influenced by the Oxford philosopher, T. H. Green, whose teachings were immensely influential at the turn of the twentieth century. Green's thought influenced a whole generation of social reformers and politicians, especially in the Liberal Party, encouraging them to abandon laissez-faire (a philosophy of state non-intervention in social and economic life) and espouse a more activist state.[26] A generation of young men from England's elite public schools were inspired to help the poor in London and elsewhere by Green's thought. Social service in the real world would contribute to a more virtuous society. The 1906 Parliamentary Liberal Party contained 23 Greenians, four of whom were in the Cabinet.[27]

Green's contribution to late Victorian and Edwardian thought and politics lies in his ability to square a circle for churchmen in the wake of Charles Darwin's scientific explanations of the origins of species and their impact on modern progressive thinkers. Science appeared to undermine the very foundations of Christian religious belief, especially among those who considered themselves 'modern' and forward-looking. What could they do to further the Kingdom of God if there were no such thing? And what would they do with all that missionary, religious emotion and zeal that they felt and contained? Green provided the answer: God is in each and everyone and in every social institution. The religious must try with all their might to perfect the Kingdom of God on earth, must work to improve themselves and purge society of all its ills. History, in fact, was a progressive development of attempts to attain societal perfection, that is, the realization of godliness in personal and social life. Believers must work to eradicate poverty and want, hunger and ill-health, illiteracy and corruption, and create a better society. In effect, Green's philosophy gave to well-born, privileged Christian men and women, suffering crises of faith and conscience because of the rise of scientific thought, a viable approach to the world that was both active and in the service of God. An outward-looking philosophy, Green suggested that happiness, 'such as goes along with being a great man', could only be attained

> by having wide thoughts, and much feeling for the rest of the world; and this happiness often brings so much pain with it, that we can only tell it from pain by its being what we would choose before everything else, because our souls see it as good.[28]

Unwittingly, Green created and strengthened the philosophical basis of a number of political movements, including 'New Liberalism' – rejection of laissez-faire, promotion of an activist state – and of the rise of more left-wing, socialistic tendencies such as the Fabian Society and the Labour Representation Committee and, ultimately, the Labour Party. Among the young men and women who were part of this movement were people like Arnold Toynbee, the great reformer (Toynbee Hall), and future Labour Prime Minister, Clement Attlee. While at Fettes, a similar impulse led Blair to run a summer camp for a boys' club and perform voluntary work in the local community.[29]

Through Macmurray, Tony Blair is a descendant of that very tradition. What is more, he knows a great deal of the history of New Liberalism, where he stands in relation to it and how his own 'Third Way' and 'New Labour-ism' is its present-day equivalent. In *New Britain: My Vision of a Young Country*, Blair acknowledges the radical character of New Liberalism, a philosophy led by 'transitional figures, spanning the period from one dominant ethic to another'.

Like them, Blair seeks to engineer 'far-reaching social reform', to preside over a political era that bears comparison with the radical Liberal governments of 1906–14, an era that saw, among other things, reform of the House of Lords. Calling for a 'crusade for change', it is clear that the hand of history bears down on Tony Blair and on his mission to modernize Britain: After all, 'Jesus was a moderniser' too![30]

His Christianity is active and alive in his political and social life. Such belief has its radical, critical side – it questions the way things are, demands change and improvement. As Blair wrote in an article in the *Daily Telegraph* in 1996, being a Christian means 'you see the need for change around you and accept your duty to do something'.[31] To Blair, Christianity is also

> a very tough religion. . . . It places a duty, an imperative on us to reach our better self and to care about creating a better community to live in. . . . *It is judgemental. There is right and wrong. There is good and bad* . . . [although] it has become fashionable to be uncomfortable about such language. *But when we look at our world today and how much needs to be done, we should not hesitate to make such judgements. And then follow them with determined action.* That would be Christian socialism.[32]

Blair's references to the utility of Jesus in everyday life suggest something of the southern US evangelical protestant.

There is also, of course, a strong strain of Gladstonian moralism in Blair's global outlook. That combined well with the rising centre-left sentiment favouring humanitarian interventionism during the 1990s, especially with reference to events in the Balkans. Activist writers like David Rieff and the International Commission on Interventionism and State Sovereignty – of which the now Harvard scholar, Michael Ignatieff, was a member, championed the cause of people suffering from the brutal excesses within states, beyond the reach of international law and the United Nations.[33] According to Rieff, such tendencies, however, have been appropriated by political forces – such as the American neo-conservatives in the Bush administration and by Tony Blair – that are far more imperialistic in their outlook who have used the rhetoric of humanitarian intervention in a range of cases – such as Kosovo and Iraq – that fall beyond the original thinking behind the strategy.

That George W. Bush should take the title of his memoir – *A Charge to Keep* – from a hymn is unsurprising. It tells us how deeply religious he is and how far his religious and racial views and his right-wing Republican politics are enmeshed. Upon Saddam Hussein's removal from power by Anglo-American forces in 2003, Bush declared that 'freedom is the almighty God's gift to every person, every man and woman who lives in this world', and, by implication, that the US and its commander-in-chief was only doing God's work.[34]

Bush's faith was renewed after his 40th birthday. He gave up alcohol and found Jesus, influenced by Revd Billy Graham. Reading a special 'one-year Bible' – with a daily reading from across the Bible, Bush also joined a men's Bible reading group. Moral personal behaviour became part of his code of conduct and his politics, although the latter had been true for sometime. If Tony Blair traces his philosophy back to John Macmurray, Bush's harks back to the very personage of Jesus Christ, which plays well with America's evangelicals.[35] According to George W. Bush, a non-Christian cannot go to heaven.[36]

Despite Bush's own Methodist affiliations, the religious right constitutes his political core support. The melding of religious fundamentalism into mainstream politics has been made possible by the right's championing of the 'cultural' issue – like abortion, school prayer, gay rights, welfare dependency – and elevating it to the level of national politics. Bush has overtly and covertly pandered to the religious right. His choice of an anti-Catholic institution, Bob Jones University, which had also until recently forbidden interracial dating, for an election campaign speech, was a good example.[37]

The religious right and racial prejudice are strongly connected. Bush's religious politics, therefore, emerge from the historically segregationist culture of West Texas and the rest of the Deep South. According to Meinig's study:

> the population of the [West Texas] region is perhaps the purest example of the 'native white Anglo-Saxon Protestant' culture. . . . And it is such in the popular mind as well as in historical fact. . . . Emancipated from the narrowest folk expressions of southern fundamentalism, it remains thoroughly within and indeed gives much leadership to the mainstream of Southern Protestant development, with Baptists and Methodists dominant, and . . . various other evangelical sects prominent. . . . The undiluted Southern background has made it a routinely segregationist society. In the past the Ku Klux Klan found strong support.[38]

The Republican voters who backed Bush are, Lind claims, 'the political and sometimes lineal' descendants of traditional 'Southern Democrats'.[39]

Lind also points out in great detail that the region that nurtured George W. Bush was saturated in the culture and politics of the Deep South, a region that bears the hallmarks of its largest 'tribe', the Anglo-Celts. The latter derived from Scottish Protestants implanted by the English on Ulster's Catholic soil to colonize Ireland. Crossing the Atlantic Ocean, some of their number engaged in the 'ethnic cleansing' of Cherokee Indians. 'The swaggering Texan', Lind suggests, 'is nothing more than the Scots-Irish frontiersman.' Having historical experience of dispossessing Catholics in Ulster and Native Americans in the US, the militaristic Anglo-Celts made disproportionate inroads into the South and into the American military. Their culture, according to Meinig, is

> individualistic and egalitarian, optimistic and utilitarian, volatile and chauvinistic, ethnocentric and provincial. . . . There is an easy acceptance of equality among one's own kind but a rigid sense of superiority over other local peoples, and a deep suspicion of outsiders as threats to the social order.[40]

Too sophisticated and well-educated 'to express overt racial and religious bigotry', modern WASP Texans nevertheless retain an imperial mind-set, a belief in their inherent superiority.

Blair's imperial mind-set

The foreign policy of the 'New Liberals' – such as almost the entire leadership of the imperialist Round Table movement and of its offspring, Chatham House – was to strengthen the bonds of the British Empire through imperial reform and alliance (and even federation) with the US.[41] The underlying rationale was founded on a racialized world-view based on Anglo-Saxon biological and cultural superiority.[42] By the Second World War, the desire among some sections of British and American elite opinion was for a Federal Union between Britain and its Dominions and the US, and the Scandinavian democracies. This was proposed on the basis that Anglo-Saxons, and one or two Nordic nations, were uniquely suited to good government, economic development and to protection of the rights of the individual. The missionary zeal that inspired domestic reform had its overseas counterpart in imperial reform and Anglo-Saxonism.[43]

The point here relating to Tony Blair is that such ideas, in an evolved and more 'sophisticated' form, are back in circulation today and are winning support in leading policy circles in Britain and the US. The Blair government's attachment – albeit an initially reluctant one – to an 'ethical dimension' in foreign policy, the number of Christian socialists in its ranks – Straw, Blunkett, Brown, Boateng, etc. – provide some indication, an echo of the 'idealism' that accompanied early twentieth-century Anglo-Saxonism. Tony Blair, in his single foreign policy speech during the election campaign of 1997, had wanted to say (on the advice of his chief of staff, Jonathan Powell): 'I am proud of the British Empire', but was prevented by aides from doing so at the last minute. In the same speech, Blair declared that he would ensure that Britain 'provide[s] leadership to the world'.[44]

At another speech, as Prime Minister, to The Lord Mayor's banquet in November 1997, Blair set out his vision – 'the big picture' – for Britain and the world, so that its 'standing in the world . . . [would] grow and prosper'. Britain's principal strength is its ability to use its historical alliances so that 'others listen'. 'I value and honour our history enormously', Blair emphasized. The fact that we had an Empire – about which 'a lot of rubbish [is] talked' – should be cause of neither apology nor hand wringing; rather it must be used to further Britain's global influence – through the Commonwealth and through the power of the English language. Britain must look outward – we are the world's second largest importer and exporter of foreign investment. What goes on in the rest of the world is, therefore, of vital importance. Britain must rebuild the special relationship with the US, which the Major government had wrecked, Blair argued.

> 'When Britain and America work together on the international scene there is little we cannot achieve.' 'We must never forget the historic or continuing US role in defending the political and economic freedoms we take for granted . . . they are a force for good in the world. *They can always be relied on when the chips are down. The same should always be true of Britain'.*[45]

A sense of opportunities spurned in the Major years presented itself again in a series of essays to which Blair contributed a Foreword. In the introductory article, Mark Leonard reiterated the critique of Bush senior's dangerous attachment to 'stability – supporting discredited regimes in Yugoslavia and Somalia and leaving Saddam Hussein in power', and thereby contributing to Al-Qaeda's emergence. 'Bin Laden is an aftershock of the mistakes made after 1989', Leonard asserts. It is time to realize that the world has changed, that 9/11 offers new opportunities to rebuild the world order, to further the concept of international community and to promote security.[46]

Within Blair's circles, the Foreign Office diplomat, Robert Cooper, offers a further insight to the new thinking about world affairs. Cooper argues that the world needs a 'new liberal imperialism', an era of (voluntary) colonial rule by the world's most advanced countries – the post-modern nations – over those nations that are defined as 'pre-modern'. The latter are a threat to their own peoples – through the brutality of their rulers – to their region – due to their expansionist urges, and, ultimately, to the world – especially the West – as they may develop weapons of mass destruction and have strong links with terrorist organizations. As ever, those 'within the empire [have] . . . order, culture and civilisation. Outside it [lie] . . . barbarians, chaos and disorder.' When dealing with the pre-modern world, Cooper advocates, we will 'need to revert to the rougher methods of an earlier era – force, pre-emptive attack, *deception'.* Of course, the aims of such imperialism are purely to benefit the peoples of the world – not any search for economic or mineral resources – according to Cooper.[47] Under Blair's 'doctrine of international community', membership carries obligations and demands sacrifices as well as rights. Such are the obligations of post-modern states, like Britain and the US, in playing a leading role in the international community.

Bush, Texas and empire

That the US must take the lead in world affairs is the established view in the American foreign policy establishment of which George W. Bush is the current political figurehead. It also chimes with the world-view of his native Texas. Here is how one historian describes it:

> Texans . . . think of their homeland as an 'empire' . . . [and] if 'empire' implies not only a relative size, but *a history of conquest, expansion, and domin-ion over a varied realm, and not only an outward movement of people, but the thrust of a self-confident aggressive people driven by a strong sense of superiority and des-tiny*, then Texans can reasonably claim a strongly 'imperial' history and character.[48]

George W. Bush is a Texan steeped in the culture, folkways and habits of mind of Texas. As a result, one cannot understand the personality, political style and beliefs of George W. Bush without reference to Texan culture. But very importantly, it is the *marriage* of the east coast establishment's globalism, Texan imperialism and New York's, predominantly but not exclusively, Jewish neo-conservatives' democratizing mission, that George W. Bush represents, recasting and strengthening the social, regional, ethnic and ideological com-position of the American foreign policy establishment.

At the White House, he proceeded to recruit many of his father's own political and national security advisers to guide him in the turbulent inter-national politics of the twenty-first century. George W.'s foreign policies, how-ever, cannot entirely be laid at his father's door: the men known as 'crazies' in Bush senior's administration (1988–92), such as Paul Wolfowitz and Richard Cheney, are no longer peripheral figures but central to President Bush's strat-egy. George W. shares (many of) their neo-conservative ideas and outlook as it fits well with Texas' 'military-tinged patriotism', linking his commitment to 'minimal government at home and a bellicose foreign policy abroad with religious fundamentalism'.[49] Support for the most right-wing elements within Israel lies at the heart of southern Protestant fundamentalism.

Condoleeza Rice, Richard Cheney, Paul Wolfowitz, Richard Perle and George P. Shultz were among the most prominent advisers to Bush during campaign 2000. Bush self-deprecatingly declared in 1999 that 'I am smart enough to know what I don't know, and I have good judgement about who will either be telling me the truth, or has got some agenda that is not the right agenda.'[50] Belonging to a new right-wing think-tank, the Project for the New American

Century (PNAC), many of Bush's advisers were, and are, radical or neo-conservatives who believe in a more 'muscular and nakedly assertive' US foreign policy, including invading Iraq to overthrow Saddam Hussein, to end 'a sense of drift' in America's engagement with the world.[51] Even the so-called moderate conservative, Condoleeza Rice, was a Bush campaign co-chairwoman in California and a senior fellow at the right-wing Hoover Institution on War, Revolution and Peace. Other Hoover advisers to Bush included Shultz, Reagan's secretary of state and Martin Anderson (a former Nixon and Reagan policy adviser). Furthermore, the 'dovish' Secretary of State, Colin Powell, is a long-time champion of 'taking out' so-called rogue states. Rather than being hijacked by anyone, Bush surrounded himself with the kind of experienced people with the expertise to accomplish his own radical conservative goals to assert American power, to challenge emerging rival powers, especially China, and to deal with so-called rogue states. His links with the Hoover Institution reflect his own conservatism and anti-communism.

As presidential candidate, Bush wrote that one of the lessons of his gubernatorial experience was that a radical programme required a sense of crisis and 'bold leadership'.[52] Bush recognized that America is 'the world's only remaining superpower, and we must use our power in a strong but compassionate way to help keep the peace and encourage the spread of freedom'. 'This is still a world of terror', he wrote in *1999*, 'and missiles and madmen. And America's military is challenged by aging [*sic*] weapons, low morale, and failing intelligence. To keep the peace, we must rebuild America's military power.' The world today requires 'tough realism. . . . Firmness with regimes like North Korea and Iraq, regimes that hate our values and resent our success.'

Blair and Bush: Soul brothers?

Tony Blair and George W. Bush share much in common, therefore, in terms of some aspects of their outlook. In the realm of foreign affairs, both developed a critique of the 'years of drift', of opportunities missed after 1989, believing that such drift led to 9/11. Both argued that previous administrations had dangerously run down their nations' military power, spurned opportunities to deal with rogue states, and presided over greater global insecurity. Their pre-9/11 ideas and approaches suited them to react in the way that they did – robustly and militarily. Both also supported 'firm' action in the Middle East.

In terms of their backgrounds, Bush and Blair share a privileged private school education within schools that were rough, tough and Calvinistic, solid examples of the philosophy of muscular Christianity. Their religiosity plays a key role in their personal and political lives, as does their sense of historical mission and duty, their determination to make a difference, to change their country's position in the world and to punish aggressors and terrorists, and to reorder the world. Their political-diplomatic styles also suggest some similarities – evangelical vigour, missionary zeal, almost Manichean division of the world into friends and enemies, good and evil. Robin Cook's view was that the Bush–Blair evangelicalism is the reason for their sticking with Iraq WMD claims and Al-Qaeda links. 'Number 10 [Downing Street] believed in the intelligence because they desperately wanted it to be true. Their sin was one of . . . evangelical certainty.'[53] Their politics – Blair's centre-right affiliations in the Labour Party and Bush's 'compassionate' conservatism – also permit a degree of shared ground, especially in their notions of strengthening communities, particularly in a moral sense.

Related to their political-historical vision and backgrounds is what appears to be a neo-imperial resurgence in Anglo-America and in the thought of Bush, Blair and their respective advisers. New Liberalism and Progressivism, it must be remembered, shared an imperial agenda.[54] Behind or with Blair stand men such as Robert Cooper, Jonathan Powell and the Foreign Policy Centre (FPC), while behind and with Bush stand men (and a woman) such as Paul Wolfowitz, Condoleeza Rice and the PNAC. The Bush–Blair neo-imperial push represents a worrying development for Third World states, where most of the world's people live, for authentic international organizations, for the citizens and taxpayers of the advanced states, and for the political culture of modern democracies that grapple with running an empire on the 'rougher' methods of a bygone era, the methods of cruelty, deception, military pre-emption and preventive war.

It must be remembered, however, that Bush's and Blair's outlooks are not identical – even in foreign affairs. They came to certain conclusions about how to react after 9/11 that unified conservative nationalism – a robust military response to rid the world of Al-Qaeda and protect America – and liberal interventionism – aiming at eliminating the underlying problems of dictatorial regimes and failed states denying human rights and democratic aspirations to their people. This was a version of what Tony Smith calls 'a pact with the devil' made by liberals with militaristic conservatives, in the vain hope of using military power to extirpate human rights abusers and ethnic cleansers. The Iraq War is slowly unravelling the pact although the liberal alternatives are effectively a continuation of the war on terror using different tactics. The goals – reordering the world to suit Anglo-American interests – remain the same. Neither do their numerous similarities exhaust reasons for the levels of cooperation between Britain and the US. There are long-term strategic, economic and other interests that push Britain towards supporting the US in world affairs, and policy is made not entirely by Tony Blair – there is a large state apparatus charged with that responsibility. But as leaders go, Bush and Blair have come closely to form, represent and lead certain important tendencies within their respective state bureaucracies, and have articulated a new vision for their countries that has mobilized both the top levels of their foreign policy-making personnel, the leaders of the opposition political parties and, to varying extents, important sections of public opinion. Most importantly, they have set the domestic and global agendas: Bush's and Blair's political replacements will find, indeed Gordon Brown has found, their own range of options for change severely limited. There appears to be a strong basis for a new, enduring bipartisan foreign policy consensus behind policies of fighting terrorism that owes its origins to the strength of cooperation between Tony Blair and George W. Bush.

Notes

[1] Doyle, Michael (1983), 'Kant, liberal legacies and foreign affairs', *Philosophy & Public Affairs* 12:2 (Summer), pp. 205-235, and 12:3 (Fall), pp. 323-353.

[2] Stelzer, Irwin, ed. (2004), *Neo-Conservatism*. London: Atlantic Books, p. 112.

[3] Rentoul, John (2001), *Tony Blair. Prime Minister*. London: Time Warner, p. 44.

[4] Kampfner, John (2003), *Blair's Wars*. London: Free Press, p. 75.

[5] Kampfner, *Blair's Wars*, p. 123.

[6] Smith, Tony (2007), *A Pact with the Devil. Washington's Bid for World Supremacy and the Betrayal of the American Dream*. New York: Routledge, pp. 172–8.

[7] Smith, *A Pact with the Devil*.

[8] *The Sunday Herald (2003)*, 'Clare Short tells Blair: you are now reaping the whirlwind', p. 23.

[9] Mickelthwait, John and Wooldridge, Adrian (2005), *The Right Nation*. London: Penguin.

[10] Parmar, Inderjeet (2005), 'Catalysing events, think tanks and American foreign policy shifts: a comparative analysis of the impacts of Pearl Harbor 1941 and 11 September 2001', *Government and Opposition*, 40, 1, pp. 1-25.

[11] Kampfner, *Blair's Wars*, p. 3.

[12] Sullivan, Andrew (2003), 'Soul brothers?' *Sunday Times*, 16 November.

[13] Woodward, Bob (2003), *Bush at War*. London: Pocket Books, p. 106.

[14] Philp, Robert (1998), *A Keen Wind Blows. The Story of Fettes College*. London: James and James.

[15] Mangan, J. A., and Walvin, James, eds (1987), *Manliness and Morality*. Manchester: Manchester University Press.

[16] Philp, *A Keen Wind Blows*, p. 20; Clarke, Peter (1999), *A Question of Leadership: From Gladstone to Blair*. London: Penguin.

[17] Philp, *A Keen Wind Blows*, p. 79.

[18] Mitchell, Elizabeth (2000), *W. Revenge of the Bush Dynasty*. New York: Hyperion, p. 51.

[19] Mitchell, *W. Revenge of the Bush Dynasty*.

[20] Goldwater, Barry (1960), *The Conscience of a Conservative*. Shepherdsville, KY: Victor Publishing, pp. 86–114.

[21] Mitchell, *W. Revenge of the Bush Dynasty*, p. 64.

[22] Wilkinson, Alan (1998), *Christian Socialism. Scott Holland to Tony Blair*. London: SCM Press, p. 42.

23 Rentoul, *Tony Blair*, p. 41.
24 Conford, Philip, ed. (1996), *The Personal World. John Macmurray on Self and Society.* Edinburgh: Floris Books.
25 Conford, *The Personal World.*
26 Hall, Stuart (1988), 'State and Society, 1880–1930', in Hall, Stuart, *The Hard Road to Renewal.* London: Verso, pp. 95–122.
27 Richter, Melvin (1956), 'T.H. Green and his audience: liberalism as surrogate faith', *Review of Politics*, 18, 4, October, 467.
28 Richter, Melvin (1956), 'T.H. Green and his audience', pp. 467, 463.
29 Rentoul, *Tony Blair*, p. 1.
30 Blair, Tony (1996), *New Britain. My Vision of a Young Country.* London: Fourth Estate, p. 15.
31 Blair, *New Britain*, pp. 57–61.
32 Bryant, Christopher, ed. (1994), *Reclaiming the Ground.* London: Spire, p. 12, emphasis added.
33 Rieff, David (2003), 'Interview: Conversations with history', Institute of International Studies, University of California, Berkeley, 11 March; www.globetrotter. berekeley.edu/people3/rieff-con3 [accessed 20 September 2007].
34 Cannon, Carl (2004), 'Bush and God', *National Journal*, 3 January, 12.
35 Cannon, 'Bush and God', p. 17.
36 Lind, Michael (2003), *Made in Texas.* New York: Basic Books, p. 108.
37 Lind, *Made in Texas*, p. 109.
38 Meinig, D. W. (1969), *Imperial Texas: An Interpretative Essay in Cultural Geography.* Austin: University of Texas Press, pp. 104–5.
39 Lind, *Made in Texas*, p. 3.
40 Meinig, *Imperial Texas*, p. 89.
41 Parmar, Inderjeet (2004), *Think Tanks and Power in Foreign Policy. A Comparative Study of the Role and Influence of the Council on Foreign Relations and the Royal Institute of International Affairs, 1939–1945.* Basingstoke: Palgrave.
42 Anderson, Stuart (1981), *Race and Rapprochement. Anglo-Saxonism and Anglo-American Relations, 1895–1904.* London: Associated University Presses.
43 Catlin, George (1941), *One Anglo-Saxon Nation.* London: Andrew Dakers; Streit, Clarence (1941), *Union Now with Britain.* London: Right Book Club.
44 Kampfner, *Blair's Wars*, pp. 4, 16–17.
45 Blair, Tony (1997), *Speech by the Prime Minister Tony Blair at Lord Mayor's Banquet.* 10 November. www.number-10.gov.uk/output/Page1070.asp [accessed 20 September 2007].
46 Leonard, Mark, ed. (2002), *Re-Ordering the World.* London: Foreign Policy Centre, pp. x–xi.
47 Cooper, Robert (2002), 'The post-modern state', in Leonard (2002), *Re-Ordering the World.*
48 Meinig, *Imperial Texas*, p. 7, emphasis added.
49 Lind, *Made in Texas*, pp. x–xi.
50 Kitfield, James (1999), 'Periphery is out; Russia and China, in', *National Journal*, 7 August.
51 Parmar, Inderjeet (2005), 'Catalysing events, think tanks and American foreign policy shifts', p. 4.

[52] Bush, George W. (1999), *A Charge to Keep*. New York: Morrow; Richter, Melvin (1956), 'T.H. Green and his audience: liberalism as surrogate faith', *Review of Politics*, 18, 4, October, 224.

[53] Bush, *A Charge to Keep*; Richter, 'T.H. Green and his audience', 221; Robin Cook (2003), *The Point of Departure*. London: Simon and Schuster.

[54] Leuchtenberg, William (1952–3), 'Progressivism and imperialism: the progressive movement and American foreign policy, 1898–1916', *Mississippi Valley Historical Review*, 39.

Chapter 14

When Remoralizing Fails?

Christopher R. Baker, Elaine L. Graham and
Peter Manley Scott

The Labour government under Tony Blair's premiership (1997–2007) taxes our
usual approaches to the interpretation of politics. In 2001 – although the prepar-
ation had been long – the West entered a period that we shall call 'post-secular'.
This is both a chronological judgement but also a judgement about a renewal in
the standing of the religions in relation to public life. We are in a new epoch and
a new condition. Blair's premiership was both caught up in this transition but
also encouraged and reshaped it. Only in extended religious-moral perspective,
we claim, can this period of New Labour be adequately understood.

Of course, with this religious resurgence comes a deepening of the processes
of secularization. It is not that secularization is a tide that is on the turn, and
we should thereafter expect for the sea of faith to come rushing in. Rather, we
have multiple processes at work, often intertwined, that have often unlooked
for and sometimes contradictory results. One thing is for sure: the 'secular'
proceduralism of the liberal polity is being tested in new ways and the true
basis of society exposed more ruthlessly by the intensification of economic
and desocializing processes. It is from the perspective of this new condition –
both religious and secular – that the 1997–2007 government requires analysis
and judgement. And that analysis is made more demanding by Blair's self-
identification as a religious believer and the deployment of moral discourses
alongside political discourses.

The standard way of telling this story is to set out Blair's religious faith and
then seek either to deduce his politics from his faith or to trace the influence
of his faith on his politics. In this concluding chapter, we offer something different. To begin, we seek to explore some aspects of New Labour's efforts at
remoralizing. In the first two sections, we analyse Blair's faith in a fresh way by
asking how Blair's positioning of himself as a 'person of faith' contributed to
the remoralizing of British politics, and how his self-presentation as a religious
person changed over a period of 15 years. In the third section we explore the
theme of the *demoralizing* of British civil society. Our position on this matter
is sceptical: although New Labour came to power determined to revivify civil
society, there is plenty of evidence – some of it presented in this volume – that
across a range of policy areas there has been a weakening of civil society.

In the fourth and fifth sections, we argue that the *moralizing* of British society remains an important effort. We also consider that such an effort is both vital to long-term social well-being and is the source of self-reflexivity. Yet, we also argue that this road to moral renewal will be long and hard, and we try to identify 'short cuts' and cul-de-sacs. The religions, we conclude, will be vital to this renewal but their contribution cannot be instrumentalized to serve the ends of social happiness nor refunctionalized to deliver outcomes established by government policy.

Blair's religion: 'Remoralizing' politics

Rather than rehearsing accounts of Blair's personal faith and its putative impact on his political beliefs and actions, we begin by asking how Blair's references to religious conviction actually functioned within the broader New Labour project. In particular, how did the language of 'faith' help to construct a particular understanding of the moral dimensions of Blair's vision? This is not so much a matter of the orthodoxy or authenticity of his beliefs, but how faith served as a form of 'discourse' in constructing New Labour's moral universe.

In this analysis, we have appropriated Callum Brown's concept of 'discursive Christianity',[1] denoting an affiliation to a world-view that constructs identity and informs the performance of the self in the world. It is elaborated in the context of Callum Brown's analysis of the decline of Christianity in twentieth-century Britain in which he challenges some of the details of conventional secularization theory, while maintaining the overall trajectory of the association of modernization with the collapse of institutional religion. While other theorists focus on institutional, ideological or statistical dimensions of secularization, however, Brown concentrates on its cultural aspects, using the concept of 'discursive Christianity' to denote a complex and multifaceted world-view associated with orthodox, mainstream Christianity that transcends patterns of belief or attendance to encompass patterns of behaviour, constructions of gender identity, respectability, political and moral outlooks. It is the attenuation of discursive Christianity – and in particular its discrediting in the eyes and lives of women after the 1960s – that lies, for Brown, at the root of religious decline.

Brown's thesis has been extensively debated and questioned;[2] but for our purposes, it is his use of 'discourse' to denote the significance of religion as a vehicle of value and meaning-making that is relevant. The concept of discourse is also associated with the work of Michel Foucault, who is concerned to analyse the distinguishing features of modern thought. His aim is to elaborate a 'history of the present'[3] by which the taken-for-grantedness of social reality is revealed as contingent and constructed: 'how that-which-is has not always been'.[4] 'How things were made' depends on the archaeology of the socially sanctioned practices or techniques (of the self, of institutional power, of the generation of knowledge) through which power and authority are mediated. Foucault explores how social institutions and practices are regulated by forms of 'discourse' or the way in which certain kinds of statements function as authoritative by virtue of their effectiveness in creating a world of meaning; the critical task is to examine the conditions under which certain forms of discourse govern thought and action. Discourses create webs of meaning which order the world in particular ways: by indicating where authority is held to lie, what constitutes truth and falsehood, what is virtuous and what is reprehensible. They are sets of generative principles by which reality is ordered, or a particular world-view constructed and rendered axiomatic.

What happens when we apply the term to Blair's interventions into the public sphere? If we interpret his statements on faith not merely as an individual apologia for personal beliefs, or even a defence of the right of religion to engage with politics, but as a strategy to create particular world-views in which religion *represents* (stands in for) an appeal to a broader, but less coherent set of values.

Why was Blair prepared to take the risk of talking about God in public? As Robert Leach has argued, the resurgence of Christian socialism, which was in many respects a minority tradition within the Labour Party until the 1980s, coincided with Labour's search for a new identity of its own.[5] Despite the organizational connections between nonconformism and the Labour movement, Christian influence within the Labour Party was never predominant and never represented a coherent, homogenous body of thinking. The election of first John Smith and then Tony Blair may therefore be regarded as something of a departure from this pattern, in that not only were both active, practising Christians but also theologically articulate and prepared to claim religion as a significant part of their political and moral formation. While Leach remains sceptical about the lasting impact of Christian socialism within New Labour, he acknowledges that its true significance may have rested in its ability to facilitate a broader revival of ethical socialism within the party's thinking at the time. As Elaine L. Graham argues in her chapter, as New Labour sought to articulate its core political principles while in opposition during the early 1990s, a strong moral tenor both afforded it with a clear and principled identity uncontaminated by the taint of dogmatic socialism, as well as distancing itself from a fading Major administration perceived as corrupt and amoral. Leach agrees, although he portrays it as symptomatic of 'a wider ideological crisis within the modern party' (2002, 15), and remains sceptical of the long-term sustainability of Christian theology to inform a convincing and broad-based ethical socialism, not least because of the impact of religious pluralism.

Blair's comments on religion in relation to politics from 1992 onwards may therefore be construed as a kind of *intervention* into prevailing political discourse, at a time of considerable volatility in terms of the relationship between values and public debate. Yet beyond the rehabilitation of one particular tradition in ethical socialism, his intentions were always more broadly directed.

This is not to say that Blair or any other self-proclaimed Christian socialist within the Labour Party was insincere or calculating in their pronouncements. However, the use of the terminology of 'discourse' alerts us to the fact that such statements are doing more than simply describing a set of convictions; they are performing a political function, by importantly providing a set of publicly articulated values that were capable of inspiring support at a time when both Labour was struggling to reinvent itself and the electorate was losing touch with the old touchstones of political affiliation or ideological loyalty. This is both about one individual professing his beliefs but it is also about being able to interpret the meanings behind the sentiments and judge the effects of introducing religious language into public life.

The personal and confessional mode struck by Blair in his references to faith was, after all, quite in keeping with the cultural mood of what Garnett et al. in *Redefining Christian Britain* term 'authenticity': a turn to experiential, subjective sources of identity, sceptical of pre-packaged dogmas or institutional affiliations. This is obvious in terms of the drift away from organized religion in favour of more detached, eclectic or 'Self-religions', but may also be consistent with changes in political demography during the 1980s. In his appeal to 'Mondeo man', Blair was aware of the loosening of class loyalties in relation to voting behaviour and thus the greater importance of appealing to individual aspiration. In that context, speaking from the heart and providing a moral and religious rationale for his policies rooted in personal conviction becomes an alternative to appeals to political theories or class solidarities with which people no longer identify.

Perhaps in this respect politics, like religion, has shifted 'from a form of social engagement focused on commitment to a bounded community, to a form of consumption, focused on individual needs which may change over time'.[6] In the absence of hard and fast affiliations to the Trades Union Congress (TUC) or long-term commitment to political parties, the personal integrity of politicians comes to matter more, so Blair may have been echoing this trend towards authenticity as emphasis on the authority of his own experience and his political principles as 'performative':[7] in the absence of political or ideological preconceptions on the part of the electorate, a politician must inspire trust and win votes through his or her personal integrity.

Blair's discourse of religious conviction was, therefore, intended to be pitched into a cultural and political context of what Anthony Giddens terms 'reflexivity', as the characteristic of late modernity. In his theorization of modernity, Anthony Giddens has developed the notion of reflexivity to describe the nature of personal identity. He summarizes reflexivity as the situation in which 'social practices are constantly examined and reformed in the light of incoming information about these very practices, thus constitutively altering their character'.[8] This element of uncertainty and the collapse of foundational thinking – 'reason has lost its foundation, history its direction, and progress its allure'[9] – Giddens terms 'radicalized modernity'. Ambitions shift from the grand narrative of emancipation towards the 'life politics' of self-actualization, as political solidarities, theories of the state, the primacy of the market are all scrutinized and dissipated. Politics becomes a kind of pragmatism in which no single agent, no one cause, can direct the course of history, although there are still 'many points of political engagement which offer good cause for optimism'.[10] The Third Way, says Giddens, is about helping citizens to '*pilot their way* through the major revolutions of our time: globalization, transformations in personal life and our relationship to nature'.[11]

Within this perspective, Blair's discursive interventions are in part about a search for a reliable and coherent public language by which he can establish his, and New Labour's, political credentials. The recurrent references to values may have originated in Blair's own theological convictions, but they were intended to appeal not to a common culture of (Christian) belief but to resonate with an electorate in search of a 'moral compass' of their own.

However, there may be different phases to this, as the relationship between 'faith' and 'politics' shifted during Blair's decade in power. It was, from the early 1990s through to the General Election of 1997, about the renewal of New Labour's political fortunes that found in the legacy of Christian socialism a valuable moral depth and direction. It then shifted to become a discourse aimed at affording substance and direction to the programme of 'remoralization'. After 9/11, however, Blair found the ground shifting beneath his feet, as professions of personal conviction, formerly the solid bedrock of his public probity, fell on the stonier ground of public suspicion of 'doing God' in the face of the resurgence of religious fundamentalism.

The discourse of remoralization

As we have indicated above, from the election of John Smith as Labour Leader in 1992 Christian Socialism experienced an unparalleled surge in prominence within the Party. As one of a cohort of new Shadow ministers publicly associated with the Christian Socialist Movement, Tony Blair contributed to a number of manifestos and publications which explored the significance of Christian values for democratic socialism. Religion, and in particular the Christian social tradition, became firmly established as a central point in (New) Labour's moral compass, and Blair found in Christianity's combination of personal responsibility with community values a powerful summary of the emergent 'Third Way' between free market individualism and State centralism.[12]

Nor was Blair afraid to admit to holding religious values. Yet in the dying days of the Major administration (and by then the Leader of the Opposition) Blair wanted such values to be understood by the electorate not as something that set him apart from the tough decisions of governance but as a measure of his realism and moral robustness.[13]

By the turn of the century, and especially after 9/11, the public role of faith and so-called faith communities had come to preoccupy government more deeply. Speaking on two separate occasions to gatherings of faith leaders and activists, Blair returned to familiar themes within the remoralizing agenda – responsible, self-reliant individuals in resilient, value-rich communities – and exhorted his audience to recognize how religious faith epitomized these virtues.[14] We can detect here the beginnings of the debate about religion as a source of 'social capital', but also Blair's continuing self-representation as the sort of person who understands what it means, in the words of Margaret Archer, to 'value values'.[15]

There is a real contrast, however, between Blair's halting, diffident public statements on religion by the end of his premiership and those of the aspiring Shadow Home Secretary of a dozen years earlier. His commendation of the unambiguous merits of religion within a healthy civil society was now overshadowed by the excesses of religious extremism and the war on terror. Religion had been one means of New Labour putting the agenda of 'remoralization' to work, enabling them to maintain their occupation of the political mainstream and moral high ground. However, especially after 9/11, Tony Blair began to realize that the discourse of 'faith' no longer worked in his favour. Rather than furnishing him with a language of political trust and personal rectitude, Blair's professions of faith begin to isolate him from a more secular and increasingly sceptical electorate. Some of this new tone of circumspection has been traced earlier in Elaine L. Graham's chapter, in Alastair Campbell's anxiety at his boss's 'doing God'. Religion is now 'best not taken too far' and Blair shies away from 'preaching' as if it will brand him, as he was later to say, as some kind of 'nutter'.[16] If this is a sign of a greater hesitancy in the face of a realization of the divisive and negative potential of religion as political discourse, then it may reflect the fact that the language of faith and the invocation of religious values on the part of religious leaders and politicians had now come to be seen as an evasion of democratic accountability rather than a means of enriching our vocabulary of civic virtue. We will return to this theme later in this chapter.

As he left office, however, and the Blair decade came to an end, we could perhaps see a shift in his own discursive synthesis of religion, remoralization and politics. Increasingly, he draws a distinction between 'good' and 'bad' religion – of whatever tradition – a conviction that leads him to the establishment of his Faith Foundation in 2008.[17] From establishing New Labour's electoral credibility, and by extension, his own integrity at a time of unprecedented volatility in terms of political affiliations, Blair's religious commitments now propel him away from party policy – indeed away from domestic politics altogether – towards a fascination with religion as a universal quest for moral values that define our very humanity.[18]

Unfulfilled promises? The demoralization of Britain and the death of civil society

In this section we reflect on the impact of the remoralization agenda on British civil society as interpreted by some of our contributors. The strengthening of civil society has been a consistent domestic policy priority over New Labour's three terms, and has been expressed in concepts such as regeneration and sustainability. As both Jess Steele and Mark D. Chapman point out, these concepts have implied a more holistic approach to the issue of poverty and disadvantage, issues that traditionally have stood at the heart of Labour values and policy, but which under New Labour have taken on further nuances associated with Third Way and communitarian influences – namely the appeal to *individual responsibilities* as well as rights, the notion of a *redistribution of opportunity* (i.e. participation in a meritocracy) rather than redistributing wealth through progressive taxation, and *partnership working* (now devolved into contractual arrangements) with private business and the third sector as a way of delivering government services and policies.

At the heart of these three strands lies the moral exhortation to participate in civil society, a participation based on rediscovering a sense of the common good. That quest for the common good is one in which faith groups themselves are perceived as being at the vanguard (see, for example, Tony Blair's speech to the Christian Socialist Movement in March 2001).[19]

However, due to a number of related factors, what was originally conceived of as an enterprise in remoralization has in fact turned out to represent the partial if not complete demoralization of British civil society.

The first factor is expressed in the case-study of the one-person peace camp erected on Parliament Square by veteran anti-war campaigner Brian Haw, and for many a symbolic reference point to the rumbling public discontent about the Iraq war and other foreign policy initiatives since 2003. It was forcibly removed in 2006 but now a simulacrous version of it has been painstakingly recreated as an art installation by British artist Mark Wallinger who was awarded the 2007 £20,000 Turner Prize for this work. Brian Haw is said to have been pleased with the copy, and Wallinger has couched the genesis of his installation as a protest against the passing of the Serious Organised Crime Act of 2006 which prohibits unauthorized demonstrations within a kilometre of the Houses of Parliament, and which in his opinion contravenes the public right to protest enshrined in the Magna Carta.[20]

Despite these 'protest' intentions however, establishment recognition (in the form of the Turner prize) for Wallinger's piece suggests a neutralizing of the political power of Haw's protest with its removal from the public space and a replica of it inserted into more privatized and rarefied cultural space of the art gallery. Wallinger's artistic representation of Haw's peace camp thus raises the complex and contested nature of any retrospective account of the impact of Blair's domestic and foreign policies on civil society.

The second factor for consideration is the recurring motif from our contributors who relate how the general pattern of early promise and potentially radical policy and reform with respect to strengthening the autonomy of civil society became neutralized by increasingly regressive and centralizing tendencies. Jess Steele, for example, highlights the narrative curve within community and urban regeneration which moves from a genuine empowerment model based on holistic, bottom-up methodologies (e.g. New Deal for Communities programme) to a more narrowly focused policy on the 'respect agenda' and the personalizing of the environmental focus on clean and sustainable communities in terms of '"asbo" youth, problem families and hostile mutterings about immigration' (p. 97)'. She reminds us that this more authoritarian shift in domestic policy coincided with the demise of the excellent instruments established in Blair's first term to help in the delivery of structural analysis and radical policy – for example, the Social Exclusion Unit, Neighbourhood Renewal Unit and the No. 10 Strategy Unit. In her view, the high point of a genuinely collaborative and empowering local community policy were the years from 1999 to 2001 (p. 107) after which was the Northern towns riots, 9/11, the war in Iraq and 7/7 and arguably the period when the Manichean, good and evil view of the world expressed in Blair's foreign policy (see Parmar in this volume) was translated into the domestic sphere. The rhetoric identifying those nation-states opposed to the Western values of liberal democracy and consumerist-based civil society was now applied to local neighbourhoods in the UK who were considered to be beyond the influence of meritocratic and government-sponsored self-help by dint of the lifestyle choices being made. In other words, poverty, ill-health, poor education, low levels of civic engagement, became interpreted in terms of personal deficiency rather than the impact of structural inequality.[21]This personalizing of structural agendas is echoed in the observations of Emily Hicks and her chapter in which she reflects on the way that the theme of the deserving and undeserving poor find contemporary resonances in the Sure Start programme and its emphasis on 'disciplining' parents into employment.

In his chapter, Mark D. Chapman makes a similar point with regard to the way the concepts of community, multiculturalism and social cohesion are coalesced around a strongly centralized and functionalist rhetoric that 'flattens' complexity and diversity and subverts notions of genuine local democracy and participation. For example, he observes that at no point is the idea of community expanded beyond very simple references to a specific geographical space. 'Despite using the word "community" 134 times throughout the document, the Government's lengthy Sustainable Communities five-year plan nowhere offers a definition of community beyond a geographical place. The closest it comes to any clarity is where it differentiates communities from neighbourhoods ("the areas which people identify with most")' (p. 127 of this volume).

However, and this is our third factor, it is the culture of management which has also ultimately eaten away at the values base supporting real bottom-up community empowerment. Gerry Stoker has written elsewhere of the paradox of the Third Way of New Labour governance[22] – especially at the local level, where this paradox is played out between the twin and ultimately irreconcilable aims of citizens as consumers and the need to produce predictable 'market' outcomes (in the form of compliance to budgets, hitting floor targets etc. and including incentives to local community groups and local authorities who outperform others in the delivery of government-sponsored legislation).

At the heart of this paradox is the notion of the 'new localism'. New localism acknowledges the changed social and political landscape mapped by Jess Steele in her chapter – that is, the decline of 'modernist' government based on representative democracy and an expert bureaucracy, and the rise of the individual citizen as consumer who is naturally sceptical of any authority, and whose political engagement has to be 'bought' with a complex system of incentives and responsibilities that give the impression of choice and local control. However, the strong managerial element that New Labour inherited from the Conservatives, whereby central government maintains control of funding streams and sets timetables and targets for reform ensures that a competitive, market-driven approach is maintained. Stoker likens this 'centrally incentivized' approach to 'a lottery in which a complex variety of prizes have been offered to successful reformers, but where the selection of winners reflects a complex mix of their capacity and chance'.[23]

Chris Baker has commented elsewhere that if this sense of community engagement, enshrined in snappy titles like 'new localism', is perceived as taking part in a lottery, then this will counteract genuine attempts at building up a sense of trust in political networks.[24] There is always a potential for tension within a system of governance that proclaims a rhetoric of local control and autonomy (namely, a horizontal approach) while applying a framework of central managerial control (a vertical approach) – a lack of trust which if Steele with her 'insider' view is correct, has corroded the sense of expectation and hope for real change especially for those most marginalized.

So what does Mark Wallinger's 'representation' of Brain Haw's peace camp and the insights of our contributors such as Steele, Stoker and Chapman tell us about the sources of demoralization rather than remoralization of Britain and civil society?

First, there are the mixed messages in the early years of New Labour concerning the relinquishing of authority and responsibility from the centre to the periphery. Even within the high water mark of Blair's first term, bold and radical ideas enshrined within the workings of the New Deal for Communities programme (for example) were mired in confusions and overelaborate bureaucracy which underestimated the ability of local communities to absorb the language and patterns of economic regeneration and public planning. Meanwhile, the years since the millennium have seen a narrowing of the rhetoric and a tighter reinforcement of the market as the mechanism to encourage or coerce (depending on your stance) civil society to deliver public services according to government targets. If Habermas was right to describe civil society as 'the force resisting the colonisation of the life-world by the functional imperatives of state and market', and therefore of prime importance to the functioning of democracy,[25] then clearly that force has been invaded even more by the norms and values of the market.

Second, the Wallinger installation represents two further dynamics contributing to the erosion of civil society. One is the fact that the 2006 anti-terrorist legislation banning any unauthorized public demonstration (however small and peaceful) within a 1 kilometre exclusion zone around the Palace of Westminster is a serious impediment to more critical or spontaneous expressions of civil protest or disobedience. The second is the subliminal way in which the agenda of cultural regeneration and its role in the rebranding of city centres creates an impact on local sites of memory and resistance (e.g. the massive regeneration of Liverpool city centre as part of its successful bid to become European City of Culture 2008 and the erasure of key sites of public gathering and free entertainment within the regeneration area).[26] While Wallinger's explicit aim was to draw attention to the draconian way in which the civil right to peaceful protest had been short-circuited in the name of public safety legislation, the implicit outcome as we have already inferred, has been the neutralizing of public protest and its withdrawal into the privatized space of an art gallery. People are now invited to engage with the issues of the Iraq war primarily via an individual gaze on a piece of art (and the detached reflexivity that implies) rather than in the unpredictable and public setting on the green directly opposite the seat of political power. The outcomes of civil society, as well as being increasingly encroached upon by the market in the Blair and Brown era, appear to be also increasingly depoliticized by the dynamics of the cultural regeneration.

Finally, we should not discount the stark fact that for all the well-intentioned initiatives enabling local autonomy and building up a strong civil society, the Blair decade has seen the very acceleration of forces of social division rather than social cohesion. This increased social and economic polarization militates against the participation of the most marginalized communities in civil society. For example, statistics from the 2005 Citizenship Survey showed that deprivation halves the propensity of citizens to volunteer formally in their community.

In the least deprived ten per cent of areas (as defined by the Index of Multiple Deprivation), 38 per cent of people had participated in formal voluntary activities at least once a month in the 12 months before interview, compared with 19 per cent of people living in the most deprived ten per cent of areas.[27]

In an article critical of the Blair social legacy,[28] Danny Dorling highlights statistical analysis of five measures of well being (including life expectancy, university education, Jobseekers Allowance/Income Support claims, poverty levels and average house prices) over a period 1997 to 2003 across a sample of 50 English cities and towns. The cities and towns are arranged into five leagues. These statistics show an increasing regional divide, with almost all Southern cities located within the Premier league or Division One. Division Two downwards is dominated by towns and cities from the North (with the exception of York which shows the characteristics of a Southern enclave). Certain cities like Blackburn, Hull, Sunderland and Liverpool are even below Division Four. Dorling then goes on to supply further detailed data under each of the five categories of well-being to highlight the statistical evidence of growing polarization. For example, under the heading of poverty, he refers to the fact that in the Eurostat 2005 data, Britain had the 25th highest level of child poverty out of 26 other European countries (only the Slovak Republic performed more poorly).[29]

The overall impact of these dynamics has been to hollow out the language of civil society. Not only have concepts such as 'regeneration', 'community', 'sustainability', remained vague and overused, causing a blurring of meanings and values, but other significant indicators of a healthy civil society such as 'diversity' and 'social cohesion' have been reduced to a tick-box formula by the injudicious mixing of market methodologies and bureaucratic outcomes.

Do these dynamics represent the death-knell of civil society? Probably not. There is always counter-evidence to show increased activity in pockets of civil society engagement, particularly over environmental issues, for example, or the growth of volunteering in the over sixty-fives.[30] There is also the suggestion that some of the Generation Y citizens of the future (i.e. those born since the early 1980s) are rejecting the feverish work-ethic of their parents in favour of the right to spend more time in travel and the search for a values-driven basis to their lives which, it is contended, leads to increased participation in voluntary or vocational work in gap years or even as part of work packages. Other evidence for the current health or otherwise of British civil society is more ambiguous, however. Official government statistics in the form of the biennial Citizenship Survey show that volunteering levels have flatlined (i.e. 2005 reported levels of volunteering are almost identical to those recorded in 2003). Although the headline figures appear high (20.4 million people in England volunteered in 2005),[31] the definitions of what volunteering involves points to a fairly low benchmark. Thus, for example, in the category of informal volunteering (defined as 'giving unpaid help as an individual to people who are not relatives at least once a month')[32] the highest category of participation (52%) was simply 'giving advice'. For formal volunteering (defined as 'giving unpaid help through groups, clubs or organisations to benefit other people or the environment'),[33]the two highest categories of participation were organizing or helping to run an activity or event (54%) or raising/handling money/taking part in sponsored walks (52%).[34]

So the thesis of an inexorable decline in civil society hastened by the Blair revolution is probably a complex and contested one. However, the emerging consensus from this book is that after ten years of Blairism, after a positive and committed start, the dynamics associated with an increasingly moralistic and market-driven Third Way have left a civil society probably more demoralized than remoralized.

Moralizing society

In the first two sections, we have noted the discursive interventions in their diversity made by Blair regarding faith. Vital here are certain values: equality of regard and, despite differences, equality of consideration; responsibility (and, later, respect); and the self in community. In the third section, we offered some comments on the health of civil society. This should come as no surprise as civil society may be regarded as the place of generation of values as well as their operation, so to speak. And civil society bears some relationship to community. At the beginning of this chapter, we offered a tentative distinction between *remoralizing* and *moralizing*. In these final two sections, we develop this distinction a little further by expanding on the theme of moralizing.

Since Blair's departure, reference to values in the New Labour programme has been maintained but has thinned a little. Gordon Brown's favourite list now includes decency, respect and toleration. Which begs an 'elephant in the room' question: why bother with a rhetoric of values at all? Why should a government not instead concentrate on effective delivery of outcomes as required by agreed policy objectives? 'It's the results, stupid!'

One answer to this question is offered by Simon Critchley: '[T]here is a motivational deficit at the heart of liberal democratic life, where citizens experience the governmental norms that rule contemporary society as externally binding but not internally compelling.'[35] One of the reasons for this state of affairs might be the reflexivity that we discussed in the first section: citizens are more and more concerned to pilot their own way, according to their own expressive desires. Some of the time they experience the administrations of government as thwarting or reshaping or encouraging those expressions. At other times – and we are presently in such a time – citizens call on governments to help them satisfy their desires: if the cost of energy and the price of food rises sharply, better and moderately off citizens are blocked from consuming in ways to which they have become accustomed – and call upon the state as 'Big Daddy' to enable them to consume again.

One aspect of the appeal to values is therefore a response to social complexity. To make a late-modern society in all its complexity work effectively requires proactive government in a permanent effort of development-and-repair. For the citizenry to be accepting of this effort requires some agreement both on the ends of society, and on procedures for realizing those ends. At this point, the appeal to values is at least intelligible, if not persuasive. For values identify both goals and ways of working.

The problem is that these values are not available; or, if available, then not widely acceptable. The values maintained by some religious subgroups, and which are found to be compelling by these subgroups, are to most others alien and abhorrent. That is, forms of furious religion, whether Christian or Muslim, are deeply motivational; there is no motivational deficit here. The difficulty, of course, apart from the body count that seems always to follow, is that these bearers of religious values are opposed to the liberal, secular state. A motivational surplus threatens the liberal secular state. This is too much for most citizens and the state, and the state tries to negotiate a middle way between too little motivation and too much; between a hollow secularity and a religious 'fundamentalism'.

The issue here is thereby different from how it is usually presented. For example, as we have reported, Leach regards it is as unlikely that theology can offer support of, let alone a basis for, the renewal of an ethical socialism, on account of religious pluralism. Theology is identified with one religious tradition, and Britain is now a multireligious country. For theology to offer such a basis appears to privilege Christianity. On our analysis the issue is different. What matters is the strength of the values (their surplus) and their capacity to overcome motivational deficit, and the substantial relation between the values and the secular, liberal polity. These are the vital issues. It is not that there is a competition between religious communities over values. (There may be but that is not pertinent here.) The issue is that the state wishes to administer even values: they must not threaten civic order by being 'too strong' and they must be containable within the procedures of the secular state. Values may aid negotiation but are not themselves a matter for negotiation.

On the view we are sketching here, the call for a return to Christian or biblical values, of the sort demanded by some bishops in the Church of England,[36] simply reinforces the competition between values, and thereby reinforces the power of the state. For if there is competition between values, and thereby between the communities that bear those values, then it is the state's power as adjudicator that is reinforced. For the state offers itself as the referee of this competition. Often the Church – especially an established church – is only too glad to be part of this competition in that it does at least mean being noticed by the state on terms acceptable to the state. Yet, as Richard Roberts puts it, there is a loss here also: we have a 'displacement of the universality of the gospel onto the rhetorical level of "serving the nation" largely through political intervention'.[37]

From the theological perspective being developed here, the issue is discovered neither in a call for (a return to?) biblical values nor a self-censorship based in a multicultural niceness. Instead, the issue is the universality of the gospel. Put differently, the issue is not that of a competition between values held by differing religious groups – with the occasional intervention by an atheist declaring a plague on all your houses. Instead, the competition is between values in the service of 'managerialism', 'inclusion' etc. and values in the service of divinity.

In that such a claim will immediately be misunderstood, we wish to proceed carefully at this point. We have already noted that the complexity of a modern society requires much administration as a response to its complexity. Through this, a motivational deficit is evident. This means in turn that there is a practical problem concerning political legitimacy. It needs only a moment's thought to realize how calamitous such a situation is – consider the demand for intelligent moral engagement that averting the worst effects of anthropogenic climate change will require. Such engagement cannot proceed by way of a motivational deficit because in all likelihood this engagement will require fresh ways of living. And confronting such a deficit is an ethical issue: in what ways should we change, and for what reasons? This is the stuff of ethics.

Faith and the public sphere

So the 'remoralizing Britain' agenda is right at least to the extent that a people's assent – if it is to be the assent of a *people*, of a *populus* – requires a collective will resourced by a shared sense of mutual obligation or, at least, answerability. What are the sources of this shared sense, and how are citizens inducted into it? (Is the implied passivity of induction enough, or should citizens be formed through it by means of a pedagogy of 'handing-on'?) As has been noted by commentators, values like toleration and decency are too thin and abstract to counter such motivational deficit.[38] And it is to its credit that the programme to remoralize Britain noted this fact and so appealed to a longer list of values and made reference to Blair's personal faith.

However, such appeals to universality are regarded with suspicion. Consider the best example from recent British history. In his lecture on 'Civil and

Religious Law in England', given in February 2008 at the Inns of Court, Rowan Williams suggested ways of connecting Islamic or Sharia law with civil law.[39] And he tried to indicate that freedom of religious conscience is a public matter that requires some adjustment in the public realm. In making this argument, the Archbishop was acknowledging a religious quality of our politics: the polity of UK 2008 is partly based in a heterogeneity of religious traditions that many of us – and especially policy makers – find uncomfortable. Yet, if these religious traditions are here to stay, and if the liberal state is not about to shut up shop, then some public negotiation between religious traditions and the state is *unavoidable* if some measure of social cohesion is to be worked for. This was argued by a *Christian* theologian and Archbishop and yet with reference to *Islam*. On the day after Rowan Williams' lecture, the BBC's Home Affairs editor Mark Easton suggested that the Archbishop's lecture was 'self-interested'. In other words, that the Archbishop's interest in concerning himself with Muslim communities was because he wanted in the end to claim some similar privileges for Christian communities. The Archbishop unmasked!

However, could it be that Williams was drawing on a particular theological resource – present differently in Judaism and Christianity – that is opposed to the religious cult? This resource is a transcending universalism in which the religious cult is placed in God's wider purposes in salvation. The cult is never denied, of course, but neither is salvation restricted to the cult. This lack of restriction would be one way of speaking of the universality of the gospel. And we should note that the unity of the civil law in England was interpreted in a very odd way. Williams argued that the law was universally applicable, but could perhaps have multiple bases and operate overlapping jurisdictions. The response by some politicians was to affirm 'one country, one law'. Yet this is not a conclusion that can be deduced from the phenomenon of the civil law itself. To affirm a single jurisdiction for a single territory takes us into the extra-legal realm of jurisprudence. Yet those advocating this 'unity' position were not pressed to disclose what interest their position served. (And the answer to that question is easy – the unity position serves the interest of the politician-as-manager.)

Yet under the present conditions of modernity, the matter of a transcending universalism is only part of the difficulty. If there are to be religious contributions to moralizing Britain, what are these contributions, and from which religious traditions will they come?

Are we to say that the ethical substance of the modern state is to be provided by a homogeneous people bound together in one religious tradition? Given that our British-European circumstance today is after Christendom, that hardly seems convincing. We have a society peopled by a range of religious traditions, and by traditions that claim not to be religious. And yet our circumstance may also be post-secular in that religious communities are still active and determined to make a political contribution. If then there should be a

religious basis to society, and yet our society is religiously plural, how shall we
understand this religious basis? This, it seems to us, is the very difficult issue
that Williams has stumbled across. First, he is maintaining that a society has a
religious basis – much to the consternation of the liberal state. And, second,
he is then raising the question of what a heterogeneous, multiple, plural religious basis might be.

Of course, the obvious objection to our line of argument is to maintain that
society does not have, and does not need, a religious basis. It is to his great
credit that Blair sensed the vacuity of this position. For where will values come
from – values that do not pose as falsely universal and mask or present sectional
interests? There are no easy answers to this question or obvious candidates.
Given our European history of fascism, *community* seems an unlikely answer.
The *state* threatens values as well as encouraging them: its work as guarantor
of values should not be confused with the work of the construction of values.
Law, as we have just seen, is not neutral. *Patriotism* – love of country – has long
been a strong purveyor of values but we are of course in a discussion of values
at present precisely because we are no longer sure what 'country' means.[40]

Moreover, the difficulty here – and it is a religious difficulty – is that without
reference to the universality of the gospel, values can quickly appear parochial. Consider the following aphorism from Samuel Taylor Coleridge:

> He who begins by loving Christianity, better than truth, will proceed by lov-
> ing his own sect or church better than Christianity, and end in loving him-
> self better than all.[41]

For Coleridge, to fail to attend to the truth is to enter a spiral that becomes
narrower and narrower until it ends in a narcissistic love of self. This movement from loving a religion to self-regard can of course be replicated in the
political sphere. As Daniel Hardy notes, it is easy enough to rewrite Coleridge's
aphorism in political terms thus:

> He who begins by loving the nation, better than truth, will proceed by lov-
> ing his own group better than the nation, and end in loving himself better
> than all.[42]

Put more sharply: without the universality of the truth there is the permanent
risk of political narcissism. And the nastiest form of such narcissism is fascism.
In this way, we may appreciate that both Christianity and the Nation are relative
to the truth. And for theology, that truth is the truth of God. Both Christianity
and the Nation may be understood as mediators of the truth of God.

Of course, theology has settled ways of enquiring about such mediations.
As Terry Eagleton has recently recommended, theology's traditional questions include: 'Who are we? Where are we from? Can there be love among

humans? What in the end do we want? What is the nature of our desire?'[43] We should note that posing questions such as these bears no relation to theocracy. For religious communities, the question should not be: how shall we achieve power? The religious question is to ask after the truth of God in our social life. In connection with justice, the religious issue might be formulated like this: What is divine justice in a (violently) disordered world, and through what actions should religious communities bear witness to this divine justice? Or, what social forms best display or perform this divine justice? To moralize in this context is thereby to begin a debate about forms of sociality.

Of course, it is possible for the liberal state, and members of the liberal polity, to hear this only 'negatively'. The analysis might go like this: The way that YHWH/God takes form in this world is by way of social events, then attempts by Western, liberal societies to ignore or sideline Christianity, and the other Abrahamic faiths, must be a mistake. This divinity is a socializing divinity, and so cannot be easily privatized. On such a view, societies neglect theistic religions – their self-understanding and practitioners – at their peril. It is certainly possible for the liberal state to hear this as a threat: a 'religious' problem to be managed.

However, another path is possible: this religious quest for the truth of God in forms of sociality should be taken not as a threat but rather an invitation to explore forms of sociality other than that provided by liberal societies. As Catholic philosopher Charles Taylor has argued, liberal society is a form of sociality and not only a procedural device. A social order is a moral order: 'It tells us something about how we ought to live together in society.'[44] We should therefore expect any society that is interested in the truth of its social life to be engaged in a vigorous debate over forms of sociality, including the liberal.[45] This is the agenda of moralizing politics that we wish to affirm. Of course, this moralizing politics is not comfortable: reference to God remains a powerful force for both social stability and instability. As German Lutheran theologian Dietrich Bonhoeffer once observed: the divine commandment can 'demand the most radical destruction simply for the sake of the one [*sc.* Christ] who builds up'.[46]

Although it may not be comfortable, and it may be hard to grasp what this moralizing work is, one thing is certain: it is not theocracy. Moralizing in this theological discussion refers to work to secure

> the overall quality of a society which at its best has a supportive and enabling culture, a culture whose root paradigms are intact and capable of comprehending both differentiation into particularities and universals which hold the human together in the ancestral sense of a *religio*, a mutual binding informed by a gospel of grace and truth.[47]

Yet, such a quality cannot be imposed because such an imposition is destructive and disabling of a culture. Such a quality must somehow be acquired or learned. And that process of learning is concerned with relating such a quality to the truth of God in social forms through efforts to renew social forms, and debating the character and quality of alternatives.

One implication here is that the Church is always a social form, and a polity is always religious.[48] Interlinked forms of sociality provide the connections here. The issue here is not: how may the polity be commandeered as a vehicle for the maintenance of religious meanings?[49] Instead, the vital question is anti-theocratic: the polity is already seen as bearer of religious meanings and does not need to be commandeered. Instead, the question is: what is the relationship between the social form of the Church (understood how?) and the social form of the polity (understood how?)? And, of course, what is given by and with both forms is God's activity in the world: God's social life in human social lives.

Moralizing society may be interpreted, with apologies to Raymond Williams, as a phase in the 'long religious revolution'. This long religious revolution – rooted in the life of biblical Israel and YHWH's claim on a covenanted people – has certain achievements to its credit. One achievement of this revolution is the separation of church and state by which the omni-competence of the state is called into question. José Casanova argues that both historically and theoretically social freedoms are begun in the freedom of religious conscience.[50] Although Casanova does not precisely say so, this must mean something like: religious conscience is based on an appeal to an alternative jurisdiction, and all other freedoms – such as freedom of association, freedom of assembly, freedom of religion – require the positing of an alternative jurisdiction. To call for a *religio* in this context is then – in part at least – a defence of the liberal polity. In its self-attested efforts to enable citizens' desiring rather than direct their lives, such a polity is one of the achievements – although not an unambiguous one – of the long religious revolution.

In the search for the truth of God in human social life, invoking a limit on the competence of the state is an important achievement in this long religious revolution. This revolution however continues, and faces a new problem. We may put the issue sharply: must a *religiously plural* polity fall apart?[51] Above, we wrote freely of the quality of a society, an intact, enabling culture, and the capacity to negotiate universals and particularities. Yet how is that now possible when reference to a gospel of grace and truth is rendered problematic by the presence in one society of many religious traditions? British society, we sometimes say, is post-Christian. Is not the very notion of a 'gospel of grace and truth' itself outdated?

A theological response at this point cannot be content with a gesture to the Christian nature of nations in Western Europe. It is not enough to say that the history of Europe is Christian, and that this historical legacy should be respected. That is, an adequate response must be religious-theological, and not only historical. We do not have space to offer a full response. However, in these closing remarks, we stress two vital matters that are part of the response to the question: must a religiously plural polity fall apart?

First, in relation to a gospel of grace and truth, how might toleration be understood? In our references to a gospel, have we ruled out toleration? Or, if that is too strong, have we not provided the conditions for the growth of intolerance? Our answer to this objection is to insist on an earlier point: a religion is always relative to the truth of that religion and, in theological perspective, that truth is held, so to speak, by God. In this sense, a true religion must always work to extend its cultural-community basis. It will never succeed of course in that some of its vitality is derived from its roots in a community. But that is not its only source. The sources of a religious tradition are to be found in God's diverse activity to which any particular religious tradition is relative. In that relativity is to be found epistemic uncertainty and there also resides toleration. (Liturgical performance is a good example: in worship, religious communities claim to be bound into divinity and yet in granting worth to divinity (worship is the granting of worth) also acknowledge their distance from God.) A religiously plural polity need not fall apart through intolerance.

Second, if a religion should always work to question its cultural-community basis, how might that be achieved? To begin an answer, we should not think of the religions as represented by a cluster of competing communities who offer strong proposals to overcome motivational deficit. That is to reduce these communities to their cultural identifiers and to set them in competition with each other. That Rowan Williams exposed this myth of competition was the beauty of his lecture on Sharia law: he spoke as the leader of an *established* church in a post-Christian nation for the expansion of civil law to incorporate religious traditions of law *other than* the Christian. Of course, this exposure infuriated the commissariat of the liberal state as the lecture declared one of the state's tasks to be an invention that in turn legitimized its power.

Additionally, Williams's choice of the law was a good one for the law is one of the practices in a polity's 'broken middle', to borrow Gillian Rose's phrase. Put differently, it is in this middle that exchange and negotiation within a polity are carried on, and in which certain notions of social life are invested. If law is one of these areas, then others include the creation and distribution of wealth, the security of embodiment (including health), the quality of administrative bureaucracy (including the security of information) and our multidependencies on nature. It is these inescapable areas – this is our suggestion – that religious traditions might commit themselves to developing. And these areas are *theologically* inescapable for political forms of sociality are given with religious forms of sociality, and both are relative to the sociality of God. The polity would remain religiously plural but committed to renewing those practices in which all, in a diversity of ways, share.

The moralizing of a Western, post-Christendom, liberal polity-nation, it seems to us, might proceed in some such fashion. The way is not easy nor is it comfortable; nor can there be any certainty that divisiveness, and the consequent temptation to commit violence, will be avoided. That much can be learned from a careful reading of the chapters in this volume. Yet these chapters also highlight the importance of the agenda of the *moralizing* of a polity. The interaction between religion and politics will not go away. Nor should we want it to. Salvation universalizes and power concretizes; yet salvation that is not concrete is ineffective or hyper-utopian; and power that does not universalize is 'mere business' (Max Horkheimer). And who would wish to live in a polity that lives out of a fantasy or reworks all of life into technical administration? Thus the non-religious also have a stake in this moralizing agenda. We hope that the chapters presented in this volume make some contribution to the clarification of that agenda.

Notes

1   Brown, Callum (2000), *The Death of Christian Britain*, London: Routledge.
2   Garnett, J. et al., eds (2006), *Redefining Christian Britain*, London: SCM Press.
3   Foucault, M. (1977), *Discipline and Punish: The Birth of the Prison*, London: Allen Lane, p. 31.
4   Foucault, M. (1983), 'Structuralism and Post-Structuralism: An Interview with Gerard Raulet', *Telos* 55, 195–211, 206).
5   Leach, Robert (2002), 'The historical and contemporary significance of Christian socialism within the Labour party', [online], Political Studies Association, 5–7 April, available at: www.psa.org.uk (accessed 20 May 2008).
6   Garnett et al., *Redefining Christian Britain*, p. 63.
7   Garnett et al., *Redefining Christian Britain*, pp. 73–112.
8   Giddens, A. (1990), *The Consequences of Modernity*, Cambridge: Polity Press, p. 38.
9   Bryant, Christopher G. A. and Jary, David (2000), 'Anthony Giddens', in G. Ritzer, ed., *The Blackwell Companion to Major Social Theorists*, Oxford: Blackwell, p. 683.
10 Giddens, A. (1994), *Beyond Left and Right: The Future of Radical Politics*, Cambridge: Polity Press, p. 21.
11 Giddens, A. (1998), *The Third Way: The Renewal of Social Democracy*, Cambridge: Polity Press, p. 64, emphasis added.
12   [T]he values of democratic socialism, founded on a belief in the importance of society and solidarity with others, are closely intertwined with those of Christianity – hardly surprising in view of the Christian beliefs of many of the Labour Party's historical and present-day members . . .
        However, it is also a powerful compass for the direction of change in our country. The new agenda in politics will reach out past old debates between economic ideologies of State control and *laissez-faire* and embrace different issues. . . . These issues must derive from some political values and we are as well to be sure of what they are.
        A return *to what we are really about, what we believe in*, would be a healthy journey for our country as well as the Labour Party.

It would also help us comprehend more fully the importance of personal responsibility in our lives and its relationship to society as a whole. . . . It places a duty, an imperative on us to reach *our better self* and to care about creating a *better community* to live in. (Blair, Tony (1993), 'Foreword' in Christopher Bryant, ed. *Reclaiming the Ground: Christianity and Socialism*, London: Hodder & Stoughton, pp. 10–12, emphasis added).

13   I can't stand politicians who wear God on their sleeves; I do not pretend to be any better or less selfish than anyone else; I do not believe that Christians should only vote Labour; and I do not discuss my religious beliefs unless asked, and when I do, I discuss them personally . . .

Christianity is optimistic about the human condition, but not naive. It can identify what is good, but knows the capacity to do evil. I believe that the endless striving to do the one and avoid the other is the purpose of human existence. Through that comes progress. (Blair, Tony (1996), 'Why I am A Christian', *Sunday Telegraph* 7 April).

14   'The values at the heart of politics are best expressed in the idea of "community"; a belief in the equal worth of all; and the responsibility of all to play their part: "Opportunity to all; responsibility from all".' (Blair, Tony (2000), 'Values and the Power of Community', Tübingen, pp. 4–5).

Today's theme of faith in politics is I suppose, at its most basic level, about the importance of values in politics and public life. Politics without values is sheer pragmatism and values without politics can often be ineffective, so the two have to go together. . . . Your local and your social activity is driven by your values and beliefs in the spiritual dimension of your faith. And the one thing I'm sure of is that, as the world around us becomes ever more transformed by globalisation and technology, to make sure there is some guiding sense of values becomes ever more important. . . . So I think this concept of values and value-driven politics is more important than ever before. And it is based, certainly for me, on the concept of community. (Blair, Tony (2001), *Faith in Politics*, ed. Graham Dale, London: Christian Socialist Movement, pp. 12–13).

15   Archer, Margaret (2007), *Making Our Way through the World: Human Reflexivity and Social Mobility*. Cambridge: Cambridge University Press, p. 230.

16   BBC Television (2007), *The Blair Years*. 2 December. See also Elaine L. Graham, this volume, p. 5.

17   In this world, religious faith, crucial to so many people's culture and identity, can play a positive or a negative role. . . . In this context, interfaith action and encounter are vital. They symbolise peaceful co-existence. That is my primary argument. However, I then go further, and argue that religious faith is a good thing in itself: that, so far from being a reactionary force, it has a major part to play in shaping the values which guide the modern world, and can and should be a force for progress. (Blair, Tony (2008), 'Faith and Globalisation' lecture, Westminster Cathedral, 3 April).

18   'Faith is not something separate from our reason, still less from society around us, but integral to it, giving the use of reason a purpose, and society a soul, and human beings a sense of the divine.' Ibid.

19   Faith communities play a fundamental role in supporting and propagating
        values which bind us together as a nation . . . looking outwards to the need
        of others, beyond your own immediate members is the prime expression of
        your beliefs and values. And in carrying out this mission, you have developed
        some of the most effective voluntary and community organizations in the
        country. (Blair, Tony (2001), *Faith in Politics*, ed. Graham Dale, London:
        Christian Socialist Movement, pp. 12–13.)

20   Higgins, Charlotte (2007), 'Wallinger takes Turner prize with recreation of Par-
        liament Protest', *Guardian* (4 December), available at www.guardian.co.uk/
        uk/2007/dec/04/art.artnews (accessed 12 June 2008).

21   BBC website (2007) 'Blair calls for lifestyle change' (26 July). For example, in a
        speech on public health in Nottingham, Blair argued that, from the perspective
        of the limited resources of the NHS to continue to fund illnesses linked to obes-
        ity, smoking and alcohol abuse public health problems were

        not, strictly speaking, public health problems at all. They are questions of indi-
        vidual lifestyle – obesity, smoking, alcohol abuse, diabetes, sexually transmitted
        disease . . . these are not epidemics in the epidemiological sense – they are the
        result of millions of individual decisions, at millions of points in time. http://
        news.bbc.co.uk/1/hi/uk_politics/5215548.stm (accessed 12 June 2008).

22   Stoker, G. (2004), *Transforming Local Governance: From Thatcherism to New Labour*.
        Basingstoke: Palgrave Macmillan.

23   Stoker, *Transforming Local Governance*, p. 69.

24   Baker, C. (2007), *The Hybrid Church in the City – Third Space Thinking*. Aldershot:
        Ashgate, p. 60.

25   Habermas Jurgen (1987) *The Theory of Communicative Action Volume II: System and
        Lifeworld*. Cambridge: Polity.

26   Bradbury, John and Glasson, Barbara (2006), 'Liverpool – the lived experience
        of culture' in *Cities of Culture: Whose Vision, Which Agenda?* – the report of pro-
        ceedings from the inaugural conference of the Core Cities Theological Network
        held at Scargill House 12–14 September 2005, [online] Core Cities Theological
        Network, available at: www.cctn.org.uk (accessed 12 June 2008).

27   Department of Communities and Local Government (DCLG) (2006), *2005 Citi-
        zenship Survey – Active Communities Topic Report*, HMSO, p. 8.

28   Dorling, Danny (2006), 'Inequalities in Britain 1997–2006: the dream that
        turned pear-shaped', in *Local Economy*, vol. 21, no 4, pp. 353–61.

29   Dorling, D. (2006), p. 359.

30   Halpern, David (2005), *Social Capital*, Cambridge and Malden, MA: Polity Press,
        p. 203.

31   DCLG, HMSO, p. 2.

32   DCLG, HMSO, p. 4.

33   DCLG, HMSO, p. 6.

34   DCLG, HMSO, p. 7.

35   Critchley, Simon (2007), *Infinitely Demanding: Ethics of Commitment, Politics of
        Resistance*. London: Verso, p. 7.

36   The interventions of Michael Nazir-Ali, Anglican Bishop of Rochester UK, are
        here exemplary. See his 'Breaking Faith in Britain', *Standpoint Magazine* (June 2008),

to be found at www.standpointmag.co.uk/breaking-faith-with-britain (accessed 4 June 2008).

37 Roberts, Richard R., 'A postmodern church? Some Preliminary Reflections on Ecclesiology and Social Theory', in D. Ford and D. Stamps (eds), (1996), *Essentials of Christian Community*. Edinburgh: T & T Clark, p. 192.

38 Billings, Alan, 'Thought for the Day', BBC Radio 4, 'Today programme', 2 June 2008. www.bbc.co.uk/religion/programmes/thought/documents/t20080602.shtml (accessed 2 June 2008).

39 www.archbishopofcanterbury.org/1575 (accessed 9 February 2008).

40 This explains Gordon Brown's interest in 'Britishness'.

41 Coleridge, S. T. (1996), *Aids to Reflection*, cited in Daniel W. Hardy, *God's ways with the world*. Edinburgh: T & T Clark, 'God and the Form of Society', p. 174.

42 Hardy, 'God and the Form of Society', p. 175.

43 Terry Eagleton, 'Monotheism and Violence', in Hoelzl, M. and Ward, G. (eds) (2008), *The New Visibility of Religion*. London: Continuum, p. xx.

44 Taylor, Charles (2007), 'The Moral Order: The Transition to Political Modernity', in Michael Hoelzl and Graham Ward (eds), *Religion and Political Thought*. London: Continuum, pp. 259–67 (p. 259).

45 It follows that where atheism is unprepared to engage in an argument of the diversity of social forms, it functions as an apologist for the regnant social order; at the present time, this would be the liberal state.

46 Bonhoeffer, Dietrich (1970), *No Rusty Swords*. London: Fontana, p. 163.

47 Roberts, 'A Postmodern Church', p. 179.

48 This claim is also true, *mutatis mutandis*, of other religious traditions.

49 This is theocracy's question.

50 Casanova, José (1994), *Public Religions in the Modern World* (Chicago and London: University of Chicago Press).

51 And fall apart into what – religious warfare, fascism?

Index